ARTHURIAN LITERATURE

IV

Contents of previous volumes

I

Chrétien de Troyes and England
Constance Bullock-Davies

The *Vera Historia de Morte Arthuri* and its place in Arthurian Tradition
Richard Barber

An Edition of the *Vera Historia de Morte Arthuri*
Michael Lapidge

Malory and the Archaic Mind
Derek Brewer

From Logres to Carbonek: the Arthuriad of Charles Williams
Karl Heinz Göller

II

Geoffrey of Monmouth and Gildas
Neil Wright

The Round Table: Ideal, Fiction, Reality
Beate Schmolke-Hasselmann

The Tradition of the Troubadours and the Treatment of the
Love Theme in Chrétien de Troyes' *Chevalier au Lion*
Fanni Bogdanow

Kairo-ko: A Dirge
Toshiyuki Takamiya and Andrew Armour

Twentieth-Century Arthurian Literature: an annotated bibliography
Mary Wildman

III

The Prologue of Crestien's *Li Contes del Graal*
Claude Luttrell

The Presentation of the Character of Lancelot: Chrétien to Malory
Derek Brewer

The Briar and the Vine: Tristan Goes North
M. F. Thomas

Vengeance and Love in 'The Book of Sir Launcelot and Queen Guinevere'
Irene Joynt

ISSN 0261-9946

Arthurian Literature IV

EDITED BY RICHARD BARBER

Advisory editors
Tony Hunt
Toshiyuki Takamiya

D. S. BREWER · BARNES & NOBLE

First published 1985 by D. S. Brewer
an imprint of Boydell & Brewer Ltd
PO Box 9, Woodbridge, Suffolk IP12 3DF
and Barnes & Noble
81 Adams Drive, Totowa, NJ 07512, USA

British Library Cataloguing in Publication Data

Arthurian literature. — 4
   1. Arthur, *King* — Periodicals   2. Arthurian
romances — History and criticism — Periodicals
3. English literature — History and criticism
— Periodicals
820.9'351   PR149.A79
ISBN 0-85991-163-2
ISSN 0261-9946

The Library of Congress has cataloged this serial
   as follows:

Arthurian literature. — 1- — Woodbridge, Suffolk:
D. S. Brewer; Totawa, N.J.: Rowman and Littlefield,
c1981- v.; 24cm.
Annual.

1. Arthurian romances — History and criticism —
Periodicals.
PN685.A68   809'.93351 — dc19   83-640196
                            AACR 2   MARC-S

Bibliographical note   Due to an oversight, the date of publication was omitted
on vols I to III. For the record, the years of publication were as follows: I – 1981,
II – 1982, III – 1983.

Printed and bound in Great Britain by Short Run Press Ltd, Exeter

CONTENTS

I   An Early Text of Geoffrey of Monmouth's *Historia*   1
Regum Britanniae and the Circulation of Some Latin
Histories in Twelfth-century Normandy
David N. Dumville

II   Was Mordred Buried at Glastonbury? An Arthurian   37
Tradition at Glastonbury in the Middle Ages
Richard Barber

Appendix: The Discovery of the Holy Cross of Waltham
at Montacute, the Excavation of Arthur's Grave at
Glastonbury Abbey, and Joseph of Arimathea's Burial
James Carley

III   Uther and Igerne: A Study in Uncourtly Love   70
Rosemary Morris

IV   Manuscripts, Readers and Patrons in Fifteenth-century   93
England: Sir Thomas Malory and Arthurian Romance
Carol Meale

V   Ernest Chausson's 'Le Roi Arthus'   127
Tony Hunt

VI   UPDATE: Geoffrey of Monmouth and Gildas Revisited   155
Neil Wright

VII UPDATE: The Manuscripts of Geoffrey of Monmouth's   164
Historia Regum Britanniae: Addenda, Corrigenda, and
and Alphabetical List
David N. Dumville

VIII UPDATE: Additions to Twentieth-century Arthurian   172
Literature

I

AN EARLY TEXT OF
GEOFFREY OF MONMOUTH'S *HISTORIA REGUM BRITANNIAE*
and the circulation of some Latin histories
in twelfth-century Normandy

David N. Dumville

It is now common ground among students of Geoffrey of Monmouth that the textual history of his *Historia Regum Britanniae* remains quite unknown.[1] Early attempts to make some headway with the classification of the vast number of surviving manuscripts (currently standing at 211)[2] of this long text culminated in the editions by Edmond Faral and Acton Griscom, published in 1929.[3] One of Griscom's helpers, Jacob Hammer, who subsequently took up the task of attempting a critical edition, later commented that Faral and Griscom had scarcely scratched the surface of the text-historical problem. Their analysis had rested on the detailed investigation of very few copies of the *Historia*. It had also been controlled by a belief that the varying dedicatory forewords provided a sufficient basis for textual classification; but, as Hammer pointed out, these sections could have a history very different from the accompanying copies of the text itself.[4] Death claimed Hammer long before he could complete and publish his critical edition; yet it is apparent from his interim publications that a traditional process of collation and text-historical analysis had proved the only adequate method of establishing the interrelationships of the many copies.[5] In short, the weakness of the

---

1 Hammer, 'Remarks', p. 525; cf. now Wright, *The Historia*, introduction.
2 See Dumville, 'The manuscripts', with addenda, corrigenda, and an alphabetical listing, below, pp. 164-71.
3 Faral, *La légende* (text at III. 63-303); Griscom & Jones, *The Historia*.
4 For Hammer as one of Griscom's helpers, see Griscom & Jones, *ibid.*, p. x; Hammer, 'Remarks', p. 525.
5 See his remarks, quoted below (p. 165) from a letter written in 1939, about the Longparish manuscript; also 'Remarks', p. 525, and elsewhere in his many papers published in the 1930s and 1940s.

1929 editions, suspected almost from the first, was demonstrated by collation of more manuscripts. Among the results of such collation was the discovery of a number of variant versions of the *Historia*;[6] the necessity of organising separate publication of these versions seems seriously to have dislocated Hammer's programme; and the published results were far from happy.[7] Notwithstanding the evidence for such textual diversity, the image has persisted of a remarkable homogeneity of text among the 90% of manuscripts constituting the so-called 'vulgate' text of the *Historia*. Yet it is among these many 'vulgate' copies that the answers to essential questions about the early history — and indeed the origins — of Geoffrey's *Historia Regum Britanniae* must lie.

The aim of the present paper is to study one small part, of the textual history of the 'vulgate' *Historia*, which seems to have something to say about the early diffusion of the work and which may indeed even contribute to our understanding of the difficult problems attending interpretation of its author's motives. One of the few manuscripts of the *Historia* to have achieved some notoriety is now resident in Switzerland: Bern, Burgerbibliothek, MS. 568.[8] It forms part of a small group of copies which are textually very closely related: together they form the subject of this paper. But before examining their evidence we must turn instead to the Norman abbey of Le Bec to consider one of the mid-twelfth-century products of its scriptorium: this is perhaps the most notorious of *Historia*-manuscripts — Leiden, Bibliotheek der Rijksuniversiteit, MS. BPL 20.

THE LEIDEN MANUSCRIPT

This Leiden book, comprising 107 folios, is a composite of two distinct manuscripts distinguishable by their separate series of quire-signatures. The first (and possibly the earlier), now fos 2-59, is acephalous owing to the loss of the initial two quires. It contains the *Gesta Normannorum Ducum* in the recension written perhaps during 1139 at Le Bec by Robert of Torigni (fos 2r-32v),[9] Einhard's *Vita Karoli Magni* (33r-38v), the *Vita Alexandri Magni* (38v-47r), *Epistola Alexandri Magni ad Aristotelem* (47r-51v), *Abbreuiatio Gestorum Regum Franciae*

6 For the standard account, see Hammer, *Geoffrey*, introduction.
7 *Ibid.*, where Hammer's text departs repeatedly from sound editorial principles. See the review by Frappier; cf. Dumville, 'The origin'.
8 Now described, and its text published, by Wright, *The Historia*.
9 For the date, see van Houts, *Gesta*, pp.36-51, with reference to Chibnall, 'Orderic Vitalis and Robert of Torigni', where the case for 1139 seems perhaps less securely established than van Houts suggests.

2

(52r-59r), and *Genealogia Comitum Flandriae* (59v). The copy of *Gesta Normannorum Ducum* is perhaps Robert's original copy of his recension: at any rate, it spawned a numerous and influential progeny.[10] The second manuscript (now fos 60-106) contains Geoffrey's *Historia* (60r-101v), divided into ten books and with the dedicatory prologue to Robert of Gloucester, as well as the *Historia Brittonum* in one of the sub-versions of the pseudo-Gildas recension (101v-106r)[11] and a brief excerpt from the *Historia Ecclesiastica* of Orderic Vitalis (106v).[12] The two manuscripts were already united in the possession of Le Bec by the 1150s at the latest, as is apparent from their appearance as a single codex in the Bec library-catalogue prepared not later than that decade.[13] The catalogue-entry reappears verbatim as a contents-table on fo 1v, a prefixed flyleaf, in mid-twelfth-century Bec script.

Leiden MS. BPL 20, fo 1v

In hoc uol[umine conti]nentur:

Historię [Norm]anorum libri octo, uide[licet] ab aduentu Hastingi in regnum Francorum usque ad mortem primi Henrici regis Anglorum et ducis Normannorum.

Item uita Caroli Magni imperatoris Romanorum et regis Francorum.

Item uita Alexandri Magni regis Macedonum.

Item epistola eiusdem de situ Indię ad Aristotelem magistrum suum.

Item abbreuiatio gestorum regum Francię ab egressione eorum a Sicambria usque ad principium regni Ludouici iunioris regis Francorum et ducis Aquitanorum.

Item hystoriarum de regibus maioris Britannię usque ad aduentum Anglorum in eandem insulam libri XII, in quorum septimo continentur

Le Bec library-catalogue

In uno uolumine:

Historie Normannorum libri septem, uidelicet ab aduentu Hastingi in regnum Francorum usque ad mortem primi Henrici regis Anglorum et ducis Normanorum.

Item uita Caroli Magni imperatoris Romanorum et regis Francorum.

Item uita Alexandri Magni regis Macedonum.

Item epistola eiusdem de situ Indie ad Aristotilem magistrum suum.

Item abreuiatio regum Francie gestorum ab egressione eorum a Sicambria usque ad principium regni Ludouici iunioris regis Francorum.[14]

Item historiarum de regibus maioris Britannie usque ad adventum Anglorum in insulam libri XII, in quorum septimo continentur prophetie Merlini,

---

10 The standard account is now by van Houts, *Gesta*.

11 For this text see now *The Historia Brittonum*, ed. Dumville; this version is discussed in volume 5.

12 See Chibnall, *The Ecclesiastical History*; the extract is of VIII. 21 (Chibnall, IV. 264-7).

13 See appendix II for the date of this catalogue.

14 The cataloguer or its Mont-Saint-Michel copyist has suppressed *et ducis Aquitanorum*; when he wrote (after 1152), this title belonged to Henry II, no longer to Louis VII (as noted by Delisle, *Mélanges*, p.175, n.1).

| prophetię Mellini, non Siluestris, sed alterius, id est Mellini Ambrosii. | non Siluestris, sed alterius, id est Merlini Ambrosii. |
| Item exceptiones ex libro Gildę sapientis historiographi Britonum, quem composuit de uastatione suę gentis et de mirabilibus Britannię. | Item exceptiones ex libro Gilde sapientis historiographi Britonum, quem composuit de uastatione gentis sue et de mirabilibus Britannie. |

Indeed, the script of the whole codex, represented by a number of hands, and the decorated initial on fo 60r, have been recognised as work emanating from the scriptorium of Le Bec.[15] This book's early copy of Geoffrey's *Historia* can therefore be assigned a point of origin and early provenance. But by sometime in the last quarter of the century, the book may have reached England, for a Reading manuscript of that date appears to be the first of an English progeny.[16] That it spent the rest of the middle ages in England seems likely; it bears an *ex-libris* inscription, now fragmentary, on 1v which seems also to indicate an English provenance.[17]

When, in the late nineteenth century, it became known to scholars that this book had been in the library of Le Bec in the twelfth century,[18] it seemed natural to suppose that here was the very manuscript of Geoffrey's *Historia* which Robert of Torigni showed there to an astonished Henry of Huntingdon in January 1139.[19] Yet to accept this conclusion requires us to suppose that by the time of Henry's arrival at Le Bec the scriptorium had executed a copy of this recently published work.[20] Unless we pick up J. S. P. Tatlock's hints that Geoffrey might have worked at Le Bec itself,[21] we are bound to wonder why Robert of Torigni would not have shown Henry the copy which the abbey had received from its source, whether Geoffrey himself or a third party. And if the *Historia* was as recent a publication as Tatlock thought,[22] the equation is rendered yet more uncertain.

Some further evidence on the point may be derived from a collateral

---

15 Cf. the discussions by Avril, 'Notes', p.211, and 'La décoration', p.234; van Houts, *Gesta*, pp.229-31; and Hermans & van Houts, 'The history of a membrum disiectum', pp.80-1.

16 van Houts, *Gesta*, pp.239-41 (her MS. F7); one is bound to wonder whether Reading might not also have been the point of origin of BL MS. Cotton Nero D.viii (her MS. F11, *ibid.*, pp.244-6).

17 van Houts, *Gesta*, pp.229-30.

18 See Delisle, *Mélanges*, pp.167-94.

19 See Henry's *Epistola ad Warinum*, most conveniently in Delisle, *Chronique*, I.97-8. For this (mistaken) interpretation, see Tatlock, *The Legendary History*, pp.311-12 and 433 n.2.

20 Cf. below, p.23.

21 Tatlock, *ibid.*, p.444, n.36.

22 *Ibid.*, pp.433-7, arguing for late 1138 (especially p.434).

witness. The textual history of the other content of Part II of Leiden BPL 20, namely the ninth-century *Historia Brittonum*, is now better established than that of its later relative, Geoffrey's *Historia Regum Britanniae*. By bringing the evidence of the *Historia Brittonum* to bear on our problem, we may gain elucidation: the recension attributed to Gildas seems to have been created in midland England in the early years of the twelfth century; there followed a rapid and massive multiplication of copies, which led to the development of a number of distinct sub-groups of this recension, as well as conflations with other recensions.[23] One of these sub-groups is attested principally in Norman manuscripts, among which Leiden BPL 20 is to be numbered. Three copies of the *Historia Brittonum*,[24] with Leiden BPL 20 as their chief representative, introduce the text with an extraordinary rubric: 'Incipiunt Excerptiones De Libro Gilde Sapientis quem composuit De primis habitatoribus Brittannie que nunc Anglia dicitur et De Excidio eius'. We may compare with this the rubric which introduces Geoffrey's *Historia* in Leiden BPL 20 (fo 60r): 'Incipit prologus Gaufridi Monimutensis ad Rodbertum comitem Claudiocestrie in Hystoriam de regibus Maioris *Brittannie que nunc Anglia dicitur*, quam historiam idem Gaufridus nuper transtulit in latinum'. Whatever one makes of the word *nuper* here, there can be little doubt that a relationship exists between these two rubrics. Geoffrey's *Historia*, as the first and the major text in the manuscript, might perhaps be considered the primary witness in this matter. But, in fact, the text-history of the *Historia Brittonum* indicates that the formula derived from an earlier copy of that work. What is apparent, then, is that we have evidence for the modelling of the title of the Le Bec copy of Geoffrey's work on that already known for a related text, and for the production of a joint copy. That is not all, however. In a manuscript now at Rouen — MS. U.74 (1177) — is a copy of the pseudo-Gildasian *Historia Brittonum* with a rubric, and indeed a text, recognisably immediately ancestral to that of the Leiden sub-group. The Rouen manuscript itself is, however, later in date than the Leiden book. The Rouen title reads: 'Incipit liber Gilde sapientis de primis habitatoribus Britannie que nunc dicitur Anglia, et de excidio eius'. The title has been expanded in the Leiden sub-group to give greater specification: 'Incipi*unt Excerptiones De* Libro Gilde Sapientis *quem composuit* . . .'. This is almost certainly a learned expansion, based on knowledge of the existence of a much longer text attributed to

[23] Dumville, *The Historia Brittonum*, V.
[24] Leiden, UB, MS. BPL 20; London, BL, Cotton Nero D.viii; Évreux, Bibliothèque municipale, MS. 41.

Gildas;[25] the Rouen title, on the other hand, implies that the *Historia Brittonum* is Gildas's *De Excidio*. Other aspects of the Leiden BPL 20 text of the *Historia Brittonum* (notably glosses and subheadings) indicate modification in the light of modern (pseudo-)learning, while the physical condition of the text, showing much efficient correction, perhaps hints at its status as a lightly revised version of the work. One must suspect that its copy of Geoffrey's *Historia* has suffered a similar fate.

THE ROUEN MANUSCRIPT

Rouen, Bibliothèque municipale, MS. U.74 (1177), was probably written at the Norman Benedictine abbey of Jumièges ca 1200; certainly it was of later mediaeval Jumièges provenance. Alongside its slightly more primitive copy of the pseudo-Gildasian *Historia Brittonum*, it contains a text of Geoffrey's *Historia*, a copy which will demand our further attention. I now present a summary table of its contents.

1r-59ra14:	Geoffrey of Monmouth, *Historia Regum Britanniae*.
59ra14-62ra4:	Extracts from Bede, *Historia Ecclesiastica* (I. 15, 23, 25, 26, 34; II. 1-3), on the origin and christianisation of the Anglo-Saxons; these continue directly the text of Geoffrey's *Historia*, without any indication of a textual division.
62ra4-166r:	Henry of Huntingdon, *Historiae Anglorum Libri Decem*. Rubric reads like one of the Le Bec catalogue-entries.
166v-171r:	Extract from the Chronicle of Robert of Torigni, covering the years 1147-1157.
171r-172v:	Bec continuation, for the years 1157-1160, of the Chronicle of Robert of Torigni.
173r-275r:	Bede, *Historia Ecclesiastica Gentis Anglorum*: c-type text.
275v:	blank
276r-278r:	Two fragments of Book X of the *Historia Anglorum* of Henry of Huntingdon. These are leaves replaced by fresh copies, fos 160-1 and 166r.
278v-282va20:	Bede, *De Temporibus*.
282va21-288r:	Bede, *De Natura Rerum*.
288v:	blank
289r-297v:	*Historia Brittonum*, in the pseudo-Gildasian recension.
298r/v:	blank

---

[25] We may note the same realisation at work in the apparent modification of the rubric in what appears to be the 'Gildasian'-recension archetype — Oxford, Bodleian Library, MS. Bodley 163 (*S.C.* 2016) — where (on fo 228r) the rubric 'Incipiunt Gesta Brittonum a Gilda sapiente composita' is glossed 'Gilda minor'.

299r-302r: Incomplete copy (stopping in the middle of §21) of Bede's
               De Temporibus.
302v: blank, except for two later scribbles.

This manuscript from Jumièges may be subdivided in a number of ways. Like Leiden BPL 20 it contains Geoffrey of Monmouth and the pseudo-Gildasian *Historia Brittonum*, but not at all in close physical proximity. The Le Bec library-catalogue, dating from the mid-twelfth century,[26] does, however, offer further helpful evidence about the manuscript's possible antecedents. As its item 80, in the section headed *Libri Bede presbiteri*, we find the following.

In alio [uolumine]   historia Anglorum libri V.
               De temporibus liber I minor.
               De naturis rerum liber I.
               Liber Gilde sapientis de excidio Britannie.
               Vita sancti Neoti, *que in capite ponitur.*

As far as is known, this book — like so much of the mediaeval library of Le Bec — has perished.[27] (It seems to have survived into the seventeenth century, for it was probably from that copy that Mabillon printed *Vita II S. Neoti*.[28]) But its apparent relationship to Rouen MS. U.74 (1177) allows the hypothesis that this lost Le Bec book was ancestral to part of that now at Rouen. In the latter book we find: fos 173r-275r — Bede, *Historia Ecclesiastica*; fos 278v-282v — Bede, *De Temporibus*; fos 282v-288r — Bede, *De Natura Rerum*; fos 289r-297v — pseudo-Gildas, *Historia Brittonum*.

The equivalence is impressive but not absolutely exact. It has always seemed odd that the volume contained fragments of Bede's *Historia Ecclesiastica* (fos 59r-62r), Henry of Huntingdon's *Historia Anglorum* (fos 276r-278r), and Bede's *De Temporibus* (fos 299r-302r) when it also included complete copies of these works.[29] One element of these duplications (that of Bede's *Historia*) can be explained by the complex antecedents of the Jumièges book.[30] In principle that could be true also in the case of Henry's *Historia*; but a close look at these will show that they are fragments, not deliberately chosen excerpts. And the partial duplication of Bede's *De Temporibus* seems inexplicable on any theory of overlapping exemplaria.

The fragments duplicating parts of Henry's *Historia* provide the

---

26 See appendix II below.
27 Porée, *Histoire*, I. 524-42, and II. 409-13, 554-6, on the library and its fate.
28 Mabillon, *Acta Sanctorum*, IV. 2, pp. 323-36; Lapidge, *apud* Dumville & Keynes, *The Anglo-Saxon Chronicle*, XVII, Introduction, n. 97.
29 Omont, *Catalogue général*, I. 295-7.
30 See below, pp. 15-16.

key to what has happened but threaten, in the process, considerably to complicate the reconstruction of the Jumièges volume's antecedents. Fos 276r-277v and 278r contain two separate fragments of Book X of the *Historia Anglorum*, which begin, end, and begin again with no evident textual reason. The last page in fact contains the end of Book X (and therefore of the whole *Historia Anglorum*), relating events of A.D.1147. The verso bears the opening of Bede's *De Temporibus*. A look back to the complete copy of Book X earlier in the manuscript shows what has probably happened. The book's scribe-compiler originally in this section followed his exemplar where Bede's *De Temporibus* followed immediately upon Henry's *Historia Anglorum*. Only one surviving copy known to me displays such a relationship (Cambridge, University Library, MS. Gg.2.21 [1451], a French book of the second half of the twelfth century).[31] But that at least one other such volume did exist is shown by the catalogue of volumes bequeathed to Le Bec by Philippe de Harcourt, bishop of Bayeux, in 1164.[32] Item 95 of that list reads as follows.

In alio [uolumine] historia Henrici de Anglia,
et liber Bede minor de temporibus
et de natura rerum.

In the Jumièges volume this model was no longer seen as satisfactory when the possibility was perceived of extending Henry's account nearer to the present day. The two outer bifolia (now fos 276-279) of the quire comprising the end of Henry's *Historia* and the beginning of Bede's *De Temporibus* were therefore removed and replaced by a corresponding number of blank leaves on which were copied the same portions of Henry's text; these are now to be found on fos 160-161 and fo 166r. On completion of the recopying, the revising scribe then added an extract from Robert of Torigni's *Chronicon*, for the years 1147-1157,[33] followed by a Bec continuation of Robert's work covering the period December 1157 to 1160.[34]

This continuation of Robert's *Chronicon* is attested in other manuscripts.[35] No copy from Le Bec survives, but three others are known, their provenances restricted to a narrow geographical area at whose centre stands Le Bec itself. Copies survive, or are attested, from Le Bec,

---

31 Hardwick & Luard, *A Catalogue*, III. 53-4; this volume has been studied in detail by Miss Sarah Foot (Newnham College, Cambridge) who intends to publish on the subject; I am grateful to Miss Foot for various points of information, as will appear, below.
32 On Philippe, see also below, pp. 24-6.
33 Delisle, *Chronique*, II.143-5; for the text of annals 1147-1157 see I. 242-310.
34 *Ibid.*, II.137-46 and 165-80; this copy (Delisle's H) is slightly incomplete.
35 *Ibid.*, and see appendix I below.

Lyre, Saint-Wandrille, Évreux, and Jumièges. Apart from the (slightly incomplete) version in Rouen MS. U.74 (1177), another twelfth-century Jumièges book, Rouen MS. Y.15 (1132), contains a copy, in Delisle's opinion the best to survive.[36] However, neither of these two Jumièges copies can derive from the other, with the result that one must postulate a third which served as exemplar for both the extant Jumièges copies.[37]

We must suppose, therefore, that discovery of the availability at Jumièges of a copy of Robert's *Chronicon* supplemented by the *Continuatio Beccensis* caused our volume's sequence of texts to be reorganised. The separation of Bede's *De Temporibus* from Henry's *Historia* permitted also, it would seem, the interpolation of Bede's *Historia Ecclesiastica* (fos 173r-275r), whether from another part of the book or from a separate source. And the second, incomplete, copy of Bede's *De Temporibus* (fos 299r-302r)[38] must perhaps be reckoned as part of an abortive attempt to replace the original copy of that text (back to back with the end of Henry's *Historia* on fo 278) with a new one no longer physically tied to discarded sheets of Henry's *Historia*.

All this might suggest that item 80 in the Le Bec library-catalogue was a derivative of part of the Jumièges manuscript, in which the pattern of texts was first established thus. But such a hypothesis is nullified by the evidence of chronology, for the Le Bec catalogue is clearly much anterior in date to the writing (and revision) of Rouen MS. U.74 which was executed late in the twelfth century or possibly in the early thirteenth.[39]

How, then, is one to decide on the precise nature of the antecedents of this part of Rouen MS. U.74 (1177)? The equation of item 80 in the Le Bec catalogue with an ancestor of fos 173-297 is exceptionally neat. But to the extent that this sequence of texts seems to have been created in Rouen U.74 itself, it is difficult to admit of an earlier manuscript providing a single exemplar for this portion of the book. Under such circumstances we must imagine the primitive Rouen U.74 being compared with another book which suggested a reorganisation of its contents.

A good deal more can be said about the text of Henry of Huntingdon's *Historia Anglorum* in Rouen MS. U.74, albeit with the reser-

---

[36] Delisle, *ibid.*, I. xiii-xvii and II. 137-46, 165-80.

[37] *Ibid.*, II. 145.

[38] It finishes in § 21 with the words *Esdra legem* (ed. Jones, *Bedae Venerabilis Opera*, VI. 3, p. 606, line 6).

[39] For the later date, see Mynors *apud* Colgrave & Mynors, *Bede's Ecclesiastical History*, p. lxi.

9

vation that, since Thomas Arnold's edition[40] provides almost no help to one wishing to classify individual manuscripts of the work, all text-historical remarks must be viewed as very provisional until the completion of the work of re-edition which Diana Greenway[41] has recently undertaken. The copy in Rouen MS. U.74 is in ten books, extending in its account of English history to A.D.1147. It therefore belongs to a well recognised recension of Henry's work, in which Books VIII-X are new matter.[42] Further help in classification may be gained by reference to the rubric which introduces this copy (fo 62ra4-7): 'In uolumine hoc continetur historia Anglorum nouiter edita ab Henrico Huntendunensi archidiacono libri .x.'. This is most unlike a normal introductory rubric, resembling nothing so much as a contents-list on the flyleaf of a twelfth-century Le Bec manuscript (reproducing an entry in the library-catalogue of Le Bec), or even of a Mont-Saint-Michel book of the second half of the twelfth century.[43] This rubric helps to identify relatives of Rouen U.74: three are known to me – Cambridge, University Library, MS. Gg.2.21 (1451), a French book of the later twelfth century; Exeter, Cathedral Library, MS. 3514, a Welsh book of the mid-thirteenth century;[44] Paris, Bibliothèque nationale, MS. latin 6042, a Norman book of the second half of the twelfth century.[45]

The Paris manuscript forms a convenient starting point. It was written after 1151, for its incomplete copy of the canons of that year's Council of London is in the hand of one of the main scribes of the book.[46] Léopold Delisle gave it as his opinion that the book was copied (no doubt at the behest of Robert of Torigni) for Mont-Saint-Michel, probably 'a little after the middle of the twelfth century'.[47] In his view, the exemplar of this copy of Henry's *Historia Anglorum* was that which Robert of Torigni used at Le Bec when making his *Chronicon*,[48] and BN lat. 6042 was a faithful copy. It was left unclear whether BN lat. 6042 was actually written at Le Bec or

---

[40] *Henrici Archidiaconi Huntendunensis Historia Anglorum.*

[41] Institute of Historical Research, University of London. The edition is to appear in the series 'Oxford Medieval Texts'.

[42] Arnold, *ibid.*, pp.xiii-xvi.

[43] For Le Bec contents-lists, cf. above, pp.2-6; for Mont-Saint-Michel, see Nortier, *Les bibliothèques*, chapter 3, especially p.70.

[44] Ker, *Medieval Manuscripts in British Libraries*, II.822-5.

[45] Brooke, *The English Church & the Papacy*, p.103; cf. Whitelock *et al.*, *Councils & Synods*, I.2, pp.821-6, which seems to opt for a slightly earlier date.

[46] The identity was pointed out to me by Sarah Foot (cf. n.31 above).

[47] Delisle, *Chronique*, I.lv-lxi ('un peu après le milieu du XIIe siècle', p.lix).

[48] *Ibid.*, especially pp.lx-lxi.

at Mont-Saint-Michel, but there was a hint that he favoured the latter possibility.[49]

The other important content of this group of copies of Henry's *Historia* is a collection (or series of collections) of episcopal (and abbatial) lists.[50] They are not to be found in Rouen MS. U. 74, but each of the other three manuscripts has varying collections, as may be seen from the following table.

BN lat. 6042	CUL Gg. 2. 21	Exeter 3514
		1. Canterbury
1. Rouen		
2. Coutances		
3. Séez		
4. Bayeux		
5. Avranches		
6. Lisieux		
7. Évreux		
8. Mont-Saint-Michel (abbots)		
9. Le Bec (abbots)		
10. Langres		
Autun [not in contents-table]		
11. Chartres		
12. Winchester		
13. Le Mans	Le Mans	2. Le Mans
14. Poitiers	Poitiers	3. Poitiers
15. Nantes	Nantes	4. Nantes
16. Canterbury	Canterbury	
<Amiens> (erased?)	Amiens	5. Amiens
*17. [Beauvais	Beauvais	6. Beauvais
*18. Sens	Sens	7. Sens
*19. Paris	Paris	8. Paris
*20. Orléans	Orléans	9. Orléans
*21. Senlis	Senlis	10. Senlis
		11. Jumièges (abbots)
*22. Tours		12. Tours
*23. Angers		13. Angers
*24. Jumièges (abbots)]		
		14. Saint-Wandrille (abbots)
25. Reims		
26. Laon		
27. Châlons-sur-Marne		
28. Thérouanne		
29. Vermandois		
30. Noyon-Tournai		
31. Amiens		
32. Arras-Cambrai		
33. Auxerre		

---

[49] *Ibid.*, pp. lix-lxi; cf. the situation envisaged in respect of the *Gesta Roberti Wiscardi* by Mathieu, 'Le manuscrit 162 d'Avranches ou Robert'.

[50] Delisle, 'Anciens catalogues', is the fullest available study of French episcopal lists; the texts in our manuscripts have not been fully published.

It seems clear from such a distribution of evidence that the original collection of lists associated with this text of Henry's *Historia* comprised the thirteen which immediately preceded it in BN lat. 6042 (fo 2v and lost succeeding folio) and which with minor variations do precede in CUL Gg. 2. 21 and Exeter 3514. For whatever reason, the last three lists (Tours, Angers, abbots of Jumièges) were lost in the tradition from which CUL Gg. 2. 21 derives. And the Exeter manuscript embodies a reorganisation (as befits a British copy) by which Canterbury has been moved to the head of the series; but it also gives away its Norman history, in as much as an extra list, that of the abbots of Saint-Wandrille, concludes the series − it is presumably to that abbey that we should look for the source of this copy of Henry's *Historia*.[51]

In BN lat. 6042 the original series of thirteen lists is surrounded (on fos 1v-2r, 121v-122v) by an additional twenty-two lists of French sees and abbeys (two: Mont-Saint-Michel and Le Bec) in a plurality of hands; these additions seem most likely to have been made (at Mont-Saint-Michel) in the 1170s.[52] Delisle thought that Robert of Torigni was probably responsible for this collecting activity;[53] no doubt he was correct. But the question remains as to when and where the original series of thirteen lists was assembled and where it was first prefixed to a copy of Henry's *Historia*. Sarah Foot has established that the dates of the last bishop in each list would agree with a compilation-date of 1148/9,[54] and those of the last-named abbot of Jumièges (Eustachius, 1142-53) would not conflict with that.[55] In view of the Norman associations of the manuscripts of this group, it is perhaps surprising that no Norman see is included. Beginning at Le Mans, the series describes a (very incomplete) circle, clockwise, around the boundaries of Normandy, finishing at Angers. To that extent, Jumièges is − twice over − the odd man out: it is both the only abbey and the only Norman institution (diocese of Rouen). Two alternative conclusions seem possible: either the series was intended to complement another series, listing the bishops of Norman sees, or it was drawn up outside Normandy, received at Jumièges (where the

51 It is something of a mystery why the abbatial list of Jumièges has been transposed to its present odd position in Exeter 3514. The Exeter book contains other Norman texts, but we are inhibited from connecting them with Saint-Wandrille by the codicological evidence that pp. 223-450 (lists and Henry) are earlier than the rest of the book: Ker (cf. n. 44), II. 822, 823-4.
52 Delisle, *Chronique*, I. lv-lxi; I am indebted to Miss Sarah Foot for more precise information on this matter on which she proposes to publish.
53 Delisle, *ibid*.
54 See the work referred to in n. 31.
55 Laporte, 'Les listes', p. 459.

local abbatial list was added) and circulated thence; one would be happier making the latter argument, however, if CUL Gg.2.21 had the Tours and Angers lists which conclude the collection in the other two manuscripts.

Much turns on the evidence of CUL MS. Gg.2.21. Its list of Le Mans bishops (shared with BN lat. 6042) is much more detailed, giving chronological details,[56] than that in the Exeter manuscript. Since the manuscript is not obviously Norman and since its Early Modern provenance was Le Mans itself,[57] it is tempting to take this as evidence for the book's origin at Le Mans. However, if the series of twelve lists (Le Mans – Angers) originated there, the form in CUL Gg. 2. 21 might simply reflect the original, subsequently abbreviated in the Norman transmission of the collection. In the latter case, the argument for a Le Mans origin for CUL Gg.2.21 would be weakened (though not destroyed). But since it cannot itself be the source of the other copies, we must still hypothesise an original copy which had the order beginning with Le Mans. It would therefore be most economical to suppose that the series originated in that diocese.

If we were to make the supposition – by no means the sole requirement of logic – that the series of lists was joined to the source-copy of Henry's *Historia Anglorum* where it originated (*ex hypothesi*, at Le Mans), we could tentatively represent the tradition as in Figure I (p.14). This stemma could be modified in two ways without changing the basic supposition. The hypothesised Le Bec (lost) copy (which could conceivably be item 132 in the mid-twelfth-century library-catalogue) depends solely, for its place in the stemma, on Delisle's premise that BN lat. 6042 is a faithful copy of the copy of Henry's *Historia* used at Le Bec by Robert of Torigni in 1148 x 1154.[58] If we reject that premise, and admit that BN lat. 6042 could be a collateral relative of any Le Bec copy of Henry's *Historia*, then there is no reason to admit the Le Bec copy of that work (as used by Robert, and presumably item 132 in the library-catalogue) to this stemma. The library of Le Bec might have received it quite independently of the transmission of the collection of texts most fully represented today by CUL Gg. 2. 21. Secondly, it is far from certain that Philippe de Harcourt's copy has been correctly placed in the stemma. He collected widely – in England, France, Normandy, and Italy – during

---

56 Delisle, 'Anciens catalogues', pp.441-3.
57 As evidenced by the ownership of J. B. Hautin: cf. Hunter Blair & Mynors, *The Moore Bede*, pp.25-6.
58 Delisle, *Chronique*, I. lv-lxi.

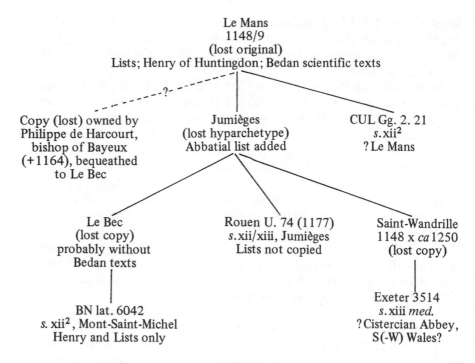

FIGURE I

a busy career,[59] and his copy (whose extreme limits of date must have been 1147 x 1164) of Henry's *Historia* with its two following Bedan scientific texts may have been ancestral to the hypothetical Le Mans collection or may have been derivative of the lost Jumièges hyparchetype; without the discovery either of his manuscript or of a much more detailed description of it, we cannot go further.

The stemma would be fundamentally altered, however, if we were to reject the basic premise on which it was constructed. If the series of lists was associated with the Henrician and Bedan texts as an act separate from that of creation and circulation of that series, then a much simpler stemma, displaying greater ignorance, must be drawn (Figure II).

Either of these reconstructions (but especially the former) would seem to place more stress on the place of Jumièges in the circulation of all these texts than has been customary. It would be possible to

59 Cf. Mathieu, 'Le manuscrit 162 d'Avranches et l'édition princeps', p.124(-5), n.3; Winterbottom, *Problems in Quintilian*, p.27, n.3; Marshall *et al.*, 'Clare College MS. 26', pp.376-7. On the career of Philippe see further Gleason, *An Ecclesiastical Barony*, pp.26-43, 63, 87, 92-3, 100-5.

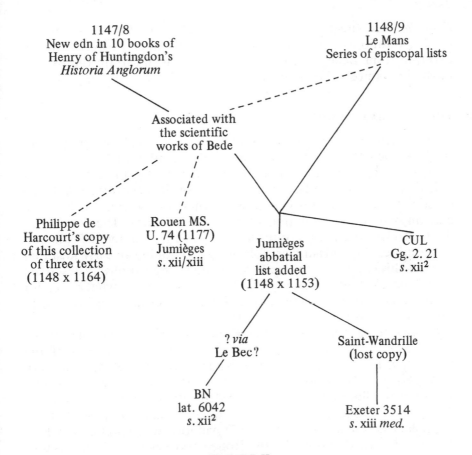

FIGURE II

rewrite the stemma to give Le Bec the central place in the Norman distribution, but a highly complex and uneconomical history (accompanied by a striking lack of direct evidence) would result; until such direct testimony is forthcoming, it would perhaps be better to leave Jumièges at the centre of the stage.

We turn at last to the first element in Rouen MS. U. 74 (1177), namely Geoffrey's *Historia Regum Britanniae* and its Bedan appendix. There are three immediately noteworthy features of this copy of Geoffrey's *Historia*. First, it lacks §§ 1-5, beginning simply with 'Eneas post troianum bellum . . .' (§ 6). It is introduced by a rubric (fo 1ra1-2) — 'Incipit historia Anglorum edita a Gaufrido Monemutensi iussu Alexandri Linconiensis episcopi' — clearly indicating total ignorance of §§ 2-4; the deduction must rest solely on a reading of the preface (§§ 109-110) to the *Prophetia Merlini* embodied in the

Historia. And the text is continued directly (fo 59ra14) — with no more indication of a break than a new paragraph — by a series of excerpts from Bede's *Historia Ecclesiastica* to illustrate the Roman mission to convert the pagan Anglo-Saxons.[60]

THE BERN MANUSCRIPT

All these features can be explained by reference to another manuscript-copy of Geoffrey's *Historia* — Bern, Burgerbibliothek, MS. 568, a complex object, probably of Norman (and possibly of Fécamp) origin, written perhaps in the last quarter of the twelfth century. A detailed description of this codex may now be found elsewhere;[61] I therefore limit myself to consideration of the main features. The copying of the Galfridian text was scriptorium-work, with a number of collaborating scribes. Jacob Hammer, following (no doubt) an early idea that parts of this copy were in significantly later script, foolishly described it as a patched-up manuscript.[62] There is no reason whatsoever for crediting this view. All the scribal performances are consistent with a date in the last third of the twelfth century.

Of the three features, of the Rouen MS. U.74 text, mentioned above, only one — the Bedan appendix — is shared directly with the Bern copy. But the other two are explicable by a single fact. In Bern 568, §§1-5 of Geoffrey's *Historia* have been written on the second leaf of a bifolium constituting an independent quire preliminary to the body of the text. It is therefore open to us to suppose that the exemplar of Rouen MS. U.74 (1177) had lost such a preliminary leaf. This would explain both why the Rouen text begins with 'Eneas post . . .' (§6) and why its scribe evinced such ignorance of the information with which §§2-4 would have supplied him.

Jacob Hammer noted the close textual relationship between Bern MS. 568 and London, British Library, MS. Arundel 237, another twelfth-century copy of Geoffrey's *Historia*.[63] Differently from Rouen MS. U.74 (1177), the Arundel manuscript also illustrates the separable nature of §§1-5 in this branch of the textual tradition. Here again the text opens with §6 ('Eneas post . . .') which, it is clear from a late mediaeval foliation, has long been the beginning of the manuscript. Unfortunately, after the end of the eighth quire (fo 64v), the remainder of the text has been lost. It is, therefore, impossible to

---

60 I. 15, 23, 25, 26, 34; II. 1-3. For similar (but not identical) groups of excerpts, see Laistner & King, *A Hand-list*, pp.103-11.
61 Wright, *The Historia*, introduction.
62 'Remarks', p.525.
63 *Ibid.*; cf. Ward [& Herbert], *Catalogue of Romances*, I. 241.

know whether this copy finished with the Bedan appendix; in default of a complete collation with the Bern and Rouen manuscripts, the precise relationships must remain uncertain; but it is clear that in many of its readings it preserves a somewhat better text than the Bern copy of Geoffrey's *Historia*.[64] The principal interest of this copy, for the present purpose, is a note written at the head of fo 1r in a hand of the fourteenth or fifteenth century:[65] 'Require prologum folio .3. ante finem istius libri; qui incipit sic, "Dum mecum [multa]"'', 'Find the prologue, which begins with "Dum mecum [multa]", on the third last folio of this book'. The concluding leaves have, of course, been lost; but here is further evidence that in this branch of the text-history the prefatory matter was separable and subject to dislocation.

The absence of §§ 1-5 from the line of transmission represented by Rouen MS. U.74 (1177) may be put down to an accident resulting from their physical separability or to prudence on the part of a copyist mindful of the political troubles of the mid-twelfth century and the implications held by the dedications to King Stephen and Earl Robert.[66] What is clear, however, is that §§.1-5 had been lost before the scribe of the Rouen copy began to transcribe his exemplar, for his rubric displays a total innocence of their existence.

We may conclude, then, that the unique survival in Bern MS. 568 of the double dedication to King Stephen and Earl Robert is no indication that the branch of the textual history which it represents failed to circulate, as has sometimes been concluded.[67] We know already, notwithstanding our limited comprehension of Galfridian text-history, that at least three manuscripts have existed in this form: Bern 568, its exemplar, and BL Arundel 237; a slightly less restrictive view of the tradition would allow the hypothetical reconstruction of a further one or two copies.

It is clear, then, that in the second half of the twelfth century there was in circulation in Normandy[68] a text of the *Historia Regum Britanniae* among whose characteristics was (or had been) a joint-dedication to King Stephen and Robert, earl of Gloucester, with physically distinct presentation of §§ 1-5.[69] This text was quite

---

64 Hammer, 'Remarks', p. 525; cf. Wright, *The Historia*, introduction.

65 Ward [& Herbert], *Catalogue of Romances*, I. 241.

66 Davis, *King Stephen*, for the period in general; see pp. 78-9 on Normandy's 1144 crisis and its results.

67 Tatlock, *The Legendary History*, pp. 436-7.

68 And perhaps in England, depending on the origin of BL MS. Arundel 237.

69 It is curious that § 5, the description of Britain, is part of this matter, and one wonders about its significance for the work as a whole. It is worth noting that there are other surviving manuscripts which begin only with § 6: see the list of manuscripts in Griscom & Jones, *The Historia*, pp. 550-72.

distinct from another which circulated in Normandy and England in the same period, with Le Bec and Leiden MS. BPL 20 as the earliest known points of reference.[70] What, then, can be said of the version found in the Bern, Arundel, and Rouen manuscripts?

THE BERN VERSION OF THE *HISTORIA REGUM BRITANNIAE*

Jacob Hammer reserved some harsh words, not merely for the Bern manuscript, but also for its version of the *Historia*. By comparison with the printed vulgate text of Geoffrey's *magnum opus*, the Bern version was — he alleged — characterised by revision intended to portray Geoffrey's Saxons in a better light than the author had originally intended.[71] His remarks may be quoted *in extenso*.

While giving the variants of the Bern, both Faral and Griscom failed to call attention to one peculiar feature: Geoffrey is violently anti-Saxon. For Saxon *proditio* the Bern and Arundel MSS substitute *audacia, propositum* or *consilium*; the Saxon Eopa (or Eapa) who agreed to poison king Aurelius Ambrosius and who is referred to as "unus ex Saxonibus vocabulo Eopa," is called here simply "unus vocabulo Eopa." For *proditores* we find *homines* or *exterminatores*; for *nefandus Hengistus* we read *bellator Hengistus*; for *prodere* we read *occidere* (twice), *relinquere* or *vulnerare*. Such uncomplimentary references as *mentitae fidei Saxones* or *proditioni solitae indulgentes* are omitted entirely and once we find *reliquerunt* for the more insulting *fidem mentientes*. But the job of white-washing the Saxons was not thoroughly done, because the corrector either neglected or forgot to eliminate two references to "the accursed race" of the Saxons and one to their treason. This must be a case of "bonus dormitat Homerus." Now Professor E. Windisch states: "dass ein Mann, der Galfred heisst, die Saxones von sich aus so genannt habe (= nefandus populus), ist unwahrscheinlich: der Ausdruck ist im Stile des Gildas und Nennius und könnte im *liber vetustissimus* gestanden haben."[72] Gildas and Nennius, it is true, were anti-Saxon and Geoffrey may have followed suit. But since we have no *liber vetustissimus* and since the text of the Bern MS was not known in 1912, when Windisch wrote, another explanation for this changed attitude towards the Saxons is necessary. It does not seem probable to me that a scribe with Saxon sympathies is responsible for this not entirely successful attempt to whitewash the Saxons; such a scribe would have done his job more thoroughly. The responsibility for those textual changes rests in my opinion with Geoffrey. To promote his interests he did not hesitate to rededicate his work. He was ready, as will be seen below, to remove a patron's name altogether from the dedication when circumstances dictated such a course. It was, therefore, not beyond Geoffrey, who shortly after the appearance of his work rededicated it to Stephen and to Robert, to take into consideration the fact that Matilda, the daughter of the late king Henry the First, was the former wife of the German

---

[70] Leiden, UB, MS. BPL 20; London, BL, MS. Cotton Nero D.viii; Leiden, UB, MS. Voss. lat. F.77; Firenze, Biblioteca Laurenziana, MS. XVII.dextr.6.

[71] Hammer, 'Remarks', pp.525-6.

[72] Windisch, 'Das keltische Britannien', p.129, n.1.

emperor, Henry the Fifth. By doing so he wanted to be on both sides of the fence. I shall be glad to accept any other explanation which fits the facts.

As it stands, this is hardly a conclusive or even a convincing line of argument. It is not clear in which direction the changes have been made. And that the process is not consistent or complete seems terminal to this line of approach. It may have been noticed, one could aver, that Geoffrey's generally anti-Saxon line could have been made occasionally more pointed by sharpening some of his blander vocabulary. And that we see Geoffrey's hand in the revisions witnessed by the variations, between the Bern version and the printed text of the *Historia*, is an interesting idea, but no more than that; we shall require a full view of the text-history before any such notions can be seriously discussed or entertained. It must be said, however, that Hammer's view, that the very inconsistency of the variations favours authorial rather than scribal intervention in the text, seems to stand common sense on its head.

For the moment, then, we are thrown back on the prefatory chapters and must ask what information they can supply to us about the origins of the version represented principally by the Bern text. If we discount any notion that the combination of dedicatory chapters occurs by virtue of a scribe's scholarly or antiquarian instincts, we can apply some basic historical facts to interpretation of this version.

Chronology is the simplest of the matters to be discussed in this respect. The absolute outer limits of composition are — arguing solely from §§ 3-4 — December 1135 (the accession of King Stephen) and October 1147 (the death of Earl Robert).

The interrelationships of the various forms of the dedicatory chapters (§§ 3-4) present a much more complex and frustrating problem. Of the three known forms (to Earl Robert alone, to Earl Robert and Count Waleran, to King Stephen and Earl Robert) it is alone clear that one of the two versions which place Earl Robert in leading position must be original: the evidence which appears conclusive (and which could be undone only by production of contrary text-historical information displaying its absence from an early version of the *Historia*[73]) is the apostrophe of Earl Robert — as *consul auguste*, not by name — in § 177. That *consul* cannot be a suitable appellation for King Stephen seems self-evident; and that Robert is known as a patron of letters further suggests his appropriateness as the dedicatee of Geoffrey's work.

---

[73] Tatlock, *The Legendary History*, p. 427, n. 21, is in fact referring to the First Variant Version, for which see (for the moment) Hammer, *Geoffrey*.

19

Accepting that both the principal versions of §§ 3-4 were Geoffrey's work, Tatlock argued that the single dedication (to Robert) must be original and that the two double-dedications arose from the desire (or necessity) to offer presentation-copies.[74] While this argument embodies an unfortunate contradiction — those receiving presentation-copies (the second dedicatee in each case) would be Earl Robert and Count Waleran, not (as Tatlock apparently intended) Stephen and Waleran —, it undoubtedly points the way forward.

The dedication to King Stephen presumably results from the preparation of a special copy for presentation to him, no doubt (as Griscom thought) on one of his many visits to Oxford.[75] Some would think that a joint-dedication to Stephen and Robert must have important chronological implications, being possible only until June 1138 when Robert renounced his allegiance to Stephen and the civil war began;[76] but reasons will be given below for ruling out such a deduction.[77] The description of Robert as *altera regni nostri columna* (§ 4) is appropriate enough for either such an important descendant of King Henry I or the leader of Matilda's party. On the other hand, the double-dedication to Robert and Waleran is difficult to explain in terms of the careers of the two men,[78] and the possibility may emerge from a tentative history of the circulation of the text that the Robert-Waleran dedication could have originated in the circle of Count Waleran himself. The order would then be (i) Robert, (ii) Stephen-Robert, (iii) Robert-Waleran. But textual evidence might make this hypothetical sequence very difficult to sustain.[79]

A very different hypothesis is also possible, however. This would reject the notion that the king could be described, by implication, as *columna regni*.[80] A form of § 4 which described the second dedicatee as *'altera* regni nostri columna' would therefore be appropriate only in combination with a primary dedication to Earl Robert. The Robert-Waleran double-dedication would therefore have to be antecedent to that to Stephen and Robert; the latter would be a reworking of the

---

74 Tatlock, *The Legendary History*, pp.436-7. It is perhaps doubtful that the Robert-Waleran double-dedication could be original in view of the internal apostrophe of a single *consul*: see below, p. 27.

75 Griscom, 'The date of composition', pp.141, 152-5; cf. Tatlock, *The Legendary History*, p.437, n.17, who points out that Griscom's precision is wrong-headed.

76 Davis, *King Stephen*, p.37, on the immediate political situation.

77 See below, pp. 25-7.

78 Cf. n.82 below.

79 It is exceedingly difficult to see the Robert-Waleran double-dedication as a rewriting of the Stephen-Robert version. (Nor is the single dedication to Robert likely to have derived from the dedication to Stephen.)

80 Cf. Griscom, 'The date of composition', pp.150-1.

former,[81] giving the order (i) Robert, (ii) Robert-Waleran, (iii) Stephen-Robert. This assumes continued acceptance of the (by no means wholly conclusive) argument that the single (rather than the Robert-Waleran) dedication is primary; and the difficulty of explaining the circumstances of the Robert-Waleran double-dedication remains.

This discussion makes it plain, I think, that the chronological limits for the writing of the *Historia* remain December 1135 (unless we insist that, if the single dedication to Earl Robert is original, it carries with it no necessary implication that King Henry I has already died[82]) and January 1139 when Robert of Torigni showed the work to Henry of Huntingdon at Le Bec. For the Bern version, however (since it was not necessarily that version which Henry saw), the later terminus remains the death of Robert in October 1147.[83]

It was once thought that the Bern manuscript itself was (on the evidence of its palaeography) testimony to the earliness of the version, perhaps even that it might have been the presentation-copy for Stephen.[84] But the codicology and the palaeography of the volume both make this impossible. The Bern copy of the *Historia* gives the impression — although this is scarcely susceptible of proof — that it was written hastily and carelessly; and the quality of the parchment is not always good.[85] On these grounds alone it is an unlikely presentation-copy. Some play has been made with the fact that the script of §§ 1-5 is rather different from what follows: but in fact this argument has been overdone, for the scribe is found elsewhere in this copy of the *Historia* but writing a less formal grade of minuscule.[86] That this prefatory matter occurs on an independent bifolium[87] is significant for the textual history of the version rather than for the Bern manuscript itself.[88] And finally, in respect of codi-

---

81 In fact, Griscom (*ibid.*, pp.146-54) shows conclusively that the Stephen-Robert double-dedication is a rather crude rewriting of that to Robert and Waleran.

82 Robert became earl of Gloucester in 1120, and Alexander succeeded to the bishopric of Lincoln in 1123. These are in fact the only absolutely secure evidence for the *terminus post quem*. On the relationship of Robert and Waleran *ca* 1130, see the remarks of Griscom, *ibid.*, pp.138-9; cf. Tatlock, *The Legendary History*, p.436, but also Madden, 'The Historia Britonum', p.309.

83 The Robert-Waleran double-dedication remains problematic (above, pp.20-1).

84 Cf. Griscom, 'The date of composition', p.152 and n.2.

85 I agree with Griscom, *ibid.*, p.136. I am greatly indebted to Dr Christoph von Steiger (Burgerbibliothek, Bern) for his many kindnesses in connexion with my studies of this manuscript since 1972.

86 Against Griscom, *ibid.*

87 Not a single leaf, as Griscom, *ibid.*, pp.134-5, 136.

88 See above, pp.16-18.

cology, it is apparent that this copy of the *Historia* was physically prefixed to an already existing copy of Aelred of Rievaulx's *Vita Edwardi* (composed in 1162/3). The hypothesis that the Bern manuscript was a presentation-copy for Stephen or Robert is therefore quite incredible. The evidence of palaeography has also been confusingly deployed. W. L. Jones described Bern MS. 568 as being 'certainly as old a MS. of the History as any we know' but quoted the opinion of that excellent palaeographer, George Warner, to the effect that the handwriting of the several scribes was to be dated 'somewhere about 1160'.[89] Griscom wrote that 'all the hands are contemporaneous and closely resemble those appearing in facsimiles of handwriting dating before the middle of the twelfth century'.[90] But Griscom persistently confuses the dating of the versions of the text with that of the manuscripts which attest to those versions.[91] And he even went so far as to conjecture that Bern MS. 568, fo 18r/v, is in Geoffrey's own hand![92] The script can now be seen, in fact, to belong to the last third of the twelfth century; the evidence of its physical union with an already extant copy of Aelred's *Vita Edwardi* confirms this chronology. And it is at least as likely (on the evidence of script) that it was written in Normandy (perhaps at Fécamp) as that it is what Griscom's hypothesis would require, an Oxford manuscript.

The Bern version of the *Historia* is therefore datable to before October 1147 and is a version of a text which is itself datable (between *ca* 1130[93] and January 1139 and) most probably before 1138. It is now known from three manuscripts, two of which seem to have been written in Normandy by *ca* 1200. Its relationship to the original form of the *Historia* remains for the moment uncertain.

The next stage of our enquiry must be to attempt some deductions as to the history of this version between its point of origin in Stephen's reign and its appearance in the surviving copies. To the extent that nothing is known about the origin of BL MS. Arundel 237, this effectively means tracing the prehistory of the version in Bern MS. 568 and Rouen MS. U.74 (1177).[94] Their extreme closeness suggests very strongly that they derive from a common exemplar, but one which

[89] Jones, 'Geoffrey of Monmouth', p.67.
[90] Griscom, 'The date of composition', p.136.
[91] *Ibid.*, pp.136-8.
[92] *Ibid.*, p.152, n.2.
[93] Tatlock, *The Legendary History*, pp.435-6.
[94] Collation of their texts displays the exceptional closeness of Rouen and Bern, and the superiority in some respects of Arundel. See Figure III. See also now Wright, *The Historia*, introduction.

must have lost the bifolium containing §§ 1-5 between the copying from it of Bern (at Fécamp?) and, probably about a quarter-century later, Rouen (probably at Jumièges). It is of course possible that more copies intervened, but this minimal genealogy would in fact suffice to explain the evidence.

The common exemplar can be given only an approximate *terminus ante quem*, perhaps *ca* 1160, or at any rate the 1160s as a whole. What can be said about the two or three decades of the version's prehistory which must still be accounted for?

We know that during the twelfth century there was extensive circulation of historical and pseudo-historical texts between Norman churches, particularly the Benedictine foundations. Robert of Torigni, first at Le Bec and then at Mont-Saint-Michel, has always seemed to be the central figure, but we must not assume that he was the sole driving force in this intellectual movement. Apart from the surviving and hypothesised members of the Bern group, we have independent evidence for the former existence of three copies of the *Historia Regum Britanniae* in Normandy in the quarter-century 1139-64. The first was the copy shown by Robert of Torigni to Henry of Huntingdon at Le Bec in January 1139: for the moment at least, we know little of its characteristics.[95] The second is the extant book, Leiden UB MS. BPL 20, written at Le Bec itself and containing a version which, I have suggested, shows signs of revision by Robert himself. If this were the same as the copy shown to Henry in 1139, we should have to suppose that Robert had reacted with remarkable rapidity to the availability to him of a copy (now lost or unidentified) which he then caused to be copied in his house-scriptorium and whose text he subjected to some revision; the script and decoration of the Leiden manuscript would in any case perhaps sit better with a slightly later date. It is curious that the Leiden manuscript has the single dedication (§ 3), to Robert of Gloucester; in view of the sometime position of Waleran of Meulan as patron or lay protector of the monastery of Le Bec,[96] one might perhaps have expected to find there a copy with the Robert-Waleran double-dedication. One is left to wonder whether a dedication to Waleran might have been suppressed in the period 1139 x 1141 when Waleran was King Stephen's right-hand man or even after 1144 when he was no longer obviously the 'second pillar of the realm' in a Normandy now dominated by the house of Anjou.

---

[95] Close, critical investigation of the Letter to Warinus must be the first step in this process.
[96] Farrer, *An Outline Itinerary*, p.138, no.648, of July-August 1131.

The third copy known to have been in the Le Bec library at this period was bequeathed thither by Philippe de Harcourt, bishop of Bayeux (*ob.* February 1164). It is item 44 in the catalogue of Philippe's bequest, being recorded thus:

Vita Alexandri
Historia Britonum.

That this book yet survives is most unlikely, but in its association with the *Vita Alexandri* it conforms to a known pattern. *Historia Britonum* is the usual title given to Geoffrey's work in mediaeval library-catalogues and need not provoke thoughts of the pseudo-Nennian work.

Philippe de Harcourt had had a long and varied career before he was made bishop of Bayeux in 1142; but the constant element in that career is his relationship with a patron, Count Waleran of Meulan, and (more generally) with that Beaumont family. His career in England (as dean of Lincoln) began at about the time, 1129, when Waleran had been released from imprisonment and restored to favour by King Henry I;[97] he rose with Waleran, and, at the time when the latter's influence was dominant with King Stephen, Philippe was made Chancellor of England (June 1139 to March 1140) and then nominated by Stephen for the bishopric of Salisbury.[98] When Waleran withdrew to Normandy in 1141 to protect his patrimony, Philippe (whose consecration had been blocked by Henri de Blois, bishop of Winchester and papal legate) seems to have withdrawn also, being soon rewarded with preferment in Normandy.[99] Throughout his career as an ecclesiastical office-holder in Normandy, he seems to have had links with Le Bec, these ties (which no doubt originated in the context of Waleran's relationship with the abbey) culminating in his splendid bequests.[100]

The possible sources of Philippe's copy of Geoffrey's *Historia* are therefore many and various. He could have obtained it from Le Bec in the first place. The book may already in his lifetime have been widely in circulation in France and Normandy, and therefore reasonably readily available, especially to a widely travelled bishop. Philippe held office for at least a decade in the diocese of Lincoln,[101] where that Bishop Alexander then held sway (1123-48) who was a patron

97 *Ibid.*, p.124.
98 Davis, *King Stephen*, pp.32 and 47.
99 Greenway, *John Le Neve, Fasti Ecclesiae Anglicanae 1066-1300*, III. 8, 114, 152, 153, 154, on Philippe's offices and dates.
100 Porée, *Histoire*, I. 93, 402, 416, 525.
101 See n.99 above.

24

of Geoffrey of Monmouth and Henry of Huntingdon. But a further possibility may seem the most promising, and could perhaps lead us back to the Bern version of the *Historia*.

The motives for the double-dedication to Stephen and Robert have remained obscure. If we assume (and it is difficult to do otherwise) that Geoffrey himself was responsible for adapting it from the Robert-Waleran double-dedication, we have to conclude further that Geoffrey wished his book to come to the attention of the king or at any rate his principal ministers. If he did this simply in hopes of preferment, the act can hardly be dated later than mid-1138 when Robert defied the king. But if the *Historia* carried a message directed to the two sides in an impending (and subsequently actual) civil war, the *terminus ante quem* becomes less clear. The original double-dedication to Robert and Waleran could then hardly post-date 1141 when Waleran left the king to return permanently to Normandy. But it would be difficult, on this hypothesis, to deny the possibility that the Stephen-Robert dedication could be as late as 1147. We shall return to the question of the purpose of the *Historia*.

Dedication to the king, for whatever motive, would almost certainly involve the submission of a presentation-copy to him or, more likely, to one of his court-officials. That we do not have that copy (unless perhaps it be BL MS. Arundel 237) is regrettable. We are therefore obliged to conjecture what its history might have been. Stephen is known to modern historians, whether rightly or wrongly, as a warrior-politician, not as a patron of letters.[102] In the absence of a royal library, we may suspect, an interested court-official would end up in possession of any presentation-copy of a literary work dedicated to the king.

On two counts we might suppose that Philippe de Harcourt would have had the chance of access to presentation-copies of the *Historia*. As a principal dependant of Waleran of Meulan he might have come into possession of a copy presented to Waleran before 1141. But as the king's chancellor in 1140/1 he could have had the opportunity to acquire the original copy dedicated to Stephen and Robert (especially if it had not been well received by Stephen!).

As far as we have been able to observe it, the circulation of the Bern version was Norman. Yet it was in Normandy that Stephen's power was completely and irreversibly broken within the first decade of his reign. It is difficult to know what conclusion, if any, to draw from this juxtaposition of the facts. The lack of an observed English

---

102 Madden, 'The Historia Britonum', p.301; cf. Griscom, 'The date of composition', p.152.

25

tradition of this version implies that it gained no circulation at all until it was carried into Normandy, but that — once there — it belonged to a library accessible to a Benedictine transcriber. The hypothesis that Philippe de Harcourt was the agent of transmission solves a number of problems. He could have had access to the presumed original, his base of operations was transferred to Normandy in 1141/2, he gained a position in the Norman hierarchy, he retained his role as a man of letters and collector of books, and he bequeathed his library to Le Bec whence any of the texts which he owned could have been disseminated. There may have been other such men, but they must have been few at best.

If the hypothesis should be admissible — though not, of course, provable without more direct evidence — then the further conclusion could follow that the version had been created by 1141 at the latest. Given the secondary nature of the dedicatory chapters (§§ 3-4) in the Bern version, these very hypothetical conclusions would point to a greater likelihood that the work, with the double-dedications, was composed before the outbreak of civil hostilities, than that it is to be seen as a reaction to such strife.

Such arguments, though speculative, are nonetheless a necessary background to consideration of the purpose of the *Historia Regum Britanniae* and the bearing of the dedicatory prefaces on that issue. Only one question need concern us here. Can the *Historia* be seen — as has been persuasively argued[103] — as an exemplum constituting, in effect, an appeal to two sides in a potential or actual civil war to see the advantages of unity in the light of the dire consequences of former occasions of internecine conflict? Much evidence may be — indeed, has been — drawn from the text to support such a reading; but it would be fair to say that quite different readings ('mockery and mischief', for example)[104] might deserve comparable prominence, given the present state of scholarship, for literary critical study of Geoffrey's work has scarcely begun.

For the immediate purpose, the importance of this reading of the *Historia*, as an appeal for national unity, is that, as long as such a view remains a possibility, it inhibits us from arguing that the mutual friendliness or hostility of the dedicatees is relevant to the question of dating. From the moment in 1120 when the succession to King Henry I began to look uncertain, the prospect of civil war and the principal protagonists therein must have been a frequent topic of

---

103 Cf. Schirmer, *Die frühen Darstellungen*, pp. 7-40, and Pähler, *Strukturuntersuchungen*.
104 Brooke, 'Geoffrey of Monmouth', p. 82.

conversation. By the time of Henry's death late in 1135 it must have been clear who those protagonists would be. On the appeal-for-unity reading, then, at any date down to the withdrawal of Waleran in 1141 or the death of Robert of Gloucester in 1147, the respective double-dedications would make sense.

If that interpretation should be rejected, however, the traditional criteria for dating the *Historia* would begin to reassert themselves.[105] It would become crucial to know at what point hostilities had come to be perceived as inevitable. But here experts in the subject have differed.[106] Professor R. H. C. Davis, a biographer of King Stephen, has given his view that by the beginning of 1138 hostilities must have been universally expected.[107] That would confine both of the double-dedications within a very narrow time-span — 1136 and 1137, in effect. If the single dedication to Earl Robert was original, the *terminus post quem* could in theory be made considerably earlier, but the double-dedications would still be constrained within 1136-7. If the single dedication, occurring in the great majority of manuscripts, were a later development, it would have to reflect either Geoffrey's rapidly throwing in his lot with the anti-Stephen cause (which would in itself be a denial of the appeal-for-unity reading) or rapid accommodation to local political realities in the centre from which the principal manuscript-tradition was early disseminated. This latter view would require much indulgence: on the whole it seems easiest to suppose that the single dedication to Robert was original and usual, and that the double-dedications require special circumstances to explain them. If so, then the publication of the *Historia* itself can hardly be placed later than 1137 and might just conceivably considerably antedate 1135. But interpretation, of the passage in which the *consul* is apostrophised, in the light of the events of 1135 seems not without merit.[108] On these arguments, publication of the *Historia* is indeed to be confined to the period 1136/7.

What we lack at the moment is a knowledge of how the various branches of the vulgate *Historia* developed. Too many manuscripts and too little study of them have together retarded our appreciation of the circulation of this late mediaeval best-seller. Means have yet to be found for differentiating the mass of manuscripts with the single dedication, although my remarks above on Leiden BPL 20 perhaps

---

[105] Cf. the discussions of Griscom, 'The date of composition', and Tatlock, *The Legendary History*, pp.433-7.

[106] Brooke, 'Geoffrey of Monmouth', p.87.

[107] 'In 1138 it would surely have been clear to all that civil war was on the way': in a letter of 23 July, 1981, quoted by kind permission of Professor Davis.

[108] Cf. Tatlock, *The Legendary History*, pp.426-7.

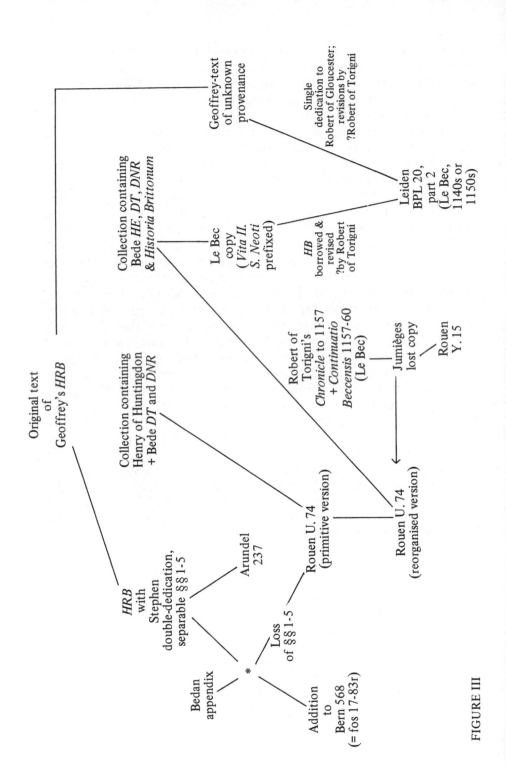

FIGURE III

point to one possible line of approach.[109] It is clear, from the evidence of the Bern group, that to classify copies by the presence or absence of dedicatory or preliminary matter is foolhardy.[110] In the unlikely event that copies with the single dedication derive in any number from a copy or copies with a double-dedication, that must have been the Robert-Waleran pair. Hammer has pointed out that even the eight copies with that double-dedication are not textually homogeneous as a group.[111] Under all these circumstances it is apparent that the witnesses to the Bern version attest the only text which can so far be assigned a definable history. As it stands, it cannot (given §§ 3-4) be the original text of the *Historia*. But whether that conclusion must be true also of the body of its text is a matter for considerable discussion; where it differs in substance from the standard printed texts, are those variations to be associated with the change of dedication or do they have a textually longer pedigree?

Answers for all these problems can come only by intensive study of the manuscripts and text-history of the *Historia*. But what is the student of the *Historia* to do in the meantime? It seems clear that the cause of Galfridian scholarship would be best served by a straightforward edition of the one identifiable version; and this version has a pedigree which must carry it back into the reign of Stephen (before October 1147, the death of Earl Robert) and possibly into the first two years of that reign. It is, in other words, the nearest thing to a fixed point in Galfridian text-history; as a result, it requires sympathetic and critical consideration.[112] Other aspects of the textual tradition can then be defined in relation to this fixed point. Discussion might centre on whether the text reported to Warinus Brito by Henry of Huntingdon was a copy of the Bern version or not. It would be interesting to know how the version certainly at Le Bec *ca* 1150 (in Leiden BPL 20) related to both of these fixed points. One could continue with such suggestions. But the first requirement is a new text of this early version so that students of Arthurian literature may begin to become familiar with the problems to which its existence draws attention.

---

[109] See pp. 2-6 and 23 above.
[110] See pp.16-18 above.
[111] 'Remarks', p.525.
[112] That it is now receiving from Mr Neil Wright: see his *The Historia*.

APPENDIX I

The date of Robert of Torigni's Chronicle

Robert of Torigni was a monk of Le Bec from 1128 to 1154; within that period he was Prior from 1149 to 1154. In the latter year he became abbot of Mont-Saint-Michel, an office which he held until his death in 1186.[113] One of the more considerable figures of intellectual history in twelfth-century Normandy, Robert gained fame as much for his revision and extension of the works of other writers as for his own original composition;[114] but his considerable abilities as an administrator were also at the service of learning and he seems to have been responsible for encouraging both considerable scriptorial activity at Le Bec and the circulation of texts, particularly historical texts, among the Benedictine monasteries of Normandy. On all these counts he is of great interest in the present context. His hand must be seen in a further dimension of intellectual activity, the execution and maintenance of the elaborate library-catalogue of Le Bec, the extant text of which is discussed in appendix II.

Among his works of revision and continuation is to be numbered the extension and supplementation of the world-chronicle of Sigebert of Gembloux, which came to be known as the 'Chronicle of Robert of Torigni'.[115] In a masterly survey of eighteen manuscript-witnesses to this Chronicle, Léopold Delisle sought to show how the tradition of the work may be defined in terms of three principal recensions. Notwithstanding such extensive treatment by a master of the subject, the dating and development of Robert's Chronicle remain rather obscure. Since the question impinges upon, and is touched by, some of the issues of textual transmission studied above, it has seemed worthwhile to pursue the matter further here.

Although we possess some seven manuscripts of what Delisle has called the first recension,[116] there is some impressive evidence that none of these fairly represents Robert's original Chronicle. What might have provided the most primitive text — London, British Library, MS.

---

113 For an account of Robert of Torigni, his career and writings, see Delisle, *Chronique*, II. i-xix.
114 The Chronicle is such an adaptation of an earlier work; cf. also his version of the *Gesta Normannorum Ducum* (van Houts, *Gesta, passim*).
115 Edited by Delisle, *Chronique*.
116 Delisle's MSS. ABHJLSW.

Arundel 18 — is in fact so defective that the whole of the Chronicle has been lost from it. But this manuscript has a rubric which describes Robert (as author of the Chronicle) as *Beccensis monachus* and refers therefore to the years before 1154 when he succeeded to the abbacy of Mont-Saint-Michel, or perhaps indeed to the period before 1149 when he became Prior of Le Bec.[117] A further indication that he first wrote the Chronicle before his move to Mont-Saint-Michel is provided by a letter directed by Robert in 1183 to the abbot of Le Bec: it accompanied a copy of the part of his Chronicle covering 1154-1182, the extent of this copy being determined by what he thought was at Le Bec, namely coverage to the end of 1153.[118] (He left for Mont-Saint-Michel in 1154, presumably before the annal for that year had been written.) In fact, Le Bec must have had a copy extending into 1157, given the evidence of the *Continuatio Beccensis*, 1157-1160, which was written in 1160/1.[119]

Further, in the preface to the Chronicle, Robert wrote that he was bringing the Chronicle to 1150 (this date is found in MSS. BHJFLM* according to Delisle, being corrected only in the third-recension version represented by MSS. BoCaM^C where we read '1182' instead).[120] Here we might think that we have discovered the original date of composition. Reference to Delisle's MS. S (written in the second half of the twelfth century and probably at Savigny) whose text, though somewhat abbreviated and interpolated, probably represents the earliest *surviving* form of the Chronicle, shows that here it has a rather different version of the preface, avoiding a concluding date.[121] It is open to us to deduce that the date '1150' arises merely from a subsequently influential copy having been made in that year.

At all events, it seems to be clear that the original endeavour antedates 1150 and perhaps Robert's succession to the office of Prior in 1149. A further piece of evidence suggests much the same, though less precisely. Robert tells us, at the end of his preface, that he drew on Henry of Huntingdon's *Historia Anglorum*. In MS. S we read that Robert has used 'historiam eiusdem de regibus Anglorum, incipiens eam a Iulio Cesare et texens usque ad mortem regis Henrici'.[122] In the other copies, the same statement is made, if rather more wordily:[123]

---

117 *Ibid.*, I. iii-iv.
118 *Ibid.*, I. xlii-xliii; II. xviii and 340-1.
119 *Ibid.*, II. 137-46, 165-80.
120 *Ibid.*, I. 96 and n.1.
121 *Ibid.*, I. 94-5 and note.
122 *Ibid.*, I. 95, note.
123 *Ibid.*, I. 97.

et historia predicti Henrici archidiaconi, quam composuit de regibus Anglie, incipiens eam a Iulio Cesare, et texens ordinatim usque ad mortem predicti regis Henrici, id est usque ad millesimum centesimum tricesimum quintum annum dominice incarnationis.

He used an edition of Henry of Huntingdon's *Historia Anglorum* which brought the story down to A. D. 1135. 1135 and 1150 seem therefore to be the termini for the composition of the Chronicle, unless we should wish to hypothesise that an earlier, lost recension would not have been indebted thus to Henry.[124] If we could determine by what date Robert had received the new edition of Henry's *Historia*, extending in ten books to 1147, we should be able to give further definition to the dating. Le Bec owned a copy of the ten-book version by the time when the twelfth-century library-catalogue assumed its present form (where item 132 reads 'In alio historia Henrici de gente Anglorum libri X');[125] this may have been an antecedent of Paris, B.N., lat. 6042 (or even that book itself), which latter was certainly in Robert's hands at Mont-Saint-Michel by the 1170s.[126] At the moment, further precision as to date eludes us. However, incorporated in the earliest *surviving* version of Robert's Chronicle are excerpts from the 1147 edition of Henry's *Historia*.[127] If we are not to date the original Chronicle to 1147 x 1150 (and explain away the reference to the '1135' edition of Henry's *Historia*), we must suppose that some substantial changes were made to the text, with the aid of Henry's edition of 1147, in or antecedent to the common ancestor of all extant copies of the Chronicle.

If it can be agreed that the earliest surviving text rests on a recension created in 1147 x 1150,[128] yet which was not the original version of the Chronicle, we can proceed to the question of the maintenance and circulation of the work thereafter. What has been seen as a represen-

---

124 But that would be perverse; it could perfectly well have been so, but − in the absence of evidence − there is no sense in making such an extravagant conjecture.

125 Omont, *Catalogue général*, II. 393.

126 Delisle, *Chronique*, I. lv-lxi.

127 *Ibid.*, I. 117-19.

128 We find Henry's ten-book *Historia* travelling with a collection of episcopal lists datable to 1148/9 (see above, pp. 9-13). Given the existence of a copy of the ten-book text in the Le Bec library-catalogue (item 132), we may wonder whether Robert gained rapid access to such a manuscript. Unfortunately the text-history (see Figures I-II and pp. 13-15 above) gives insufficiently precise help in this regard. The date for the episcopal lists does not therefore bear seriously on the present question: if Robert had gained both texts together, he is unlikely to have received the ten-book *Historia* before 1149, but that is all.

tative of the most primitive form of the text, Delisle's MS. S, brings the Chronicle down to the year 1156 for which it had originally a single sentence.[129] However primitive the underlying form of the text, the extant copy represents an abbreviated text made at Savigny later in the twelfth century. The single-sentence entry for 1156 in fact corresponds to the first two entries in other manuscripts,[130] and it is most notable that Delisle's MS. M (Avranches, Bibliothèque municipale, MS. 159), made under the author's supervision at Mont-Saint-Michel and used as the basis for the revised edition of 1182-6, originally ended on fo 206v at this very point (concluding . . . *subsecutus est*).[131] This suggests recognition of a major stratum-line in the continuing revision, augmentation, and circulation of the Chronicle. Other copies of Delisle's 'first recension' extend to the end of the annal for 1157 – one, MS. H (London, B.L., Harley 651) to within one sentence of the end (to . . . *militibus Templi*),[132] the others (MSS. BJ and presumably LW)[133] to the very end (. . . *et uocatus est Richardus*). All this evidence suggests that, at least in the decade up to 1157, repeated modifications of the Chronicle, perhaps on a year-by-year basis, were the rule. After 1157 a local continuation was made at Le Bec for 1157 *ex.* -1160, being found now in Chronicle MSS. JLW.[134] At Mont-Saint-Michel, where the author now resided, only bursts of activity in 1169 (the 'second recension') and 1182 (the 'third recension') seem clearly attested.[135] Perhaps the text-historical evidence is sufficient to suggest that in the concluding four or five years of his life Robert once again took a close, continuing interest in his Chronicle.[136]

---

[129] Delisle, *Chronique*, I. iv-vii and 296, n. 5.
[130] Compare Delisle, *ibid.*, I. 296, n. 5, with I. 296-7 (main text).
[131] *Ibid.*, I. xlv-liii (at pp. l-li) and 297 & n. 3.
[132] *Ibid.*, I. vii-viii and 310.
[133] *Ibid.*, I. ix-xiii and xiii-xvii on MSS. B and J; LW are close relatives of these, but Delisle does not specify the precise point at which their texts end.
[134] *Ibid.*, II. 137-46, 165-80, where Chronicle MS. W becomes *Continuatio* MS. V.
[135] On these recensions, see Delisle, *ibid.*, I. xxiii-lv.
[136] *Ibid.*, I. xlii-lv.

BIBLIOGRAPHY

ARNOLD, Thomas (ed.)   *Henrici Archidiaconi Huntendunensis Historia Anglorum. The History of the English, by Henry, Archdeacon of Huntingdon, from A.C. 55 to A.D.1154, in Eight Books* (London 1879)

AVRIL, F.   'La décoration des manuscrits au Mont Saint-Michel (XIe-XIIe siècles)', in *Millénaire monastique du Mont Saint-Michel*, II, ed. R. Foreville (Paris 1967), pp. 203-38

AVRIL, F.   'Notes sur quelques manuscrits bénédictins normands du XIe et du XIIe siècle', *Mélanges d'archéologie et d'histoire (École française de Rome)* 76 (1964) 491-525 *and* 77 (1965) 209-48

BECKER, Gustav (ed.)   *Catalogi Bibliothecarum Antiqui* (Bonn 1885)

BROOKE, C. N. L.   'Geoffrey of Monmouth as a historian', in *Church and Government in the Middle Ages*, edd. C. N. L. Brooke *et al.* (Cambridge 1976), pp. 77-91

BROOKE, Z. N.   *The English Church and the Papacy from the Conquest to the Reign of John* (Cambridge 1931)

CHIBNALL, M.   'Orderic Vitalis and Robert of Torigni', in *Millénaire monastique du Mont Saint-Michel*, II, ed. R. Foreville (Paris 1967), pp. 133-9

CHIBNALL, Marjorie (ed. & transl.)   *The Ecclesiastical History of Orderic Vitalis* (6 vols, Oxford 1969-80)

COLGRAVE, Bertram & MYNORS, R. A. B. (edd. & transl.)   *Bede's Ecclesiastical History of the English People* (Oxford 1969)

DAVIS, R. H. C.   *King Stephen 1135-1154* (London 1967)

DELISLE, L.   'Anciens catalogues des évêques des églises de France', in *Histoire littéraire de la France*, t. 29 (Paris 1885), pp. 386-443

DELISLE, Léopold (ed.)   *Chronique de Robert de Torigni, abbé du Mont-Saint-Michel, suivie de divers opuscules historiques de cet auteur et de plusieurs religieux de la même abbaye* (2 vols, Rouen 1872/3)

DELISLE, Léopold   *Mélanges de paléographie et de bibliographie* (Paris 1880)

DUMVILLE, David & KEYNES, S. (gen. edd.)   *The Anglo-Saxon Chronicle. A Collaborative Edition* (23 vols, Cambridge 1983-)

DUMVILLE, David N. (ed.)   *The Historia Brittonum* (10 vols, Cambridge 1985-)

DUMVILLE, D. N.   'The manuscripts of Geoffrey of Monmouth's *Historia Regum Britanniae*', *Arthurian Literature* 3 (1983) 113-28

DUMVILLE, D. N.   'The origin of the *C*-text of the Variant Version of the *Historia Regum Britannie*', *Bulletin of the Board of Celtic Studies* 26 (1974-6) 315-22

FARAL, Edmond (ed.)   *La légende arthurienne. Études et documents* (3 vols, Paris 1929)

FARRER, William   *An Outline Itinerary of King Henry the First* (Oxford 1919)

FRAPPIER, J.   [Review of J. Hammer (ed.), *Geoffrey of Monmouth* (1951)], *Romania* 74 (1953) 125-8

GIBSON, Margaret   *Lanfranc of Bec* (Oxford 1978)

GLEASON, Sarell Everett   *An Ecclesiastical Barony of the Middle Ages: the Bishopric of Bayeux, 1066-1204* (Cambridge, Mass. 1936)

GREENWAY, Diana E.   *John Le Neve, Fasti Ecclesiae Anglicanae 1066-1300*, III, *Lincoln* (London 1977)

GRISCOM, A.   'The date of composition of Geoffrey of Monmouth's *Historia*: new manuscript evidence', *Speculum* 1 (1926) 129-56

34

GRISCOM, Acton & JONES, R. E. (edd.)   *The Historia Regum Britanniae of Geoffrey of Monmouth with Contributions to the Study of its Place in Early British History* (New York 1929)

HAMMER, Jacob (ed.)   *Geoffrey of Monmouth,* Historia Regum Britanniae. *A Variant Version* (Cambridge, Mass. 1951)

HAMMER, J.   'Remarks on the sources and textual history of Geoffrey of Monmouth's *Historia Regum Britanniae* with an excursus on the *Chronica Polonorum* of Wincenty Kadlubek (Magister Vincentius)', *Bulletin of the Polish Institute of Arts and Sciences in America* 2 (1943/4) 501-64

HARDWICK, C. & LUARD, H. R. (edd.)   *A Catalogue of the Manuscripts preserved in the Library of the University of Cambridge* (6 vols, Cambridge 1856-67)

HERMANS, J. M. M. & VAN HOUTS, E. M. C.   'The history of a membrum disiectum of the Gesta Normannorum Ducum, now Vatican, Reg. Lat. 733 fol. 51*', *Mededelingen van het Nederlands Instituut te Rome*, N.S., 9/10 (1982/3) 79-94 and 219-26

HUNTER BLAIR, Peter & MYNORS, R. A. B. (facs. edd.)   *The Moore Bede. Cambridge University Library MS. Kk. 5. 16* (Copenhagen 1959)

JONES, C. W. (ed.)   *Bedae Venerabilis Opera, Pars VI: Opera Didascalia,* 3 (Turnhout 1980)

JONES, W. L.   'Geoffrey of Monmouth', *Transactions of the Honourable Society of Cymmrodorion* (1898/9) 52-95

KER, N. R.   *Medieval Manuscripts in British Libraries* (4 vols, Oxford 1969-   )

LAISTNER, M. L. W. & KING, H. H.   *A Hand-list of Bede Manuscripts* (Ithaca, N.Y. 1943)

LAPORTE, J.   'Les listes abbatiales de Jumièges', in *Jumièges. Congrès scientifique du XIIIe centenaire, Rouen, 10-12 juin 1954,* I (Rouen 1955), pp.435-66

MABILLON, J. (ed.)   *Acta Sanctorum Ordinis Sancti Benedicti,* t.IV. 2 (Paris 1680)

MADDEN, F.   'The Historia Britonum of Geoffrey of Monmouth', *Archaeological Journal* 15 (1858) 299-312

MARSHALL, P. K., *et al.*   'Clare College MS. 26 and the circulation of Aulus Gellius 1 7 in medieval England and France', *Mediaeval Studies* 42 (1980) 353-94

MATHIEU, M.   'Le manuscrit 162 d'Avranches et l'édition princeps des Gesta Roberti Wiscardi de Guillaume d'Apulie', *Byzantion* 24 (1954) 111-30

MATHIEU, M.   'Le manuscrit 162 d'Avranches ou Robert de Torigni et Robert Guiscard', *Sacris Erudiri* 17 (1966) 66-70

NORTIER, Geneviève   *Les bibliothèques médiévales des abbayes bénédictines de Normandie* (2nd edn, Paris 1971)

OMONT, Henri   *Catalogue général des manuscrits des bibliothèques publiques de France, Départements,* I-II (Paris 1886/8)

PÄHLER, Heinrich   *Strukturuntersuchungen zur 'Historia Regum Britanniae' des Geoffrey of Monmouth* (Bonn 1958)

PORÉE, [-]   *Histoire de l'abbaye du Bec* (2 vols, Évreux 1901)

SCHIRMER, Walter F.   *Die frühen Darstellungen des Arthurstoffes* (Köln 1958)

TATLOCK, J. S. P.   'Geoffrey of Monmouth's *Vita Merlini*', *Speculum* 18 (1943) 265-87

TATLOCK, J. S. P.   *The Legendary History of Britain. Geoffrey of Monmouth's Historia Regum Britanniae and its Early Vernacular Versions* (Berkeley, Cal. 1950)

VAN HOUTS, Elisabeth Maria Cornelia   *Gesta Normannorum Ducum. Een Studie over de Handschriften, de Tekst, het Geschiedwerk en het Genre* (Groningen 1982)

WARD, H. L. D. & HERBERT, J. A.   *Catalogue of Romances in the Department of Manuscripts in the British Museum* (3 vols, London 1883-1910)

WHITELOCK, D., *et al.* (edd.)   *Councils and Synods with Other Documents relating to the English Church*, I, *A.D. 871-1204* (2 parts, Oxford 1981)

WINDISCH, E.   'Das keltische Britannien bis zu Kaiser Arthur', *Abhandlungen der königlich sächsischen Gesellschaft der Wissenschaften, phil.-hist. Klasse*, 29 (1912), Heft 6

WINTERBOTTOM, Michael   *Problems in Quintilian* (London 1970)

WRIGHT, Neil (ed.)   *The Historia Regum Britannie of Geoffrey of Monmouth*, I: *A Single-manuscript Edition from Bern, Burgerbibliothek, MS. 568* (Cambridge 1984)

WAS MORDRED BURIED AT GLASTONBURY?
ARTHURIAN TRADITION AT GLASTONBURY
IN THE MIDDLE AGES

Richard Barber

British Library MS Cotton Titus A xix is a composite manuscript of unknown origin, one quire of which contains on ff.16r-23r a collection of material relating to Glastonbury and to the death of Arthur, as well as a wider range of Glastonbury legends and history culled from a variety of sources. My interest in this manuscript was originally aroused by the presence in it of a copy of the *Vera historia de morte Arthuri*, to which the late Dr Neil Ker drew the attention of Michael Lapidge and myself.[1] But the Glastonbury collection as a whole is a noteworthy one, containing as it does a further 'eclectic' account of Arthur's burial in addition to the unusual version of his death recounted in the *Vera historia*. This anthology was clearly assembled by someone with a strong interest in the Glastonbury traditions at some point in the middle or late fifteenth century. It is possible that the manuscript is autograph; there is a degree of correction and variation in the single hand of the Glastonbury section to support such an idea. The texts appear to be handled with some freedom: rephrasing, changes of verbal order and occasional abbreviation of the original being copied are not uncommon. If the manuscript is indeed autograph, the first name of the scribe and editor is given in an outraged comment on the piece which is the main topic of the present essay: 'Ego henricus non concedo . . .'

There are six entirely Arthurian pieces in the anthology, which comprises some sixteen items in all, of which the majority are part of the standard Glastonbury traditions, going back to the interpolated edition of William of Malmesbury and repeated in either Adam of

---

1 See Michael Lapidge, 'Additional Manuscript Evidence for the *Vera Historia de Morte Arthuri*', *Arthurian Literature* II (1982), 163-168. I am grateful to Dr Lapidge and Dr James Carley for reading the paper in draft and for their helpful comments. All remaining errors are of course my own responsibility.

Domerham or John of Glastonbury. Why then was this collection assembled? The presence of the *Vera historia* implies an attitude of mind which did not accept uncritically the received tradition as a kind of gospel; the compiler seems to be thinking in terms of comparison and collation, and it is interesting that the only fourteenth century chronicle which makes use of the unusual account of Arthur's burial found in the Cotton Titus A xix collection is the Jervaulx chronicle usually known as 'John of Brompton',[2] which has a not dissimilar approach, fusing together various accounts in a way that is the despair of the modern historian anxious to evaluate the source material behind an often fascinating but *prima facie* unreliable text. The Glastonbury texts in Cotton Titus A xix may well represent a collection intended to form the basis of a new history of the early years of the monastery; they look like a miscellany assembled with a purpose rather than a mere commonplace book compiled out of curiosity.

The 'Glastonbury quire' (so designated by Michael Lapidge)[3] contains items concerned with the early history of Glastonbury culled from a variety of sources, as follows:

1. 'Quedam narracio de nobili rege Arthuro [in sacramentum altare non pleno] credente qualiter confirmatus fuit in fide et factus vere credens et quare mutavit arma sua'   ff.16r-16v

The words in square brackets have been crudely deleted. This is a free version of John of Glastonbury, ch. 34;[4] a noteworthy addition is that Arthur has his dream in 'camera sororis sue nomine morgan cognomento la faye sita supra montem proximum iuxta Wirehalle' instead of in the nunnery there. The excerpt is given a formal pious ending, and notes the date of Arthur's death and his burial in the cemetery at Glastonbury, as if it had been reworked as a piece for reading on a suitable occasion.

2. Hec est vera historia de morte Arthuri   ff.16v-17v

This version of the *Vera historia* has been described by Michael Lapidge in *Arthurian Literature* II.[5]

---

2   See Antonia Gransden, *Historical Writing in England II: c.1307 to the Early Sixteenth Century* (London 1982), 56-57. John Taylor, *The Universal Chronicle of Ranulph Higden* (Oxford 1966), 144, calls 'John of Brompton' 'one of the more ambitious compilations of this period'.

3   *Arthurian Literature* II (1982), 164-5.

4   James Carley's new edition of John of Glastonbury, *The Chronicle of Glastonbury Abbey* (Woodbridge 1985) was unfortunately not available in time to cite page references: I have therefore referred to this text by chapter number, as the chapters are relatively brief.

5   The text is examined on pp.164-7.

3. 'De invencione corporis regis Arthuri <quam> Giraldus Cambrensis archidiaconus landavensis narrat.'   f.17v-f.18r
This is not taken from Gerald of Wales' original account in *De principis instructione* but is an almost perfect copy of Ralph Higden's *Polychronicon*, book vii.[6]
4. Untitled excerpt   f.18r
A relatively close version of the account of Arthur's burial as found in the chronicle of Margam Abbey.[7]
5. 'Incipit tractatus de sancto Joseph de Arimathia extractus de libro quodam quem invenit Theodosius imperator in Ierusalem in praetorio Pilati'   f.18r-19r
A fairly close copy, with altered ending, of John of Glastonbury ch. 18, from which the heading is also taken.
6. 'Hec scriptura reperitur in gestis incliti regis Arthuri'   f.19r-v
A copy of John of Glastonbury, end of ch. 20, from which the heading is taken: it is a passage citing Arthurian romance as evidence for Joseph of Arimathea's coming to Britain. The text continues with ch. 21, including the heading for that chapter, but an item on king Arviragus from ch. 20 is inserted before the genealogy showing Arthur's descent from Joseph of Arimathea.
7. 'Incipit quomodo xii discipuli sanctorum Philippi et Jacobi apostolorum primo ecclesiam Glastonie fundaverunt.'   ff.19v-20r
Taken from ch. 1 of William of Malmesbury's *De antiquitate Glastonie ecclesie*.[8] A generally close copy.
8. Untitled   f.20r
A summary of John of Glastonbury, ch. 1, or possibly of the lost church lection on which this is assumed to have been based,[9] ending with a note on the dimensions of the old church.
9. Untitled   ff.20v-21r
The life of St Benignus, in a form which is comparable to John of Glastonbury, chs. 29-30, but told in a totally different style, ending with a prayer to St Benignus. The tree which grows from Benignus' staff when it is planted in the earth is said to be a yew, and its precise location is given, details not apparently found elsewhere.
10. Untitled   f.21r-f.22v
An abbreviated account of the early history of Glastonbury based loosely on William of Malmesbury, *De antiquitate glastonie ecclesie*

---

6 Both are printed in Appendix below.
7 Printed in Appendix below.
8 See John Scott, *The Early History of Glastonbury: an Edition, Translation and Study of William of Malmesbury's* De antiquitate Glastonie Ecclesie (Woodbridge 1981), 42-47.
9 J. Armitage Robinson, *Two Glastonbury Legends* (Cambridge 1926), 57.

ch. 1, followed by a list of the saints who visited Glastonbury or whose relics were kept there; this list is from an unidentified source, and ends with the statement that John Chinnock (abbot 1375-1420) renovated the chapel where the relics brought by Joseph of Arimathea were kept, and a note on Arthur:

'Hic requiescat rex Arthurus flos britonum <et> Guennora regina de quibus tales extant versus:

Hic iacet Arthurus flos regum gloria mundi

Quem morum probitas commendavit laude perenni

Arthurus iacet hic coniunx tumulata secunda

Que meruit celos virtutum prole fecunda.

The text continues with a list of royal visitors and burials at Glastonbury.

11. 'De translacione sancti Dunstani a Cantuaria ad Glastoniam

f. 22v

An abbreviation of *De antiquitate* ch. 23.[10]

12. 'De venerabili cruce que quondam locuta est.' f. 22v

Copied from *De antiquitate* ch. 26: 'nu' is modernised to 'now'.[11]

13. 'De alia cruce de qua cecidit diadema' f. 22v

Copied from *De antiquitate* ch. 27-28.

14. 'De quadam ymagine beate Marie' ff. 22v-23r

Copied from *De antiquitate* ch. 29.

15. 'De ymagine antiquioris capelle' f. 23

A summary of the incident in John of Glastonbury, ch. 17.

16. 'De reliquiis Sancti David' f. 23

A summary of *De antiquitate* ch. 16, followed by an excerpt from ch. 40 on churches founded in the isle of Avalon.[12]

Items 1, 2, 3, 4, 5, 6, and the end of 10 are Arthurian in content. They represent the bulk of the material on Arthur himself to be found in the Glastonbury chronicles; the most notable exception is the episode concerning Yder, given by John of Glastonbury in ch. 33, where Arthur fails to arrive in time to help Yder in his combat against three giants. Yder kills all three, but dies of his wounds, and Arthur endows Glastonbury with the necessary lands for the maintenance of eighty monks to salve his conscience. The other items which one might expect to find are the story of the abduction of Guinevere by king Melwas, as told in Caradoc of Llancarfan's *Life of St Gildas*,[13] where

10 Scott, *The Early History*, 72-73.
11 For items 12-14 see Scott, *The Early History*, 78-81.
12 Scott, *The Early History*, 64-65 and 94-95.
13 Ed. Theodore Mommsen, *Monumenta Germaniæ Historica, Auctores Antiquissimi*, III, 107-10. J. S. P. Tatlock, *The Legendary History of Britain* (Berkeley and Los Angeles 1950), 188 describes it as 'almost certainly written at Glaston-

Guinevere is taken to Glastonbury, and is only restored to Arthur through the good offices of the abbot; and the tale of Arthur's killing of Gildas's brother. Although John of Glastonbury used Caradoc's *Life* for the latter story, he ignores the tale of Guinevere's abduction, which does not appear in any of Glastonbury's own versions of its history which have come down to us. Much more remarkable is the presence of the *Vera historia de morte Arthuri*, which actually contradicts Arthur's supposed burial at Glastonbury. The inclusion of this piece would tend to indicate that the selection was compiled elsewhere than at Glastonbury.

What is noteworthy about the whole group of excerpts, and also about the Glastonbury traditions about Arthur in general, is that they scarcely cross paths with the great romance cycles, and only draw marginally on Geoffrey of Monmouth. Once again, we are reminded that the Vulgate version of the romances is not the exclusive and authorised version of Arthur's story that it might sometimes seem to be: at Glastonbury, and in the manuscript with which we are concerned, the traditions about Arthur are strongly localised and with more than a hint of lost tales like those of which Ailred of Rievaulx complained.[14] The origin of this material is clearly Celtic, but the form in which it is preserved is interesting: these fragments, notably the story contained in the first item above (which is paralleled in the opening scene of *Perlesvaus*),[15] represent a stage in the evolution of Arthurian romance of which little remains — the Latin versions of Celtic or traditional local stories. How extensive these Latin versions were must remain a matter for conjecture, but it is possible that the

bury abbey', but gives no supporting details. See also his article, 'Caradoc of Llancarfan', *Speculum* XIII (1938), 141, where he argues that Caradoc must have been at Glastonbury at the time of writing because of the references to the abbey in the *Life*.

14 See G. G. Coulton, *Five Centuries of Religion* (Cambridge, 1923) I, 359.

15 Ed. William A. Nitze and collaborators, *Le Haut Livre du Graal: Perlesvaus* (Chicago 1932, 1937): text I, 26-38; commentary II, 104-120. Translation in Nigel Bryant, *The High Book of the Grail: a translation of the thirteenth century romance of* Perlesvaus (Cambridge 1978), 20-27. I hope to examine the question of the relationship of the *Perlesvaus*, John of Glastonbury and the variant text represented by Cotton Titus A xix and Digby 186 in a forthcoming article in *Arthurian Literature*. There is a further possible manuscript containing the three items in the Digby MS, British Library MS Cotton Cleopatra D VIII, which I have not yet had an opportunity to examine. Dr Carley points out a further link between the *Perlesvaus* and the Arthurian traditions at Glastonbury which is relevant to the present topic: the head of Loholt, Arthur's son, is sent to Glastonbury for burial after he is slain by Kay in an episode reminiscent of the death of Yder as recounted by John of Glastonbury. For this passage see Nitze, I. 270-4 and II. 304-6, and Bryant, 174-5.

claims of the romance writers to have used Latin texts should not be totally dismissed; they may well have taken incidents like these from Latin sources and woven them into the larger tapestry of their stories.

But we digress from our main theme. The material in Cotton Titus A xix is clearly Glastonbury-related; it is equally clearly a summary of most of the Glastonbury traditions about Arthur, as the only 'external' Arthurian item is the *Vera Historia*, and nowhere is there material from the myriad other possible sources. What information can we deduce about the compilation from the manuscript itself and from the texts used? On f.18r, the scribe names himself in a note at the head of the page: 'ego Henricus . . .'[16] Otherwise, as Michael Lapidge has pointed out,[17] there is little information to be gleaned from this composite and rebound manuscript, apart from a clear association of other texts in it with York and its neighbourhood.

The question is complicated by the presence of copies of three of the texts in Bodleian MS Digby 186, an even more composite manuscript than Cotton Titus A xix, which consists of assorted parchment and paper items from the thirteenth to the sixteenth century bound together. Some of the items have York connections: the first item, injunctions of the legate John about the reformation of St Mary's, York, in 1206, can only have come from that house. A series of prophecies follow, including those of John of Bridlington (a text too common to claim any specific Yorkshire connection) and then, in a late fifteenth century hand, the following items also found in Cotton Titus A xix:

1. 'Quaedam narratio de nobili rege arthuro in sacramento altaris non pleno credente qualiter confirmatus fuit in fide et factus vere credens et quare mutavit arma sua.' A later hand has noted 'Haec fere omnia (ad verbum) recitantur a Gulielmo Malmesbury in libro de antiquitatibus Glastonbury.'

2. 'Hec est vera historia de morte Arthuri.' This breaks off at Arthur's death, in the middle of the first sentence of a new paragraph. ('Igitur prefati tres episcopi spiritum . . .'[18] The text contains all the corrections made by hand T_1, and we therefore are dealing either with a direct copy of Cotton Titus A xix, or a more accurate copy of a common original.

3. 'De origine gigantum in Albion.' This piece is copied in Cotton Titus A xix separately, and much later in the manuscript, than the Glastonbury material.

16 See text in Appendix below.
17 *Arthurian Literature* II (1982), 165.
18 *Arthurian Literature* I (1981), 88, l. 75.

This is followed by topographical material on Berwick and Newcastle, further prophecies, a chronicle, various notes, and an incomplete text of John Acton's commentary on the *Constitutiones legatinas Othonis*, Acton being a canon of Lincoln.[19]

The texts in Cotton Titus A xix show that the compiler used the two major Glastonbury histories, William of Malmesbury's *De antiquitate glastonie ecclesie* and John of Glastonbury's *Cronica*, but I have not been able to identify specific manuscripts of these which he might have used, largely because he handles his material with considerable freedom, and many passages are no more than paraphrases. Of the sixteen items listed above, six are closely copied from the *De antiquitate* (7, 11, 12, 13, 14, 16): one is a free version from the same source (10). John of Glastonbury is treated with less respect: there are three items closely copied (5, 6, 15), and three where the versions are so different that they could represent John's source rather than rewritings of his text (1, 8, 9). The other Arthurian items are all concerned with Arthur's death and burial, a crucial question for a Glastonbury historian: one is the *Vera Historia*, and the other two are from the *Polychronicon* and a source also used by the Margam chronicle. None of these items help us to pinpoint the compiler's place of activity closely. Copies of William of Malmesbury's work in its various thirteenth-century recensions were by no means uncommon: the most recent editor lists four main MSS and a further eleven with parts or excerpts from William's work.[20] John of Glastonbury's work was also reasonably well circulated; seven major manuscripts have survived.[21] The *Vera Historia*, in Michael Lapidge's words, had 'perhaps a wide circulation but infrequent copying'.[22] The *Polychronicon* was perhaps the major historical reference work of the fourteenth century; the fact that Gerald of Wales's account of the discovery of Arthur's tomb was taken from this source rather than from the original would indicate that the *De principis instructione* was not available to the compiler, but the latter seems to have been a fairly scarce text.[23] This leaves us with the text otherwise found only in the Margam chronicle as the rarest of the works, and it is with this that I shall chiefly be concerned. I hope to show that it was not as rare as is supposed, and

---

[19] The manuscript was no. 63 in Thomas Allen's collection, which Sir Kenelm Digby bought. For a full description see William D. Macray, *Catalogi codicum manuscriptorum bibliothecae Bodleianae: pars nona, codices a viro clarissimo Kenelm Digby . . . donatos complectens* (Oxford 1863) cols 196-199.

[20] Scott, *The Early History*, 34-39 and 184.

[21] Carley, *The Chronicle of Glastonbury Abbey*, preface, section 1.

[22] *Arthurian Literature* II (1982), 168n.

[23] BL Cotton Julius B. xiii is the only surviving copy.

that it is a crucial text for Glastonbury's Arthurian connections.

The Margam chronicle has long been used by historians as a major source for the events of John's reign, containing as it does important evidence on the death of Arthur of Brittany. It survives in a unique MS, Trinity College, Cambridge, O. 2. 4 (1108).[24] A note in M. R. James's catalogue of 1900 refers to a Trinity College, Dublin, MS (507) with the same astronomical diagrams; but the connection between the two texts has only recently been investigated. The Dublin text (up to 1191) is an abbreviation of the Margam text, condensing longer entries, and haphazardly deleting some, but not all, entries of local interest to Margam only. Dr Martin Brett, in an as yet unpublished paper, has shown that we are dealing with a set of interrelated annals, whose textual history is highly complex.[25] A lost original (A) was the source of the Margam annals and of a second lost manuscript (B) from which the Trinity College, Dublin, annals and the *Annals of Abbey Dore*[26] were derived. There is also a version which used both this text and the independent Tewkesbury annals. But beyond the lost original of this group, we can trace sources used by both (A) and the Coggeshall chronicle;[27] in the Coggeshall chronicle this material appears as interpolations in the main text. This material is related in turn to the annals produced at Hyde (formerly the New Minster, Winchester) and Waverley. The problem is further complicated by the independent use of outside material by varying combinations of the differing groups of annalists.

We are in fact confronted by the problem of how these annalists set about their work. With such a complex set of texts, it is of course dangerous to draw general conclusions, and what follows must of necessity be a hypothesis, to be tested carefully as work on the annals proceeds. The central influence in all this seems to be the Cistercian order: Waverley, Margam, Abbey Dore, Coggeshall, and Jervaulx were all Cistercian houses. Cistercian writers, although prohibited by the Rules of their order from literary undertakings ('libros facere') without the consent of the general chapter, began to compile histories of the

24 It is printed in H. R. Luard (ed.), *Annales Monastici I: Annales de Margan . . . Theokesberia . . . Burton . . .* (Rolls Series 36, London 1864) 3-40.
25 I am most grateful to Dr Martin Brett for communicating a summary of his work in a letter, and to Dr David Dumville for drawing my attention to Dr Brett's paper. I must also thank Thomas Power, librarian of Trinity College, Dublin, for making available a microfilm of the manuscript at short notice, and for the information that Professor Marvin Colker of the University of Virginia was also working on the MS.
26 Ed. R. Pauli, *Monumenta Germaniæ Historica, Scriptores*, XXVII, 526.
27 Ralph of Coggeshall, *Chronicon Anglicanum*, ed. Joseph Stevenson (Rolls Series 66, London 1875) 36.

foundation of their abbeys and brief sets of annals in the thirteenth century, and a Cistercian monk wishing to start such a set of annals would have had little difficulty in borrowing an existing set as a basis from a sister house.[28] This material was then supplemented by information from other sources as and when it became available, often through magnates or officials with local connections: in the case of Ralph of Coggeshall, he had access to important news about Richard I on crusade which must have come from a member of his entourage, while in the case of the Margam annalist, it seems that he was able to learn from William de Briouze what he knew about Arthur of Brittany's death.[29] A further source, and one which particularly complicates the issue of interrelationships between the chronicles, were the newsletters which first appear in large numbers at this period. In 1202 and 1212 there are examples of this: that of 1212, a letter from the archbishop of Narbonne about the Spanish triumph over the Moors at Las Navas de Tolosa, is a particularly good example of how the medium could be used. Furthermore, there is evidence of very deliberate use of the medium to spread news through the monastic network: the archbishop's letter was to be read out to the assembled Cistercian abbots at the annual general chapter enjoined by the rules of their order.[30] It is also easy to underestimate the degree of correspondence between monasteries: perhaps the most dramatic evidence of communication between far-flung houses are the mortuary rolls which survive from the tenth century onwards. Here we find documents passed from monastery to monastery, each adding their tribute to the deceased, for years on end, between France, England, the Low Countries and Germany; a roll might go from Glastonbury to a neighbouring priory or – more dramatically – direct from Glastonbury to Ely.[31]

I would like to suggest that communication of this sort, probably in the form of a newsletter rather than a verbatim report, lies behind the accounts of Arthur's supposed exhumation at Glastonbury, variously dated by the chroniclers to 1189 and 1191. The original document would therefore be a newsletter sent out by the monks of Glastonbury to inform the world of their discovery; it would be nice

---

[28] On the literary activity of the Welsh Cistercians, see F. G. Cowley, *The Monastic Order in South Wales 1066-1349* (Cardiff 1977), 146-164.

[29] See W. L. Warren, *King John* (Harmondsworth 1966) 98-9, and W. Greenway, 'The Annals of Margam', *Transactions of the Port Talbot Historical Society* I (1963) 28-30.

[30] *Annales Monastici* I, 32.

[31] See Léopold Delisle, *Rouleaux des morts du IXe au XVe siècle* (Société de l'Histoire de France, Paris 1866) 192, 339.

to believe John Bale's report that the abbot himself, Henry de Sully, wrote a treatise entitled 'De inventione corporis Arthuri', but Bale's statement is not corroborated by any other evidence.[32] Whatever the original text may have comprised, it no longer survives in its pristine form, but is represented by the accounts in the three major texts, of which — so I would argue — that in the Margam chronicle is the most authentic. The three major texts are the accounts given by Gerald of Wales in *De principis instructione* and *Speculum ecclesie*, that given by Ralph of Coggeshall in his chronicle, and that in the anonymous Margam chronicle.[33] In the past, only the first two writers have generally been taken into account: Gerald has acquired the reputation of being an eye-witness, while Ralph of Coggeshall is esteemed as a generally reliable historian. The Margam text, on the other hand, has a very different account at one critical point, and has either been ignored or treated as an isolated aberration. Now we can show that the Margam text was far from unknown, even if treated with scepticism, in the medieval period. First, there is the copy in the manuscript under discussion: and secondly, there is a close version of it in 'John of Brompton''s chronicle from the Cistercian abbey at Jervaulx in the late fourteenth century. So we have not one isolated manuscript, but three manuscript versions. Next, it is perfectly possible to see Ralph of Coggeshall's text as a simple abbreviation of either Margam or Margam's source, while it is difficult to argue the reverse — that Margam is an expansion of the simple version given in Coggeshall. Furthermore, Gerald of Wales's text is less likely to be itself an eye-witness account than a reworking in his high literary style of an earlier, genuine description by someone who was present.

The three versions of the Margam or 'Mordred' text carry indications that they derive from a common lost original, a thesis reinforced by what little we know about the manuscripts. The dating of the burial varies: 1189, 1191, and 1192-3 are variously given. If Brompton and Cotton Titus had been following Margam, there would have been no reason to vary the date, and it seems that the original had no precise indication of the year in which the discovery took place. Furthermore, the Trinity manuscript of the Margam chronicle contains a small but telling scribal alteration, the deletion of two letters to change 'avalon'

---

[32] John Bale, *Scriptorum illustrium maioris Brytanniae* (Basle 1557-9) II, 133. Bale confuses Henry de Sully with Henry of Blois, and claims: 'Scripsit Soliacus plura, iam prosa quam carmine: et inter alia ad avunculum regem adiutore iam dicto Geraldo: De inventione corporis Arthuri lib. 1. Reliqua eius opuscula nec tetigi unquam, nec vidi.'

[33] Printed in Appendix below.

46

into 'aval'. The Margam chronicler was likely to correct a mistake in Welsh, whereas if copies of the original were made in England, the original wording was likely to stand without alteration, and it seems likely that this read 'avalon'. The spelling of Guinevere's name in Margam, 'John of Brompton' and Cotton Titus A xix diverges widely, but this is common to almost any Latin text where her name appears: 'Guenore', 'Guenhavere' and 'Wenevore' are the attempts offered. The inscription on the cross is relatively uniform: Margam gives 'sepultus . . . Avellania', Cotton Titus omits 'sepultus'; John of Brompton reads 'Avalana'.

When we compare these three texts with Ralph of Coggeshall and the only other derivative of his version in the *Flores Historiarum*, the details in this latter account are much briefer: the episode of the crumbling hair is omitted, as is the discovery of the first two coffins. Nor is it possible to explain the fuller version by reference to the third group of accounts, those by or derived from Gerald of Wales. Gerald has been described as an eyewitness by later authorities such as John Leland in his *Assertio Arthurii*, but Gerald's accounts are deceptive and a close reading of the texts shows that Leland and other writers have been misled by them.[34] The text in *De principis instructione*, is the briefer: that in *Speculum ecclesie* is fuller, but more literary in approach — the whole episode is brought in as an example of the vanity of earthly glory. The *Speculum ecclesie* account survives only in a manuscript damaged in the Cottonian Library fire of 1731. However, it has not previously been noticed that the text of this passage was copied into the margins of one of the manuscripts of Adam of Domerham's *Historia de rebus gestis Glastoniensibus* and can therefore be recovered almost in its entirety. It is printed in the appendix below. (According to Leland, there was a copy of *Speculum Giraldi* at Glastonbury, so the copying is easily accounted for.)[35] Neither text can be dated accurately, both were written over a long period of time, between the early 1190s and about 1220, though *De principis instructione* is probably the earlier of the two.[36] The *Speculum ecclesie* text dealing with Arthur's burial cannot be earlier than 1193, as Henry de Sully is described as subsequently bishop of Worcester, and he did not become bishop until that year.

Gerald says that he has seen the cross and handled it, and that he

---

[34] John Leland, *Assertio Arturii* (f. 28b) in *Collectanea*, ed. Thomas Hearne (London 1774, reprinted Farnborough 1970) V, 52. See also Antonia Gransden, 'The Growth of the Glastonbury Legends and Traditions in the Twelfth Century', *Journal of Ecclesiastical History* 27 (1976) 355-6.

[35] John Leland, *Collectanea*, III, 360.

[36] Robert Bartlett, *Gerald of Wales* (Oxford 1982) 219-20.

was shown Arthur's thigh-bone by the abbot. I would read his whole account as the kind of description that an intelligent and privileged visitor to Glastonbury would have written, coming to the abbey between the discovery and the official translation of the relics, which the first reports of the event would doubtless have announced for a future date, because it would take time to prepare a site and a suitable tomb, and such an occasion would need to be staged in appropriate style. If Gerald had actually watched the excavation in progress, he would surely have said as much. As a distinguished ecclesiastic and courtier, he would naturally be shown the relics, and his account is overlaid with details which point to the abbey's own propaganda machine at work. The passage is introduced by a celebration of Arthur as patron of Glastonbury, which is not borne out by any material that can be safely dated to before the discovery. He recalls Arthur's devotion to Mary as found in the *Historia Brittonum*, and then goes on to quote from what I would argue was the 'official newsletter' on the discovery; but he adds that the event was 'signatum miris indiciis et miraculosis' and that the body was 'translatum' into the church — clothing the whole event in the conventional garb of a saint's 'inventio et translatio' so beloved of the twelfth and thirteenth centuries. He reinforces this with an account of the 'indicia' by which the body was found, partly by ancient inscriptions on the pyramids (which in fact related to seventh century burials) and partly by dreams and revelations, the standard stock-in-trade of such occasions.[37]

We have to account for two major discrepancies between the putative newsletter and Gerald's account: the finding of *three* bodies and the inscription on the cross. I would suggest that the two changes are related and part of the same process. The clue lies in the horrified reaction of the fifteenth century scribe of Cotton Titus to the idea that Guinevere and Mordred — 'proditores illius' — could be buried in the same tomb as Arthur. Any reconstruction must of course be hypothetical, but the original newsletter seems to have been concocted by monks who knew their local or Welsh legends better than their *Historia Regum Britannie*: and in the Welsh legends there is little evidence that Mordred was necessarily Arthur's betrayer. But the world at large was much more familiar with Geoffrey of Monmouth's version and reacted with disbelief to the initial account of the discovery, just as Henry the scribe did when confronted with the same

---

[37] Martin Heinzelmann, *Translationsberichte und andere Quellen des Reliquienkultus* (Typologie des sources du moyen âge occidental, fasc. 33, Turnhout, 1979) 79.

account three centuries later. So the burial was simplified, and reduced to that of Arthur and Guinevere, and the three separate coffins became one coffin divided into three parts — hence the curious detail of the division of Arthur's bones between two compartments of the coffin. To confirm the new version, the cross was remade; but it seems that when the fuss had died down, the original version of the lettering regained favour, because William Camden's drawing in the 1607 edition of his *Britannia* reverts to the simpler wording. If Camden's cross is that originally 'found' in the grave, then Gerald's account must be treated as highly unreliable; if we accept Gerald's account as eyewitness, then the cross is a definite forgery. It has been argued that the letter forms of the cross are decisive evidence of a pre-Conquest date,[38] and that it could even be that it is genuine. But given the level of skill of monastic copyists of antiquities — we should not call them forgers — demonstrated by Dr Antonia Gransden in a recent paper at the Society of Antiquaries,[39] an 'antique' inscription would have presented few problems, and as Aelred Watkin has pointed out, there is suitable source material not far away at Stoke sub Hamdon.[40] Without the physical presence of the cross itself, last seen in the eighteenth century, we can take the case no further. There is one further mystery attaching to Gerald's account of the burial. He alone describes the epitaph as referring to Guinevere as Arthur's *second* wife; the phrase seems to echo the tradition of the 'true and false' Guineveres which may possibly have had Welsh origins.[41] 'Secunda' could possibly be used here in its rare meaning of 'fortunate', found in classical Latin as a trope.[42] If so, this would almost inevitably point to someone like Gerald as the author of this version of the inscription.

Two other accounts of the burial must also be considered: that of Adam of Domerham, writing in 1343, who says that the grave was surrounded by curtains when the digging took place: James Carley points out a very interesting parallel for this in Appendix B below. The other is that of Alberic of Trois Fontaines, a monastery in north west France, who was relatively well informed about Welsh matters — he had a copy of Gerald of Wales's *Descriptio Kambriae* in front of him when he wrote his chronicle in the 1240s — and evidently had

38 C. A. Ralegh Radford, 'Glastonbury Abbey' in *The Quest for Arthur's Britain*, ed. Geoffrey Ashe (London 1968) 126.
39 Antonia Gransden, 'Antiquarian Studies in Fifteenth Century England', *The Antiquaries Journal*, LX (1980) 79-80.
40 See Appendix B, n.10, below.
41 See Rachel Bromwich, *Trioedd Ynys Prydein: The Welsh Triads* (Cardiff 1961) 156.
42 I owe this suggestion to Dr James Carley.

direct contacts with the west country. He claims that he was told that the newly appointed abbot dug up the whole of the old cemetery in order to find Arthur's tomb. This is belied by the excavations carried out in 1962 by Dr Ralegh Radford, which showed a quite specific disturbance of 'two, or perhaps three of the slab-lined graves belonging to the earliest stratum' of the cemetery.[43] Alberic's story reflects the idea that the discovery was an intensive and organised effort, as do the curtains round the digging mentioned by Adam of Domerham. But the archaeological evidence echoes the Margam account, with its multiple coffins, rather than the single divided wooden coffin described by Gerald of Wales.

What conclusions can we draw from the available evidence, if the reading of the various sources outlined above is correct? At some time between 1189 and 1193, the monks of Glastonbury dug between the two ancient pyramids in the old cemetery, in the hope of making some kind of discovery. The believer will argue that they actually found Arthur's body; the sceptic will declare that, finding ancient burials, they fell in with a convenient suggestion, and labelled them with the names of Arthur, Guinevere and Mordred. Finding that this did not correspond with current ideas as to Arthur's death, they hastily revised their original account, and a new version was presented to visitors within a few years of the original excavation. A close comparison of the texts describing the burial tends if anything to confirm the accepted view that the 'discovery' was carefully planned; what we can add is that the details were not so well thought out, and for a brief time it was indeed 'officially announced' that Mordred, too, was buried at Glastonbury.

43 Radford, 'Glastonbury Abbey', p.132.

TABLE Comparison of details in reports of the discovery of Arthur's burial

	Margam	Ralph of Coggeshall	Gerald of Wales	Glastonbury accounts
Number of coffins	3	1	1	2 ?[1]
Type of coffin	'sarcofagus'	'sarcofagus'	'in quercu cavata'	'sarcofagus ligneus'
Epitaph	Hic iacet inclitus rex Arthurus sepultus in insula Avellonia	Hic iacet inclitus rex Arturius in insula Avallonis sepultus	Hic jacet sepultus inclitus rex Arthurus cum Wenneveria uxore sua secunda in insula Avallonia	Hic jacet sepultus inclitus rex Arturius in insula Avallonia
Depth	Not given	Not given	16 feet	Considerable depth
Pyramid inscriptions	Illegible	Illegible	Partly legible	Once nobly carved
Incident of Guinevere's hair	Yes	No	Yes	Yes
Reason for digging	Monk had insisted on burial there	Monk had insisted on burial there	Information from King, visions, old writings	Information from King

1 'Dehinc tumbam reginam aperientes' implies a second coffin.

APPENDIX A

The major texts dealing with Arthur's burial at Glastonbury

Where a manuscript source and a printed text are cited, that manuscript has been collated against the printed text. Medieval Latin usage has been preferred to classical, and minor scribal errors have been allowed to stand.

A. The Margam version and its affiliates

Annales de Margan
Trinity College, Cambridge, MS O.2.4 f.9r
Printed: H. R. Luard (ed.) *Annales monastici* I (Rolls Series 36, London 1864) 21–22

1191. . . . Apud Glastoniam inventa sunt ossa famosissimi Arthuri quondam regis Maioris Britannie, in quodam vetustissimo sarcofago recondita. Circa quod due piramides stabant erecte, in quibus littere quedam exarate erant, set ob nimiam barbariem et deformacionem legi non poterant. Inventa sunt autem hac occasione. Dum inter predictas piramides terram quidam effoderent, ut quendam monachum sepelirent, qui ut ibi sepeliretur a conventu pretio impetraverat, repererunt quoddam sarcofagum, in quo quasi ossa muliebria cum capillatura adhuc incorrupta cernebantur. Quo amoto repererunt et aliud priori substratum, in quo ossa virilia continebantur. Quod etiam amoventes, invenerunt et tertium duobus primis suppositum, cui crux plumbea superposita erat, in qua exaratum fuerat, 'Hic iacet inclitus rex Arthurus sepultus in insula Avellania'. Locus enim ille olim paludibus inclusus insula Avallonis vocatus est id est insula pomorum. Nam aval[. .]* britannice pomum dicitur. Deinde predictum sarcofagum aperientes, invenerunt predicti principis ossa robusta nimis et longa, que cum decenti honore et magno apparatu in marmoreo mausoleo intra ecclesiam suam monachi collocaverunt. Primum tumulum dicunt fuisse Guenhavere regine, uxoris eiusdem Arthuri; secundum Modredi nepotis eiusdem; tertium predicti principis.

* Two letters deleted after 'aval'; original reading may have been 'avalon'.

British Library MS Cotton Titus A XIX f.18r   Not printed

Anno quarto regni regis Ricardi Anglie primi apud Glastoniam inventa* sunt ossa famosissimi militis Arthuri quondam regis maioris britannie, in quodam sarcophago vetustissimo recondita, circa quod piramides antique lapides stabant erecte, in quibus quedam litere erant exarate, sed ob nimiam vetustatem barbare et deformate legi non poterant. Inventa autem sunt hac occasione. Dum inter dictas piramides terram quidam effoderent, ut quendam monachum ibi sepelirent, qui hunc locum sepulture vehementi desiderio in vita sua preoptaverat et a conventu precibus impetrando optinuerat, repererunt quoddam sarcophagum, in quo quasi ossa muliebria cum capillitura adhuc incorrupta cernebantur. Quo

* Capital M in margin

amoto et aliud priore substrato sarcophagum invenerunt, in quo ossa virilia continebantur. Quod etiam ammoventes repererunt et tertium primis duobus suppositum, cui crux plumbea superposita erat, in qua exaratum fuit, 'Hic iacet inclitus rex Arthurus in insula Avalonis'; locus enim ille paludibus olim erat inclusus, insula Avalonis vocabatur, id est, insula pomorum; nam Avalon Britannice Latine pomum dicitur. Deinde predictum sarchofagum aperientes, invenerunt predicti principis ossa nimis longa et robusta, que cum decenti honore et magno apparatu in mausoleo marmoreo infra ecclesiam suam monachi collocaverunt. Primum tumulum dicunt fuisse Wenevore uxoris eiusdem Arthuri; secundum Modredi nepotis sui; tercium eiusdem Arthuri.†

† + sign at end. At top of page: + Ego henricus non concedo proditores illius cum eo sepultos quod absurdissimum esse videtur.

John of Brompton: Chronicon

British Library MS Cotton Tiberius C XIII f.187v – f.188r
Printed: Roger Twysden (ed.), *Historiae anglicanae scriptores X* (London 1652) cols 1152–4

De ossibus regis Arthuri inventis

In tempore istius regis Henrici secundi anno regni sui xiij. ossa famosissimi regis Arthuri quondam maioris Britanniae monarcha, cuius corpus quasi fantasticum et in fine tanquam ad longinqua deductum fabule britannice adhuc venturum confixerunt, apud Glastoniam in quodam vetustissimo sarcophago profunde in terra in quercu concava recondita, sunt inventa inter duas lapideas piramides in sacro cimiterio quondam erectas, in quibus litere quedam exarate erant, sed ob nimiam vetustatem barbare scripture et deformationem legi non poterant. Ossa vero predicta hac occasione inventa fuerunt. Dum inter dictas piramides terram quidam effoderent, ut quendam monachum sepe-[f.188]lirent, qui hunc locum sepulture vehementi desiderio in vita sua preoptaverat, et a conventu precibus Impetrando optinuerat, quoddam sarcophagum in quo quasi ossa muliebria cum trica come muliebris flaua et integritate pristina et colore reperta sunt, quam cum monachus unus avide cum manu attraxisset, tota statim in pulverem decidit. Amoto vero illo sarcophago, aliud priori suppositum reperiunt, in quo ossa virilia continebantur. Quod et eciam amoventes reperiunt tercium duobus primis suppositum, cui crux plumbea superposita erat, in qua exaratum fuit, Hic iacet sepultus inclitus rex Arthurus in insula Aualana: locus enim ille olim paludibus inclusus insula Aualon vocabatur, id est, insula pomorum. Nam Aualon Britannice, pomum dicitur latine. Deinde predictum sarcophagum aperientes, ossa nimis robusta et longa dicti principis invenerunt; que cum decenti honore et magno apparatu monachi infra ecclesiam suam in tumba marmorea posuerunt. Primum tumulum dicunt fuisse Guenore vxoris eiusdem Arthuri, secundum Modredi nepotis sui.
   Insuper scribitur quod iste rex Henricus a quodam historico cantore Britannico audierat, quod profunde in terra circiter xv. pedes corpus Arthuri regis in quercu concaua inueniretur. Idcirco autem tam profunde humatus fuerat, ne a Saxonibus sibi emulis facile reperiretur, et inde litere veritatis indices interius versus lapide sculpte erant. Et notandum est quod tibie Arthuri tunc ostense, tibiam et genu longissimi hominis tunc reperti tribus digitis excedebant; spacium quoque

53

interculii inter duos oculos palmalem latitudinem continebat. In cuius capite decem vulnerum cicatrices apparebant, que omnia praeter unum solum quod letale videbatur, in vnam cicatricem concurrebant. . .

[Brompton goes on to quote the Brut, and Gerald of Wales:]

Verumtamen secundum historiam Britonum, Arthurus postmodum cum Modredo confligens occisus est, et in valle Auallonis iuxta Glastoniam sepultus, cuius corpus postmodum etiam cum corpore Guenore vxoris sub anno domini M.Clxxx. tempore regis Henrici secundi repertum est, et ad ecclesiam ut predicitur translatum; sicut refert Giraldus distinctione prima capitulo 18. qui tunc vixit et ossa Arthuri contrectavit.

[He discusses the historicity of Geoffrey of Monmouth's account, asking why there is no mention of Arthur in Gildas and Bede, but concludes that heroes are only praised by their own nations.]

B. Ralph of Coggeshall's account and a derivative.

Ralph of Coggeshall: Chronicon Anglicanum

British Library MS Cotton Vespasian D X, ff.57v–58r
Printed: Ralph of Coggeshall, *Chronicon Anglicanum*, ed. Joseph Stevenson (Rolls Series 66, London 1875), 36

Quomodo ossa regis Arturii reperta sunt

Hoc autem anno inventa sunt apud Glastingeberiam ossa famosissimi Arturi quondam regis Britannie, in quodam vetustissimo sarcofago recondita. Circa quod due antique piramides stabant erecte, in quibus littere quedam exarate erant, sed ob nimiam barbariem et deformationem legi non poterant. Inventa sunt autem hac occasione. Dum enim ibidem terram effoderent ut quemdam monacum sepelirent, qui hunc locum sepulture vehementi desiderio in vita sua preoptaverat, reperiunt quoddam sarcofagum, cui crux plumbea superposita fuerat, in qua ita exaratum erat, 'Hic iacet inclitus rex Arturius, in insula Avallonis sepultus'. Locus autem ille olim paludibus inclusus, insula Avallonis, (id est insula pomorum) vocitatus est.

Roger of Wendover: Flores Historiarum

British Library MS Cotton Otho B V pt.ii f.67v
Printed: *Rogeri de Wendover liber qui dicitur flores historiarum*, ed. H. G. Hewlett (Rolls Series 84, London 1886) I, 203

[Inventio Arthuri, regis Britonum famosissimi]*

Eodem anno inventa sunt apud [Glastonia]m ossa famosissimi regis britannie Arturi in quodam vetustissimo recon[dita s]arcophago, circa quod due antiquissime pyramides stabant erecte, in quibus [litere e]rant exarate, set ob

* In printed edition, but not in MS

54

nimiam babariem† et deformitatem legi minime potuerunt. Invente sunt autem hac occasione; dum enim ibidem effoderent ut monachum quendam sepelirent, qui hunc sepulture locum vehementi desidederio† in uita sua preoptauerat, quondam reperiunt sarcophagum, cui crux plumbea superposita fuerat, in qua exaratum erat, 'Hic iacet inclitus britonum rex arthurus, in insula aualonis sepultus'. Locus autem ille paludibus undique inclusis, olim insula avalonis, id est pomorum insula, est vocatus.

† Sic in MS

C. Gerald of Wales's accounts and their derivatives

Giraldus Cambrensis: De principis instructione   dist.i

British Library MS Cotton Julius B XIII ff.107r–107v
Printed: *Giraldi Cambrensis Opera*, VIII: *De principis instructione liber*, ed. G. F. Warner (Rolls Series 21, London 1891) 126–9

De rege Arthuro nostris diebus inuento

Arthuri quoque Britonum regis incliti memoria est non supprimenda, quem monasterii Glasconiensis egregii, cuius et ipse patronus suis diebus fuerat precipuus et largitor ac subleuator magnificus, historie multum extollunt. Pre cunctis enim ecclesiis regni sui sancte dei genitricis Marie Glasconiensem ecclesiam plus dilexit et pre ceteris longe maiori deuocione promouit.

De ymagine beate Marie in eius clipeo depicta

Unde cum uir bellator extiterit, in anteriori parte clipei sui beate uirginis ymaginem interius, ut eam in conflictu pre oculis semper haberet, depingi fecerat; cuius et pedes, quociens positus in congressionis articulo fuerat, deosculari cum plurima deuocione consueuerat.

De corpore Arthuri apud Glasconiam

Huius autem corpus, quod quasi fantasticum in fine, et tamquam per spiritus ad longinqua translatum, neque morti obnoxium fabule confinxerant, hiis nostris diebus apud Glasconiam inter lapides pyramides duas, in cimiterio sacro quondam erectas, profundius in terra quercu concaua reconditum et signatum miris indiciis et quasi miraculosis, est inuentum, et in ecclesiam cum honore translatum marmoreoque decenter tumulo commendatum.

De cruce plumbea

Unde et crux plumbea lapide supposito, non superius ut [nostri] solet d[i]ebus inferiori pocius ex parte infixa, quam nos quoque uidimus, namque tractauimus litteras has insculptas et non eminentes et extantes, sed magis interius ad lapidem uersas, continebat: 'Hic iacet sepultus inclitus rex Arthurus cum Wenneuereia uxore sua secunda in insula Auallonia'.† Occurrunt hic autem notabilia plurima;

† Subheading, in style of other headings: Hic iacet sepultus etc.

habuerat enim uxores duas, quarum ultima simul cum ipso sepulta fuerat, et ossa ipsius cum ossibus uiri simul inuenta, sic distincta tamen, ut due partes sepulchri, uersus caput scilicet, ossibus uiri continendis deputate [f.107v] fuissent, tercia uero uersus pedes ossa muliebria seorsum contineret.

De trica muliebri a monacho rapta

Ubi et trica come muliebris flaua cum integritate pristina et colore reperta fuit, quam ut monachus quidam auide manu arripuit et subleuauit, tota statim in puluerem decidit.

De indiciis corpus arthuri de signis videlicet

Cum autem aliqua indicia corporis ibi inueniendi ex scripturis suis, aliqua ex litteris pyramidibus impressis, quanquam nimia plurimum antiquitate deletis, aliqua quoque per uisiones et reuelaciones bonis uiris et religiosis factas, maxime tamen et euidentissime rex Anglie Henricus secundus, sicut ab historico cantore Britone audierat anticho, totum monachis indicauit, quod profunde, scilicet in terra per xui. pedes ad minus, corpus inuenirent, et non [in] lapideo tumulo, sed in quercu cauata. Ideoque tam profunde situm corpus, et quasi absconditum fuerat, ne a saxonibus post necem ipsius insulam occupantibus, quos tanto opere uiuens debellauerat, et fere ex toto deleuerat, posset nullatenus inueniri; et ob hoc eciam littere, ueritatis indices, cruci impresse interius ad lapidem uerse fuerunt, ut et tunc temporis quod continebat occultarent, et quandoque tamen pro locis et temporibus id propalarent.

Unde dicta fuerit insula auallonia

Que nunc autem Glasconia dicitur, antiquitus insula auallonia dicebatur. Est enim quasi insula tota paludibus obsita, unde dicta est britannice emin* auallon, id est, insula pomifera. Pomis enim, que aual britannica lingua dicuntur, locus ille quondam abundabat. Unde et morganis, nobilis matrona et partium illarum dominatrix atque patrona, necnon et Arthuro rege sanguine propinqua, post bellum de Kemelen Arthurum ad sanandum eius uulnera in insulam que nunc Glasconia dicitur deportauit.

Unde Glasconia dicta

Dicta quoque quondam britannice eius* gutrin fuerat, hoc est, insula uitrea; ex quo uocabulo superuenientes postea saxones locum illum Glastingeburi uocitabant. Glas enim lingua eorum uitrum sonat, et buri castrum, ciuitas appellatur.

Unde officium* Arthuri magnitudine, uulneribusque plurimis in capite

Sciendum eciam quod ossa reperta corporis Arthuri tam grandia fuerunt, ut et illud poete completum in hiis uideri posset:
> Grandiaque effossis mirabitur ossa sepulchris.

Os enim tibie ipsius appositum longissimi uiri loci, quem et nobis abbas ostendit, et iuxta pedem illius terre affixum, large tribus digitis trans genu ipsius se porrexit. Os eciam capitis tanquam ad prodigium uel ostentum capax erat et grossum, adeo ut intercilium et inter oculos spacium palmalem amplitudinem

* Reading thus in MS

56

large contineret. Apparebant autem in hoc uulnera .x. aut plura, que cuncta preter unum maius ceteris, quod hiatum grandem fecerat, quodque solum letale fuisse uidebatur, in solidam conuenerant cicatricem.

Giraldus Cambrensis   Speculum Ecclesie   dist.ii

British Library MS Cotton Tiberius B XIII ff.25r–27r
Printed: *Giraldi Cambrensis Opera*, IV: *Speculum ecclesie…* ed. J. S. Brewer (Rolls Series 21, London 1891) 48–51 (passages supplied in round brackets, no longer legible in MS)

Trinity College, Cambridge MS R.5.33, ff.7 and 27v (passages supplied in square brackets, illegible in Cotton MS before Brewer's edition)

Cap.viii

(De monacho ….muliebrem manu tractante, in Arthuri sepulchro repertam et nimis impudenter).....accelerante

…(au).. …ante nostris in An(glia)… Henrico secun(do, contigit) ut apud Glas(ton)ense cenobium quon(da)m nobile sepulchrum Arthuri, dicto rege monente et abbate loci eiusdem Henrico (qui ad cathedram Wigorniensem translatus postea fuit) procurante, diligenter quesitum, in cimeterio sacro a sancto Dunstano dedicato, inter duas piramides altas et litteratas, in Arthuri memoriam olim erectas, multis laboribus effoderetur, et corpus eiusdem in puluerem et ossa redactum ab imis ad auram et statum digniorem transferretur, inuenta fuit in eodem sepulchro trica muliebris, flaua et formosa, miroque artificio conserta et contricata, uxoris scilicet Arthuri, uiro ibidem consepulte. Uerum ut in ipsam, inter astantes plurimos ……………… nimis ….et inuerecunde, (ut) tricam illam pre ceteris cunctis arripere posset, in imum fosse profunde se precipitem dedit. Sicut ergo prenotatus antea monachus, baratri figuram non saturandi, non minus impudens quam inprudens proteruusque spectator et profundus intrauit; sic monachus iste muliebrem tricam, firmos extricantem animos et infirmos intricantem, pre ceteris rapere cunctis, et impudice mentis indicio manu tractare curauit. Et licet capilli inputribiles esse dicantur, quia nihil in se corpulentum, nihil humidum habent admixtum, tamen simul ut erectam, et diligenter inspectam manu tenuit, multis intuentibus et obstupentibus in puluerem illico decidit minutissimum, et tamquam in athomos, sicut diuidi sic et discerni nescias, subito conuersa disparuit, et euentu mirabili ne …………………… …………
……………….(res ista pro ….alia;) namque (cunctis pre)figurauit esse caduca, et mundanam pulcritudinem omnem uanos oculos ad intuendum, seu perpetrandum illicita perstringendum, esse momentaneam et uanitati obnoxiam. Quoniam, ut ait philosophus, 'forme nitor rapidus est, et uelox, et uernalium florum mutabilitate fugacior'.

Cap.ix   De sepulcro regis Arthuri osso eius continente, apud Glastoniam nostris diebus inuento, et plurimis circiter hec notabilibus occasionaliter adiunctis.

Porro quoniam de rege Arturo et eius exitu dubio multa referri solent et fabule confingi, Britonum populis ipsum adhuc uiuere fatue contendentibus, ut fabulosis exufflatis, et ueris ac certis asseueratis, ueritas ipsa de cetero circiter hec liquido pateat, quedam hic adiicere curauimus indubitata ueritate comperta.
   Post bellum de Ke[melen apud Cornubiam, interfecto ibidem Modredo,

proditore nequissimo, et Regni Britannici, custodie sue deputati contra]
auun[culum suum Ar]thurum [occupatore, ipso]que arthuro [ibi letaliter]
uulnerato, co[rpus eiusdem] in insulam Au[alloniam], que nunc Glaston[ia
dic]itur,* a nobili matrona quadam eiusque cognata et Morgani uocata, est
delatum, quod postea defunctum in dicto cimeterio sacro, eadem procurante,
sepultum fuit. Propter hoc enim fabulosi Britones et eorum cantores fingere
solebant, quod dea quedam fantastica, scilicet et Morganis dicta, corpus Arthuri
in insulam detulit Aualloniam ad eius uulnera sanandum. Que cum sanata fuerint,
redibit rex fortis et potens, ad britones regendum, ut ducunt, sicut solet; propter
quod, ipsum expectant adhuc uenturum sicut iudei messiam suum, maiori etiam
fatuitate et infelicitate, simul ac infidelitate decepti.

Notandum (est)............................tur Quoniam enim
.............(s omnibus) sita, sicut ...elius, insule dicuntur, ..que in salo, hoc
est in mari, site noscuntur; Auallonia uero dicta est, uel ab aual Britannice, quod
pomum sonat, quia solet locus ille pomis et pomeriis habundare, uel a Uallone
quodam, territorii illius quondam dominatore. Item solet antiquitus locus ille
Britanice dici Inis Gutrin, hoc est insula uitrea, propter amnem scilicet, quasi
uitrei coloris in marisco circumfluentem; et ob hoc dicta est postmodum a
Saxonibus terram occupantibus, lingua eorum, Glastonia: Glas enim anglice uel
Saxonice uitrum sonat. Patet ex hiis igitur quare insula, et quare auallonia, et
quare Glastonia dicta. Patet et hoc quoque, quo pacto dea fantastica Morganis a
fabulatoribus nuncupata.

Notandum hic etiam, quod licet abbas prenominatus ....oque ex
litteris in illam inscriptis, quamquam antiquitatis tamen et fere omnino uetustate
deletis, maximam habuit predictum regem Henricum ad hec euidentiam.

Dixerat enim ei pluries, sicut ex gestis Britonum et eorum cantoribus historiis
rex audierat, quod inter piramides duas, que postmodum erecte fuerant in sacro
cimeterio, sepultus fuit Arthurus, ualde profunde propter metum Saxonum, quos
ipse frequenter expugnauerat, et ab insula Britannica prorsus eiecerat, et quos
Moderedus nepos eius pessimus contra ipsum post reuocauerat, ne in mortuum
etiam uindicis animi uicio deseuirent, qui totam iam insulam post mortem ipsius
iterum occupare contenderant. Propter eundem etiam metum in lapide quodam
lato, tamquam ad sepulchrum a fodientibus inuento, quasi pedibus .vii. [sub terra,
(cum tamen sepulchrum Arthuri .ix. pedibus inferius inuentum fuerit). Reperta
fuit crux plumbea, no]n superio[ri set poci]us inferiori parte lapidis inserta,
litteras has inscriptas habens: Hic iacet sepultus [inclitus] rex Arthurius in insula
auuallonia cum Wenneuereia† uxore sua secunda. Crucem autem hanc extractam
a lapide, dicto abbate Henrico ostendente, prospeximus, et litteras has legimus.
Sicut autem crux inferius lapidi inserta fuit, sic et crucis eiusdem pars litterata, ut
occultior esset, uersus lapidem uersa fuit. Mira quidem industria et hominum
tempestatis illius exquisita prudentia, qui corpus uiri tanti, dominique sui,
perpetuique loci illius patroni, ratione turbationis instantis, totis nisibus tunc
occultare uolebant, et tamen ut aliquo in posterum tempore, tribulatione
cessante, per litterarum saltem cruci incertarum et quandoque repertarum indicia
propalari posset, procurarunt.

* Words in square brackets down to this point supplied from marginal note on
  f.7. Words in square brackets from this point to end of text supplied from
  marginal note on f.27v.
† The names read *Arthurus, Gwennavera* and *Auallonia* in Trinity College,
  Cambridge MS R.5.33.

Cap.x

Quod rex Arthurus precipuus Glastoni(ensis ecclesie . . . . . .it; ideoque in e. . . . .
. .uina retri. . . .honorifi. . . .)

[Sicut itaque dictus rex] totum [abbati predix]erat, sic A[rthuri] corpus inuentum
[fuit] non in sepulchro ma[rmor]eo, ut regem decebat [ta]m eximium, non in
[saxe]o, aut pariis lapidibus exsecto, set pocius in ligneo, ex quercu ad hoc cauato,
et .xvi. pedibus aut pluribus in terra profundo, propter festinam magis quam
festiuam tanti principis humationem, tempore nimirum turbationis urgentis id
exigente. Dictus autem abbas corpore reperto, monitis quoque dicti regis Henrici
marmoreum ei sepulchrum fieri fecit egregium, tamquam patrono loci illius
precipuo, qui scilicet ecclesiam illam pre ceteris regni cunctis plus dilexerat,
terrisque largis et amplis locupletauerat. Ideoque non inmerito, set iusto quoque
Dei iudicio, qui bona proculdubio cuncta non solum in celis, uerum etiam in terris
siue in uita seu [post mortem, gloriam conferendo, plerumque remunerat. In
cenobiali de]mum [ecclesia antiqua pre ce]teris [regni totius] et authentica [corpus
Arth]uri egregie [sepultum fuit] et glorifice [sicut dec]uit, et tantum (ui) . . . .it
collocatum.

Ralph Higden: Polychronicon

Printed: *Polychronicon Ranulphi Higden. . .* ed. J. R. Lumby (Rolls Series 41,
London 1882) VIII, 60–64

1177(recte 1186)

Giraldus, distinctio xvi.

His nostris diebus corpus regis Arthuri, quod quasi fantasticum et in fine tanquam
ad longinqua deductum fabule Britannice adhuc venturum confinxerunt, apud
Glastoniam inter duas lapideas pyramides in sacro* cimeterio quondam erectas,
profunde in terra quercu concava reconditum, et signatum miris indiciis, est
inventum, et in ecclesia honorifice translatum, marmoreoque tumulo decenter
collocatum, ubi et crux plumbea lapide suppositis litteris insculptas interius ad
lapidem uersas, quas ego vidi et contrectavi, continebat sub hac forma: 'Hic iacet
sepultus inclitus rex Arthurus cum Wenevera uxore sua secunda in insula
Aualona'. Sic autem erant ossa distincta ut duae partes sepulchri versus caput
ossa viri continebant, tertia pars versus pedes ossa mulieris conclusit, ubi et, trica
come mulieris flava cum integritate pristina et colore reperta fuit, quam cum
monachus unus avide cum mano attraxisset, tota statim in pulverem decidit.
Audierat namque rex iste Henricus a quodam historico cantore Britannico quod
profunde in terra circiter xv. pedes corpus Arthuri invenirent in quercu concava.
Idcirco autem tam profunde humatus fuerat ne a Saxonibus sibi aemulis facile
reperiretur. Et ideo littere veritatis indices interius versus lapidem sculpte erant.
Et cst notandum quod tibie Arthuri tunc nobis ostense tibiam et genu longissimi
hominis tunc reperti tribus digitis excedebat, spatium quoque intercilii inter duos
oculos palmalem latitudinem continebat. In cujus capite xce vulnerum cicatrices
apparebant. Quae omnia praeter unum solum quod letale videbatur in unam
cicatricem concurrebant.

* Marginal note: Nota hic de Arturo quomodo erat sepultus.

Chronica Monasterii de Melsa

Printed: *Chronica monasterii de Melsa* ed. E. A. Bond (Rolls Series 43, London 1866) i.210, 216

An almost exact copy of the *Polychronicon* is given in the full version of the chronicle (i.210). An alternative version from Egerton MS 1461 (the abbreviated version) is printed at i.216:

Anno 23 regis Henrici, corpora Arthuri quondam regis Britonum et Weneverae uxoris suae, apud Glastoniam, inter duas lapideas piramides in sancto cimiterio quondam erectas, profundo in terra circiter xv pedibus quercu concava recondita, et signata miris indiciis, sunt inventa. Cujus Arthuri os tibiae tunc ostensum tibiam in genu longissimi hominis tunc reperti tribus digitis excedebat. Spatium quoque intercilii inter duos oculos palmalem longitudinem continebat.

(Probable derivative of Gerald of Wales's account)

Eulogium Historiarum

Printed: *Eulogium (Historiarum sive Temporis)* ed. F. S. Haydon (Rolls Series 9, London 1860, 1863) II, 363; III, 90–91

Sed et inclytus ille rex Arthurus lethaliter vulneratus est, qui illinc ad sananda vulnera sua in insulam Auallonis evectus, et ibidem de eodem vulnere interiit, regnum et coronam relinquens Constantino nepoti suo et filio Cadoris ducis Cornubiae, anno ab Incarnatione Domini DXLV. Sepultusque est in civitate Auallonis in ecclesia monasteriali; quod quidem sepulchrum tempore regis Ricardi illustris inventum est profundius sexdecim pedum, in coemeterio Glastoniensi, juxta vetustam ecclesiam, que tunc in magna ecclesia conventuali, ut decet tali regi, sepultus est mausolaeo marmoreo; quod quidem dignoscitur suum fuisse tumulum per epitaphium aureum in suo tumulo inventum in his verbis sculptum: Hic jacet inclytus rex Arthurus a Mordredo proditore occisus.

(1186) Sepulchrum regis Arthuri inventum est Glastoniae
Hoc anno inventum est sepulchrum regis Arthuri cum uxore sua regina in uno sarcophago conjuncti; corpus regis in parte superiori et reginae in inferiori, cum una tabula plumbea hanc scripturam continente: Arthurus rex cum uxore sua regina jacent hic sepulti. Inventi enim fuerunt in valle Auallonis in fundamento porticus Novi Monasterii ad profunditatem XVI. pedum consepulti propter metum Saxonum, ne aliquod inhonestum corpori mortuo inferrent, quia lethaliter eum oderant. Tempore regis Ricardi inventus fuit.

John of Tynemouth: Historia aurea

Corpus Christi College, Cambridge, MS 6, f.238r
Not printed

(1189)   Apud glastoniam corpus Arthuri regis et Wenevere uxoris sue reperta sunt in quercu concava xv pedibus sub terra. Os enim tibie eius tibiam et genus longissimi hominis tribus digitis excedebat.

D. Glastonbury's own tradition

Adam of Domerham: Historia de rebus gestis Glastoniensibus

Trinity College, Cambridge, MS R.5.33 f.27v
Printed: Adam of Domerham, *Historia de rebus gestis Glastoniensibus*, ed. Thomas Hearne (Oxford 1727), II, 341–3

De translacione Arturi

Hic de inclito rege Arturo decentius locando frequenter admonitus, (Requieverat enim, iuxta vetustam ecclesiam, inter duas piramides lapideas, quondam nobiliter insculptas, sexcentis quadraginta et octo annis) quadam die locum cortinis circumdans, fodere praecepit. Dehinc profunditate nimia a fossoribus exquisita, iam pene desperati, sarcophagum ligneum mire magnitudinis inuenerunt undique clausum. Quo leuato, ac aperto, regia reppererunt ossa, quantitatis incredibilis, ita ut os unius tibie a terra usque ad medium cruris et amplius in magno viro attingeret. Inuenerunt etiam crucem plumbeam, altera parte habentem inscriptum, Hic iacet sepultus inclitus rex Arturius in insula Auallonia. *Dehinc tumbam reginae, Arturo consepultae, aperientes, tricam muliebrem flauam et formosam, miroque artificio consertam, inueniunt.* Tacta tamen ab eis, in nichilum est penitus comminuta. Abbas igitur et conuentus, suscipientes eorum exuuias, cum gaudio in maiorem transtulerant ecclesiam, in mausoleo, nobiliter insculpto, intrinsecus bipertito, collocantes. Regium videlicet corpus per se ad capud tumbe, reginam ad pedes, scilicet in orientali parte; vbi usque in hodiernum diem magnifice requiescunt. Hoc autem ephitaphium tumbe inscribitur:

> Hic iacet Arturus, flos regum, gloria regni
> Quem mores, probitas, commendant laude perhenni
> Arturi iacet hic coniux tumulata secunda,
> Que meruit celos uirtutum prole fecunda.

... Words written over erasure

61

John of Glastonbury: Cronica

Printed: John of Glastonbury, *The Chronicle of Glastonbury Abbey*, ed. James Carley (Woodbridge 1985), 180–2

Giraldus tamen Cambrensis dicit eum [Henricum de Soliaco] fuisse abbatem tempore regis Henrici a quo frequenter admonitus est ut regem Arthurum decencius locaret atque ab imis ad statum digniorem transferret. Requieuerat enim iuxta uetustam ecclesiam inter duas piramides lapideas quondam nobiliter inscluptas sexcentis quadraginta et octo annis. Unde quadam die cortinis circumdans fodere precepit. De hinc profunditate nimia a fossoribus exquisita iam pene desperati sarcophagum ligneum mire magnitudinis inuenerunt undique clausum. Quo leuato ac aperto regia repererunt ossa quantitatis incredibilis ita ut vnum os tibie a terra usque ad medium cruris et amplius in magno uiro attingeret. Inuenerunt eciam crucem plumbeam altera parte habentem inscriptum: 'Hic iacet sepultus inclitus rex Arthurus in insula Auallonia'. De hinc tumbam regine aperientes, crines capitis sui circa ossa eiusdem integre iacentes aspiciunt ac si recenter ibidem sepulta fuisset, tacti tamen ab eis in nichilum sunt penitus comminuti. Abbas igitur et conuentus suscipientes eorum exuuias cum gaudio in maiorem transtulerunt ecclesiam in mausoleo nobiliter exsculpto intrinsecus bibertito collocantes, regium corpus per se ad capud tumbe, reginam ad pedes, scilicet in choro ante magnum altare, ubi usque in hodiernum diem magnifice requiescunt. Hoc autem epithaphium tumbe inscribitur:

> Hic iacet Arthurus, flos regum, gloria regni,
> Quem mors probitas commendat laude perhenni.
> Arthuri iacet hic coniux tumulata secunda
> Que meruit celos uirtutum prole fecunda.

E. An eclectic account

Alberic des Trois Fontaines: Chronica

Printed: Chronica Albrici monachi Trium Fontium, ed. Paul Scheffer-Boichorst, *Monumenta Germaniae Historica Scriptores*, XXIII, 871

[1193]   De corpore Arturi magni dicitur, quod circa hunc annum sit inventum in Anglia in insula Avalonis, ubi est abbatia sancti Dunstani, Glastonia vulgariter dicta, ad Sanctum Petrum de Glastenberia Bathoniensis dyocesis; et hoc factum est per industriam cuiusdam monachi eiusdem ecclesie novi abbatis, qui totum cimiterium loci diligenter excavando fecit investigari, animatus verbis que olim adhuc monachus audierat ab ore regis Henrici patris Richardi. Et inventa est tumba lapidea in profundo terre defossa, super quam lamina plumbea quibusdam versibus erat insignita:

> Hic iacet Arturus flos regum, gloria regni
> Quem probitas morum commendat laude perenni
> Hic iacit Arturus Britonum rex ultor inultus etc.

F. Summary accounts, probably either from Margam or Ralph of Coggeshall or their archetype

Chronicle transcribed at the end of 'Exchequer Domesday'

Printed: 'A Chronicle of the thirteenth century', *Archaeologia Cambrensis* Third Series VIII (1862) 276

mcxci   Apud Glastoniam inventa ossa Arturi in quodam vetustissimo sarcofago.

Annales Dorenses [Annals of Abbey Dore]

Printed: *Monumenta Germaniae Historica, Scriptores*, ed. R. Pauli, XXVII, 526

1191   Hoc etiam anno Glastonie inventa sunt ossa Arthuri regis.

Unidentified thirteenth century annals

Trinity College, Dublin MS 507 f.6v
Not printed

1191   Apud Glastoniam inventa sunt ossa famossissimi Arthuri quondam regis Britannie Maioris in quodam vetustissimo sarcofago recondita.

APPENDIX B

The Discovery of the Holy Cross of Waltham at Montacute, the Excavation of Arthur's Grave at Glastonbury Abbey, and Joseph of Arimathea's Burial [1]

James P. Carley

At some point in the last quarter of the twelfth century, probably shortly after 1177, an unidentified dispossessed secular canon from Waltham composed a tract concerning the foundation of his church: *De inventione Sanctae Crucis nostrae in Monte Acuto et de ductione ejusdem apud Waltham.* [2] From the text itself we learn that the author was born in 1119, that he entered the house in 1124, and that he heard the story of the Holy Cross from the aged sacristan Turkill, who had actually seen King Harold go into battle. According to *De inventione Sanctae Crucis* the Holy Cross was discovered in the reign of Cnut, probably c.1035. The smith at Montacute was, it seems, vouchsafed a vision concerning the location at Montacute Hill of a hidden cross. He ignored the vision, which then recurred. On the third occasion, it was accompanied by a violent twist of the arm, and the smith approached the priest, who assembled a crowd − including the great landowner Tofig the Proud [3] − to undertake an excavation. They climbed the mountain and the smith directed them to the divinely indicated spot. Next, 'incipiunt fodere, donec effossis xl cubitis mirae magnitudinis lapidem reperiunt, in cujus medio visa est quasi fissura dehiscens.' (p. 5). Here was found the miraculous cross, along with a

---

1 Dom Aelred Watkin first suggested to me a possible connection between the Holy Cross of Waltham and the excavation of King Arthur's grave. He was also the source for a number of specific points and, as in so much of my work, I owe him great thanks.

2 William Stubbs, ed., *The Foundation of Waltham Abbey* (Oxford, 1861). The church at Waltham was founded at the time of King Cnut. Harold refounded it as a collegiate church and his church was dedicated in 1060. The church was turned into a priory for sixteen Augustinian canons by Henry II, and at this time the seculars, including the author of *De inventione*, were expelled. See D. Knowles and R. Neville Hadcock, *Medieval Religious Houses in England and Wales* (London, 1971), p.178.

3 Charter evidence suggests that Tofig owned land both at Montacute and at Waltham. In this, as in many other details, *De inventione* seems remarkably accurate.

smaller cross, a bell and a book — the *Liber Niger*.[4] Tents were erected around the site until the precious relics could be moved. Tofig decided to send the smaller cross to the local church; the larger he placed in a cart to which twelve red oxen were yoked. These creatures refused to budge until he mentioned his vill at Waltham, to which they then immediately proceeded. Here Tofig founded a church dedicated to the Holy Cross.

A number of points in this account suggest parallels to the later and more famous excavation in Glastonbury Abbey's cemetery. First, there is the question of date. Although the Holy Cross was supposedly discovered in 1035, the account was not written until after 1177; it first appears, then, very shortly before the Arthurian excavation.[5] Montacute — and, by extension, Waltham — had connections with Glastonbury, which would cause the Glastonbury community to have an active interest in the story. Montacute is, of course, within a few miles of Glastonbury. Both places are characterised by prominent hills and one can be seen from the other. References to a lost charter suggest that as early as the last quarter of the seventh century Baldred made a grant of sixteen hides to Glastonbury at *Logworesbeorh* — i.e. Montacute.[6] William of Malmesbury, too, refers to the ancient name *Logweresbeorh* for Montacute and specifically links the place with the personal name *Logwor*, which occurs on one of the pyramids in the ancient cemetery — the pyramids between which Arthur's body was later to be found. Henry of Blois, abbot of Glastonbury (1126- 1171), held the deanery of Waltham in 1144 and tried to buy a gem from the cross for 100 marks. He was himself a Cluniac, and may too have at one time been prior of Montacute Priory.[7] In the account itself several points stand out. In both cases the excavators must dig to a great depth before they discover anything.[8] At Montacute they

4 BL, MS Harl. 3766 contains a transcription of a portion of this *Liber Niger*.
5 We have no evidence about where the canon was living when he composed the *De inventione* and I suppose that it is even possible that he took a copy of the tract to show the monks at Montacute.
6 See H. P. R. Finberg, *The Early Charters of Wessex* (Leicester, 1964), no. 358. For later charters concerning land held at Montacute by Glastonbury Abbey see also nos. 408, 414.
7 See K. Knowles, *The Monastic Order in England*, 2nd edn (Cambridge, 1963), p. 282, f. 3. Montacute Priory was not founded until c.1078, although *De inventione* suggests that there was a priest and sexton at the site earlier in the century. See *Medieval Religious Houses*, p.101.
8 Any ancient grave at Glastonbury would have been buried at a great depth, since in the tenth century St Dunstan had caused the level of the ancient cemetery to be raised. See C. A. Ralegh Radford, 'Glastonbury Abbey', in G. Ashe, *The Quest for Arthur's Britain*, paperback edn (London, 1971), pp.107-8.

finally come across a stone described as 'mirae magnitudinis'. According to Adam of Domerham the Glastonbury monks also find a 'sarcophagum ligneum mirae magnitudinis'.[9] Unlike other chroniclers, moreover, Adam adds the strange detail that the site in the cemetery was surrounded by curtains. This brings to mind the tent which covered the dig at Montacute.[10]

In sum, then, Glastonbury Abbey would have had a proprietary interest in Montacute doings, at least one twelfth-century abbot, Henry of Blois, knew the Holy Cross well, and it is certainly possible that the community had early access to a version of De inventione. The parallels between the two texts may even support the supposition that De inventione was some sort of vague model for the organisation of the excavation at Glastonbury in 1190/91. Beyond this, it is not possible to speculate, although it would be tempting to suggest that De inventione was an even more specific catalyst for the later dig.

These two excavations can ultimately, I think, be linked with an excavation which — surprisingly — did not take place. After the stone cross found in Arthur's tomb identified Glastonbury as 'insula Avallonia' it was only a matter of time before Joseph of Arimathea's name (taken in this context out of the French Grail Romances) came to be linked with Glastonbury, and in thirteenth-century additions to William of Malmesbury's De Antiquitate Glastonie Ecclesie it is first stated that Joseph was the hitherto unknown apostle of Christ who evangelised Britain and built the Wattled Church at Glastonbury.[11] With the Joseph legend came the Grail, which was transformed into an ecclesiastically respectable relic — two cruets containing the Blood and Sweat of Jesus. Ultimately Glastonbury produced writings by a Merlin-like figure, Melkin the Bard, which articulated in a rather cryptic prophetic form Joseph's role in early Glastonbury history.[12]

9 Thomas Hearne, ed., *Adami de Domerham Historia de Rebus gestis Glastoniensibus*, 2 vols (Oxford, 1727), 2.341.
10 Watkin points out another detail which may or may not be relevant. At St Mary's church at Stoke-sub-Hamdon, about one mile from Montacute, there is a twelfth-century tympanum on the north door with lettering almost identical to that reproduced by Camden from the lead cross found in Arthur's tomb. (Personal communication.)
11 The process by which Joseph of Arimathea emerged as evangelist of Britain and Glastonbury Abbey's founder is most clearly elucidated by Valerie M. Lagorio, 'The Evolving Legend of St Joseph at Glastonbury', *Speculum*, 46 (1971), pp. 209-31. For the additions to William's text see John Scott, ed. and trans., *The Early History of Glastonbury. An Edition, Translation and Study of William of Malmesbury's 'De Antiquitate Glastonie Ecclesie'* (Woodbridge, 1981), p.46.
12 See James P. Carley, 'Melkin the Bard and Esoteric Tradition at Glastonbury Abbey', *The Downside Review*, 99 (1981), pp.1-17.

In Melkin's prophecy it is made quite clear that Joseph's place of burial is unknown and that if the tomb is ever found great miracles will occur:

> Cum reperietur eius sarcophagum integrum illibatum in futuris videbitur et erit apertum toto orbi terrarum. Ex tunc nec aqua nec ros celi insulam nobilissimam habitantibus poterit deficere. Per multum tempus ante diem iudicialem in Iosaphat erunt aperta hec et viuentibus declarata.[13]

In 1345 — only three years after John of Glastonbury incorporated the prophecy into his history of Glastonbury Abbey — one John Blome of London obtained permission to search for the grave, and later in the century an anonymous East Anglian chronicler stated that the tomb had actually been found in 1367.[14] This latter report was, in fact, inaccurate and the monks never did discover where Joseph was buried. This is made clear by the account of William Good, who had served as an acolyte at Glastonbury Abbey as a boy and who after the Dissolution ended his days as a Jesuit priest in Rome.[15] Good's testimony is reported by Fr Edward Maihew[16] and it states that

> The monks never knew for certain the place of this saint's burial, or pointed it out. They said the body was hidden most carefully, either there (at Glastonbury), or on a hill near Montacute, called Hamden Hill, and that when his body should be found, the whole world should went their way thither on account of the number and wondrous nature of the miracles worked there.[17]

The verbal echoes to Melkin's prophecy are obvious. Maihew himself mentions that 'Memini vero cum aliquando per illum montem ipse transirem, me a fide dignis accepisse, senem quemdam qui non longe ab eo loco habitabat, sacpius, regnante Elizabetha haeretica, illum locum visitare, ibique certo in loco flexis genibus orare solitum.'[18] Interestingly, there is another reference to this same old man in the autobiography of Fr William Weston, S.J. (d.1615).[19] In 1586 Weston met a man of about eighty years of age who had once been a servant

---

13 See Carley, p.3.
14 On these accounts see Lagorio, pp.217-18.
15 On Good see J. Armitage Robinson, *Two Glastonbury Legends* (Cambridge, 1926), pp.46ff.
16 On Maihew and especially his connections with Good's narrative, see Hugh Connolly, 'Father Edward Maihew and Glastonbury', *The Downside Review*, 50 (1932), pp.502-504.
17 See Robinson, p.46. Robinson quotes Cardinal Gasquet's translation of a passage in Ussher's *Britannicarum Ecclesiarum Antiquitates*.
18 See Robinson, p.67.
19 See Aelred Watkin, 'Last Glimpses of Glastonbury', *The Downside Review*, 67 (1949), pp.83-86.

at Glastonbury Abbey and who at the Dissolution saved a Nail from the Crucifixion from the depredations of King Henry VIII's agents. This Nail, according to tradition, had been brought to England by Joseph of Arimathea himself. The Nail was later seized, so it seems, by the Anglican bishop of Salisbury, but the old man continued his practice of ascending the mountain on his knees. The place in question — that is, the one where 'St Joseph with his companions fixed the seat of his abode' — must be Montacute itself rather than Hamden Hill, since the old man's place of pilgrimage to St Joseph's shrine is described as 'situated on a high mountain; and its ancient foundations and confused ruins are still extant to be seen'.[20] The second part of the reference is to the ruined chapel of St Michael on Montacute Hill. Thomas Gerard's *Description of Somerset* (1633) also mentions this material:

> in this chappell [on Montacute Hill] was founde one of those nayles which fastened Our Saviour to the crosse, which a gentleman (Mr. H.) not farr of kept sometime and after sold for a greate sume of money to be transported beyond the seas . . . This place by some latter zealous Recusants hath bin had in greate veneration, for they believe that . . . the body of Joseph of Aremathea . . . was here interred.[21]

Finally, in Weston's account, the old man refers to 'attacks of spirits, for I have heard there wailings and groans and the mournful voices of people in grief'.[22] From this he concludes that the mountain contains some entrance to purgatory. Here, of course, one is put in mind of St Patrick's Purgatory.[23] Watkin suggests even further that this aspect of the story is reminiscent of Melwas in his role as king of the Underworld with his abode at Glastonbury and that Glastonbury Tor and Montacute Hill had close mythological parallels in pagan times.[24]

Why did the monks come to associate Joseph with Montacute? Why did they not 'discover' his remains in the Abbey cemetery? Generations of scholars have analysed the political expediency of the discovery of Arthur's body in 1190/91 — the implicit assumption being that the monks maliciously staged the whole affair, that it was a hoax in all its details — and Glastonbury Abbey has more than once

---

20 'Last Glimpses', p. 86.
21 Quoted by Watkin, 'Last Glimpses', p. 84, n. 1.
22 'Last Glimpses', p. 86.
23 Interestingly, BL, MS Harl. 3776, which contains one of the two surviving texts of *De inventione*, also has one of the versions of St Patrick's Purgatory.
24 'Last Glimpses', p. 84. Glastonbury Tor itself seems to have been portrayed as the entrance to a Celtic underworld in the *Life* of St Collen. This *Life*, which survives only in two sixteenth-century manuscripts, appears to contain elements from a much earlier oral tradition.

been dismissed as an 'officine de faux'. In fact, archaeologists are now suggesting that the excavation was legitimate to the degree that the monks really dug up an ancient burial site.[25] It seems to me equally clear that the monks were unable later to identify a second ancient burial site in the cemetery which might be conveniently associated with the even more ancient burial of Joseph. Arthur had, as it were, pre-empted the most likely spot and there was no grave to be excavated that might be attributed to Joseph.[26] If the monks really thought that Joseph had come to Glastonbury, then they must have been genuinely confused about where he was buried. Now, the story of Montacute Holy Cross was well known. One might ask, how and why did this relic get to this location? Could it be because Joseph had landed at Montacute before he came to Glastonbury? Or might he at least be buried at Montacute, and if so, might the Cross be a sign of his presence? This, it strikes me, could well have been the logic behind the speculations concerning Montacute as Joseph's burial site. It is no wonder either that excavations were never undertaken, since the monks would want to maintain the (very useful) Joseph connection exclusively for themselves, and did not wish to diffuse it to Waltham's Holy Cross and Montacute Priory, as the discovery of a grave on Montacute Hill would have done.

None of these speculations can, of course, be substantiated, especially since they deal with material which would never have been clearly articulated, let alone written, even by the monks themselves. If the arguments are correct, however, then there is an interesting symmetry to the traditions. The Holy Cross at Montacute may have served as a model for King Arthur's excavation, which led to the identification of Glastonbury as Avalon. This, in turn, caused Joseph of Arimathea to be named as Glastonbury's evangelist. Joseph, of course, needed a place of burial and was clearly not in Glastonbury's own cemetery and this led back to Montacute and explained why the Holy Cross was found there in the first place.

[25] See Radford, 'Glastonbury Abbey', pp.107-8.
[26] Melkin's prophecy makes the most of the situations but is not altogether satisfactory. Legitimate relics would certainly have been preferable.

III

UTHER AND IGERNE: A STUDY IN UNCOURTLY LOVE

Rosemary Morris

It is a commonplace of mythology that heroes should be conceived, born and brought up in striking and mysterious circumstances, as an adumbration of their future greatness. It is interesting to note that, in many cases, these circumstances are morally dubious. To cite some favourite medieval examples,[1] Gregorius and Roland (in late texts) are the children of incest; Alexander (in Pseudo-Callisthenes and its derivatives) is engendered by the sorcerer Nectanebus, who seduces the queen of Macedon by pretending to be the god Ammon; Merlin is the son of an incubus; Galahad's mother seduces Lancelot by taking on the appearance of Guinevere. St Kentigern's mother was raped by 'Ewen', who beguiled her into a lonely place by disguising himself as a woman. Christ himself was engendered in circumstances which provoke the worst suspicions in his mother's betrothed husband, and in Geoffrey of Monmouth's *Historia Regum Britanniae*, Arthur, engendered by king Uther Pendragon in the form of Arthur's mother's husband, conforms fully to the pattern. My purpose in this article is not to study the repercussions of Arthur's birthtale upon Arthur himself,[2] but to examine some medieval authors' reactions to the story of his parents.

The tendency for the circumstances of a legendary hero's birth to be disreputable can be explained in various ways: as a means of provoking astonishment in the hearer, as an avoidance of the *tradux peccati*, as evidencing an ancient tribal system of family relationships,

---

[1] Most of these are mentioned in the article by G. and U. Pörksen, 'Die "Geburt" des Helden in mittelhochdeutschen Epen und epischen Stoffen des Mittelalters', *Euphorion* 74 (1980), 257-86. The example of St Kentigern was suggested to me by Dr Tony Hunt who points out a connection with the *Yvain* story, the lonely place being near a fountain near a forest. See A. P. Forbes, ed., *Lives of S. Kentigern and St Ninian* (Edinburgh, 1874), 246-7.

[2] See my book, *The Character of King Arthur in Medieval Literature* (Cambridge and Totowa, NJ, 1982), 24-35.

and so on.[3] There is no one explanation for the medieval stories, however, for every author treats them differently, depending on his moral (and other) preoccupations. This comes out very clearly in the medieval Alexander legend. Some authors — for instance, the twelfth-century Anglo-Norman Thomas of Kent — delight in the story, finding that it endows the hero with magical glamour, while other versions (including all redactions of the Old French *Roman d'Alexandre* and the twelfth-century *Alexandreis* of Gautier de Châtillon) reject it with indignation: 'Nectanabi proles? ut degener arguar absit!' snaps Gautier.[4] I mention Alexander not only because his story reflects a medieval duality of reaction to this kind of tale, but also because (as J. S. P. Tatlock argued)[5] in its medieval Latin form it influenced Geoffrey of Monmouth's presentation of Arthur's birthtale, though it was certainly not its sole source. Now, as there is no trace of a birth-tale for Arthur before Geoffrey, I shall begin with his version (c.1135), from which all later versions derive.

In outline, the story is as follows. King Uther Pendragon sees the wife of his vassal, Gorlois, duke of Cornwall, at a feast, and falls violently in love with her. Gorlois, realising this, withdraws with Igerne to Cornwall and puts her in his impregnable castle of Tintagel. Uther besieges Gorlois in his other fortress. After a time Merlin transforms Uther into the form of Gorlois. He enters Tintagel, sleeps with Igerne and engenders Arthur. That same night, Gorlois is killed, so that Uther is able to marry Igerne.

Though Geoffrey's influence on the courtly romance was very great, he is one of the most uncourtly of writers where the relationship between the sexes is concerned. This need not surprise us, for even if his chosen genre (Latin pseudo-history) had admitted of courtesy, he was writing too early to have been touched by the vogue for 'courtly love' raging in far-away Provence.[6] Thus, when that vogue reached

---

3 Pörksen, 'Die Geburt', 276; Helen Adolf, 'The concept of sin in medieval romance', *Studies in Honour of M. Schlauch* (Warsaw, 1966), 21-8.

4 Thomas of Kent, *Roman de toute chevalerie*, ed. B. Foster and I. Short as *The Anglo-Norman Alexander*, ANTS 29-31, vol. I (London, 1976), 8-18; *The Old French Roman d'Alexandre*, ed. E. C. Armstrong *et al.*, Elliot Monographs 36-8 (reprint, New York, 1965); *Galteri de Castellione Alexandreis*, ed. M. L. Colker (Padova, 1978) I, 47.

5 *The Legendary History of Britain* (Berkeley and Los Angeles, 1950), 59-60, 314-18. References to the *Historia* are to the text in E. Faral, *La Légende arthurienne*, 3 vols (Paris, 1929), vol. III.

6 By 'courtly love', here and throughout this paper, I mean a generalised code of beliefs about love between a man and a woman which was acknowledged (though not necessarily as an immutable and inexorable law) by writers on love from the eleventh to the fifteenth century whom modern critics define,

northern France and England, the heartlands of the courtly romance, Geoffrey's uncourtly authority set up a conflict within the genre which caused some heart-searching in later authors.

All the women in the *Historia* are either victims or villains, and the more 'womanly' they are, the more they incline towards the former category. To survive in Geoffrey's fiercely politicised, man's world, a woman must have the pride, cunning and ruthlessness of a man. Indeed, the only way in which Cordaella and Rowena, for instance, are differentiated from the men whom they dominate is by their beauty which, of course, they use as a weapon. The female victims — Imogen, Estrildis, Igerne — are also beautiful, but their beauty, allied with gentleness, proves to be their doom by drawing masculine ferocity upon them. It arouses love, but to Geoffrey 'love' and 'lust' are practically synonymous. The onset of love in the man is always sudden and violent: he 'incaluit', he is 'amore captus'. No mention is made of the woman's response: in this context it is irrelevant. Morality is not entirely banished, but it is invoked by other characters (most memorably the giant Corineus, who whirls a club round his son-in-law's head while counselling marital fidelity, p.94), not by the author. However, Geoffrey is not uninterested in the effect of passion on the psyche, so long as the examination stays in a political context. And the most detailed examination is that of Uther.

It must be acknowledged that Uther, son of a murdered king, enmeshed from his earliest youth in war and treachery, has never had time to cultivate the peacetime refinements which are to be gloriously

by common consent, as 'courtly'. The most important elements of the code are as follows. The lovers live, or at least meet, in a court, so their love must be kept secret from spies and slanderers and their behaviour must conform to aristocratic social norms. Their own attitudes are also fundamentally aristocratic. The lover abrogates his male arrogance and submits to the lady as to a superior and an ideal, whatever their actual respective rank; an analogy with the feudal lord/vassal relationship is often drawn or felt. The lover must serve and obey the lady with all that is in him. Her beauty rouses passion in him, but he also sees it as a reflection of her inner and spiritual perfection. By aspiring towards this perfection, the lover elevates and improves himself. He is absolutely faithful to his lady, and he expects fidelity from her. If his efforts have made him worthy of her, she is bound to accept him. The relationship lays due, but not undue, emphasis on the achievement of sexual intimacy. Moments of fulfilment, sexual or emotional, are rare, fleeting and reached after much patient striving, but they bring intense joy which lingers in the memory. The relationship is generally, but not universally, held to be incompatible with marriage. (Cf. D. D. R. Owen, *Noble Lovers* (London, 1975), 25-34.) The above definition is an outline only, and does not seek to deny any of the subtleties introduced into the concept of 'courtly love' by medieval writers or modern critics.

fostered by his son. Geoffrey's account of the onset of passion in Uther carries psychological conviction. He first sees the beautiful Igerne at a feast in celebration of a great victory over the Saxons (a victory which, by a deft stroke of narrative irony, is due to the counsel of Igerne's husband, Gorlois). This feast is the first relaxation which Uther has known, and in his description of it Geoffrey insists on the words 'gaudium' and 'laetitia' (p. 221). What is more natural than that the king's eye, so used to scenes of blood and horror, should dwell with pleasure on the assembly of fair women, or that it should settle on the fairest of all, the only one worthy of royal attention? The passionate energy which Uther has hitherto devoted to battle and hatred is now diverted into this new channel, but its nature is unchanged: his passion remains an expression of violent will, which demands immediate physical action. Uther is unable to dissemble: 'Haec sola erat cui fercula incessanter dirigebat, cui aurea pocula familiaribus internuntiis mittebat. Arridebat ei multotiens, jocosa verba interserebat' (p. 221). There is something disarming about this naivety, but we are given little time to feel sympathy for Uther. His passion is immediately observed by the jealous Gorlois, and immediately (for, in the *Historia*, to think is to act), Gorlois withdraws illegally from court, 'cum id solum amittere timeret, quod super omnia diligebat' (p. 222). Anger strikes on anger, and Uther declares war on his (ostensibly) errant vassal, making Igerne into a small-scale Helen of Troy. In this reversion to bellicosity, Igerne's own feelings are entirely ignored.

Thus far, the story is commonplace. It could be paralleled a dozen times in fiction, or in twelfth-century reality: Tatlock cites examples (*Legendary History*, pp. 59-60). Uther's passion is realistic enough, for a brutal age: and yet, when Gorlois withdraws to Cornwall, and confines his wife to Tintagel, we have something very much like the classic 'courtly' situation of the lover, the *mal mariée* and the *gelos*. As the siege of Gorlois's castle drags on, we also have the necessary condition for courtly feeling: inaction. Uther suffers the frustrations of every courtly lover, and, like them, he knows of only one cure: 'Uror amore Ingernae, nec periculum corporis mei euadere existimo, nisi ea potitus fuero ... aut aliter internis anxietatibus interibo' (p. 222). Uther's self-diagnosis is medical rather than psychological, but the same thing could be said for other early 'courtly' sufferers — for example, Lavine and Eneas in the *Roman d'Eneas*.[7] Uther's passion is not in its essence different from courtly love, whose first stage

---

[7] Ed. J.-D. Salverda de Grave, CFMA 45, 62, 2 vols (Paris, 1925, 1929, repr. 1964, 1968), vol. II, ll. 8399-450, 8927-9108.

depends on repressed sexual desire. But Uther does not proceed to the equally essential second stage of courtliness, the conceptualisation of repressed desire and its refinement into a complex state of mind. Feeling, for Uther, must be translated into action, for inaction is death.

Uther's love, or lust, is at once intensely personal and depersonalising. No woman but Igerne will do, but he does not think of Igerne as a person at all: she is merely the sexual target. This sounds like the antithesis of courtliness, but in one way it is not so. The courtly lyricist devotes himself to a single lady, but the lady as a person is often curiously absent from the poetry which ostensibly focuses on her. She is the pretext for the lover's exposition of his feelings, and her moods are important because they establish the parameters for that exposition. It would not be difficult to turn Uther's sufferings during the siege into a courtly meditation.

In his treatise on love, Andreas Capellanus (mid 1180s) observes that as soon as a lover decides on some action, the first thing he does is to 'enrol a helper and find a go-between'.[8] He doubtless borrowed the precept from Ovid; fifty years earlier we find Geoffrey's Uther, acting on advice from a faithful retainer, following the same precept *avant la lettre*. But this is where Uther and proto-courtliness part company, for the go-between selected by Uther is no helpful old woman or sympathetic *ami*, but Merlin the magician. And Merlin is not going to put the lover's case to the lady, but to put the lover to the lady, like a supernatural horse-breeder. Not that Geoffrey makes clear (as Robert de Boron will later) that Merlin deliberately guides Uther's affair in order to engineer the conception of Arthur; but as Geoffrey's Merlin has prophesied Arthur's coming (*inter multa alia*, p.191), we are at liberty to suspect that he is consciously bringing about what he prophesied. Certainly Merlin, whose moral stance is ambiguous throughout the *Historia*, makes no criticism of Uther. According to some manuscripts he is 'commotus' at the king's sufferings, according to others he is merely 'admiratus' (p. 223). In either case he is perfectly willing to deceive Igerne by giving Uther the appearance of her husband.

Here the comparison with the Alexander romance becomes interesting. There, the seducer and the shape-shifting magician are one and the same. Geoffrey splits them, leaving the possible odium of the deception with the magician. Uther remains an ordinary man, no worse in his passions than any other man (in the *Historia* anyway), and resorting to deception only because he is desperate. In another way, too, the comparison is interesting. In the Latin Alexander

8   P. G. Walsh, ed., *Andreas Capellanus on Love* (London, 1982), 35 and note 11.

romance there are several broad hints that the woman in the case, Olympias, knows perfectly well what Nectanebus is up to and connives at it.[9] Geoffrey rejects this and insists on the completeness of the deception: 'Quid enim aliud accessisset, cum prorsus ipse Gorlois reputaretur adesse?'. He twice uses the word 'deceperat' of Uther, and in contrast calls Igerne 'credula' (pp. 223-4). To the end of her life, Igerne never learns how she has been deceived. When Gorlois is slain and his castles are captured, Uther at once marries Igerne, who passes to him as the spoils of war – and, of course, is not consulted. We could hardly be further from courtliness here; and, if Geoffrey assures us that (in defiance of probability) they lived 'non modico amore ligati', this is no mitigation of the uncourtliness, especially if we anticipate a dictum expressed by one of Andreas Capellanus's characters, namely that, in courtly terms, 'Love can in no sense play his role between married people' (Walsh, p.147).

Geoffrey treats the story of Uther and Igerne in, for him, considerable detail, and though he typically emphasises action and excitement, he is not indifferent to the emotions involved. The story is, in a way, a fanfare for Arthur, but we are reminded of this only with the bald sentence: 'Concepit quoque eadem nocte celeberrimum illum Arturum, qui postmodum ut celebris esset mira probitate promeruit' (p. 224). Geoffrey does not assign guilt to any party. Igerne is entirely innocent, and we may draw back from the rapid narrative just long enough to feel pity for her. Gorlois, though potentially in the invidious position of the *gelos*, acts honestly and bravely. Uther's nature is impulsive, not criminal, and he truly suffers for 'love'. He grieves sincerely over the death of Gorlois – while rejoicing equally seriously over Igerne's widowhood (p. 224) – and he makes *amende honorable* to his unsuspecting mistress. Merlin remains enigmatic; being only half human, he is not really subject to human morality. It is noticeable that, in Geoffrey, neither Uther nor Merlin is punished for his part in the affair, whereas in the Alexander romance, Nectanebus is killed by Alexander, who at the time does not know that Nectanebus is his father. It is curious to note that in the thirteenth-century *Mort Artu* and its derivatives, Arthur is killed by Mordred, his son conceived in incest. It seems that the vengeance-on-the-father motif skipped a generation in the Arthurian tradition – a generation of both authors and characters. Uther himself continues to escape punishment throughout the tradition, but Merlin does not: an interesting consequence of Geoffrey's splitting of the Nectanebus character.[10]

9 H.-J. Bergmeister, ed., *Die Historia de Preliis Alexandri Magni* (Meisenheim, 1975), 23, 29.
10 A. Micha, ed., *La Mort le roi Artu*, Textes Littéraires Français (Paris and

As so often in the *Historia*, Geoffrey creates a story which, while of merit in itself, invites development by later authors. Apart from expanding the narrative, they have a choice of three treatments: to moralise it, to make a courtly story out of it, or to brutalise it. I now wish to show how three types of author made this choice: twelfth- and thirteenth-century chroniclers depending closely on Geoffrey, romance authors, especially Robert de Boron, and a group of late medieval chroniclers, Boece and his Scottish followers.

Reaction to Geoffrey was not long in coming. The 'Variant Version' of the *Historia*,[11] which substantially rephrases much of Geoffrey's narrative without altering the course of events, has a tendency to moralise which comes out strongly in the Uther story. The accent is on personal responsibility: Uther's character is blackened rather than Merlin's. Geoffrey had merely remarked, of Uther's first sight of Igerne, 'subito incaluit amore illius'. The Variant Version expands: 'Rex, tamquam David in Bathsabee, subito, Sathana mediante, incaluit' (p. 221). Uther's inability to hide his passion (so different from courtly secrecy) is emphasised, but references to his sufferings during the siege are omitted, as is all idea that Merlin is 'moved' by Uther's plight. It is the distress caused to others which is focused on. Most revealing is the change in Uther's reaction to the news of Gorlois's death: 'subtristem ("somewhat sad!") se simulans, de Igerna a maritali copula soluta non modicum gaudens' (p. 225). Here is no decent man fallen victim to his own passionate nature, but a treacherous ravisher. The game of seduction is stripped of every possibility of courtliness, and its essential repulsiveness is laid bare. Deceiving a virtuous woman by magic is no better than deceiving her by other means.

The Variant Version gives an interesting, and probably early, clerkly reaction to Geoffrey's story, but the interest is limited because it had no literary influence — unless it influenced Wace. (The influence may even be the other way round.)[12] But about Wace's influence there is no doubt: it was on his rendering of the *Historia* that most vernacular romancers drew.[13] Chronologically, Wace stands at the dawn of northern *courtoisie*, so his version of the Igerne story is of special

Geneva, 1964). See F. Bogdanow, *The Romance of the Grail* (Manchester UP, 1966), 150-2. For Merlin's punishment see *Character of Arthur*, 28.

11 J. Hammer, ed., *The 'Historia Regum Britanniae' of Geoffrey of Monmouth: A Variant Version* (Cambridge, Mass., 1951).

12 R. A. Caldwell, 'Wace's *Roman de Brut* and the *Variant Version* of Geoffrey of Monmouth's *Historia Regum Britanniae*', *Speculum* 31 (1956), 675-82; for the contrary opinion, see P. Gallais, 'La Variant Version de l'*Historia Regum Britanniae* et le *Brut* de Wace', *Romania* 87 (1966), 1-32.

13 I. Arnold, ed., *Le Roman de Brut de Wace*, SATF, 2 vols (Paris, 1938-1940), vol. I, l. 8570.

interest. Indeed, there is no reason why Wace, as semi-official historian to the Angevin court, should not have met troubadours there. As we might expect, Wace is at some pains to improve both the dramatic and the psychological impact of our story. The beginning of the affair is 'courtly' in the literal sense. It takes place at court, and it is because of the elaborate arrangements for seating the barons at Uther's court feast, 'chescuns en l'ordre de s'enur' (1. 8570), that the duke and Igerne are opposite the king. Igerne well merits her position at this court, which has become imperceptibly more refined than Geoffrey's. She is not merely beautiful (and therefore a victim): 'curteise esteit e bele e sage / e mult esteit de grant parage' (8575-6). However narrowly one interprets 'curteise' at this early date, Igerne is clearly developing something of a character. An even more striking change is that Uther's love is no *coup de foudre*. He has already fallen in love with Igerne by reputation (ll. 8577-82): a very early northern use of this motif, which is later to make itself very much at home in Arthurian romance, in attachment to Gawain. This puts the whole affair on an entirely different footing. The violently impulsive warrior has become a lover for whom words and thoughts are as important as physical feelings, and who has already made trial of patience. He is now at the stage picked out by Andreas Capellanus as the very definition of love: 'the sight of, and uncontrolled thinking about, the beauty of the other sex' (Walsh, p. 33). He still (as in Geoffrey) shows Igerne marks of amorous favour, thereby breaking the secrecy essential to a successful courtly relationship, but this is because the sight of his beloved, at last before him in the flesh, overturns his self-control in a way which many a courtly lyricist would doubtless recognise.[14] The reactions of Igerne and her husband to this all-too-visible courtship are especially interesting. The former lives up to her reputation for 'sagesse':

> Ygerne issi se conteneit
> qu'el n'otriout ne desdiseit   (ll. 8595-6)

the only possible attitude for a virtuous lady importuned by royalty. The duke's reaction is the exact opposite. In a burst of wrath, he rises and departs, not just from the court, but from the very table. He behaves, in fact, like a *gelos*, and the violence of his reaction, unmatched by violence on Uther's part, tends to put the former in the wrong. His hastiness precipitates a disaster which would have been averted had the rules of courtliness been observed, for why should not

---

14 E.g. Wace's contemporary Bernart de Ventadour: see his *Chansons d'amour*, ed. M. Lazar, Bibliothèque Française et Romane, Sér. B, 5 (Paris, 1966), no. 1, stanza vi.

Uther, like many another passionate courtly lover, have schooled himself to love in patient silence?

With these much-altered preliminaries, we should expect Wace to make much of Uther's sufferings during the siege, and so he does, in a way different from Geoffrey's. No longer does Uther 'burn' or 'sicken': the cruel Ovidian metaphors, which express lust, are replaced by a vocabulary expressing the absorption of the whole personality in love:

> L'amur Ygerne m'ad suspris,
> tut m'ad vencu, tut m'ad conquis,
> ne puis aler, ne puis venir,
> ne puis veillier, ne puis dormir,
> ne puis lever, ne puis culchier,
> ne puis beivre, ne puis mangier,
> que d'Ygerne ne me suvienge;
> mais jo ne sai cum jo la tienge.   (8659-66)

The anaphora and the narrow rhetorical balances are typical of Wace's grand manner, but despite their inflexibility they express strong and not unsubtle feeling. The conquest metaphor, commonplace (and Ovidian) enough, is particularly apt: Uther, the warrior king, is utterly defeated in the *castra amoris*. And, whereas lust depersonalises, Uther's love here is personal. His confidant, Ulfin, draws attention to this when he points out the impossibility of fulfilling Uther's desire. This is due, not to the practical difficulty of entering Tintagel, but to the psychological difficulty of overcoming Igerne's natural repugnance:

> Le cunte avez grevé de guerre
> e a eissil metez sa terre,
> e lui cloëz en cel chastel.
> Quidez que sa feme en seit bel?   (8669-72)

Later in the story, we are in fact told that Igerne had always feared the king (8763). This is the real reason why Uther must take on the form of Igerne's husband. By trying to force Igerne to yield, he has broken every rule of courtliness. By accepting Merlin's stratagem, he cuts himself off from courtliness altogether, for if 'courtly love' means anything, surely it means persuading a noble and intelligent lady that one's *own self*, refined and improved by the experience of love for her, is worthy of her reasoned acceptance. However, once again it is not Uther who proposes the treacherous change of shape, but Merlin, on whom falls the chief odium.

Not surprisingly, after this abandonment of courtesy, Wace feels little inclination to dwell on either the seduction or the marriage. It is worth noting, however, that like the redactor of the Variant Version, and perhaps under his influence, Wace emphasises the insincerity of

Uther's grief for the duke (8797-800), and even adds that few believed his protestations of regret (8801), implying that the whole court knows exactly what has been going on. It is probably because of this disconcerting hint by Wace that Robert de Boron goes to such lengths to make the marriage seem just, and indeed feudally necessary. We shall return to Boron, but first I shall look briefly at two other chronicles, Layamon's *Brut* and the *Pantheon* of Godfrey of Viterbo: an ill-assorted couple, but interesting in comparison.[15]

Layamon's *Brut* (late twelfth century) is based on Wace, though it is possible to suspect the influence of Robert de Boron.[16] However, Layamon's presentation of the Uther story differs radically from Wace's, particularly in the development of character. To put it briefly, Uther is re-brutalised, in keeping with Layamon's generally harsher presentation of his material. In contrast, Igerne's gentleness and *sagesse* are emphasised, in accordance with Wace's hints. Layamon also pursues Wace's inclination to make the affair more public. The result is a complete loss of *courtoisie*.

Layamon dispenses with all Wace's subtle hints about Uther's *amor de lonh*, and returns to the *coup de foudre*. Not only the duke, but the whole court, notice's Uther's posturing (ll. 9255-6). Igerne's reaction is cryptic, in a different sense from that in Wace: 'and [heo] hine leofliche biheold, ah inaet whaer heo hine luvede' (9254). We are reminded of Chaucer's famous disclaimer about Criseyde's feeling for Diomed. As in Criseyde's case, we wonder whether the lady actually got what she wanted in the end. Layamon, however, does not pursue the subtlety; the point made is that Igerne *has* feelings, which are cruelly left out of account. Moreover, these feelings are not all for herself. When the war begins she is 'saeri, 7 sorh-ful an heorte; / þat swa moni mon for hire sculden habben þer lure' (9290-91). Here there may be an echo of the story of Troy, recently popularised in the French vernacular by Benoit de Saint-Maure. In Layamon, no one can doubt that the war is over Igerne, because he changes the circumstances of the duke's withdrawal from court. Instead of being hasty, it is preceded by elaborate negotiations. (This may be due to Boron's influence.) During these negotiations, the duke declares openly: 'ne scal he nevere on live me scende of mine wife' (9276). Such publicity,

---

[15] Layamon, *Brut*, ed. G. L. Brook and R. F. Leslie, EETS 250, 277, 2 vols (Oxford, 1963, 1978), vol. II; Godfrey of Viterbo, *Pantheon*, in *Patrologia Latina*, second series, vol. 198. Book 18 runs from col. 997 to col. 1007. See also L. Meyer, *Les Légendes des matières de Rome, de France et de Bretagne dans le Pantheon de Godefroi de Viterbe* (Paris, 1933), 196-219.

[16] See A. Micha, *Étude sur le Merlin de Robert de Boron*, Publications Romanes et Françaises (Geneva, 1980), 34.

79

together with Igerne's proven virtue (Ulfin calls her the faithfullest of wives, 9359), makes the use of deception to obtain her necessary. It is worth noting, however, that Layamon is not unaware of the subtleties of courtliness which Wace evoked. Ulfin tells Uther that that is how he *ought* to have wooed Igerne:

Ah ȝif þu luuest Ygaerne þu sculdest hit halden derne.
and senden hire sone of seoluere and of golde.
7 luuien hire mid liste 7 mid leofliche bihoeste.   (9355-7)

Uther has burnt his boats.

Thus far, the emotional effect of Layamon's narrative is all in favour of Igerne, a pitiful figure amidst sordid intrigue and slaughter. If Merlin were now to be brought in as a conjuring pander, the moral disgrace of the intrigue, which Geoffrey skimmed over and Wace glossed over, would become evident. Layamon does not want this. Not for an instant has he forgotten that all this quarrel is a preface to the appearance of Arthur, the wonder-child. When Layamon brings in Merlin, everything changes. Merlin does not come to Uther: Uther's messenger has to go to him, in a remote region untainted by the vileness of Uther's lust. After giving lofty consent to the seduction, Merlin passes on to a splendidly poetic prophecy of Arthur's future greatness, which is not cluttered with other and vaguer pronouncements, as Merlin's prophecies are in the *Historia* (9376-420). He then remarks that neither Igerne nor Uther knows anything of their child to be (9421-6). That is, Igerne and Uther are mere instruments. The innocence of the former and the guilt of the latter are both irrelevant in the light of the greater purpose. Whose purpose? The only answer must be 'Destiny's'. In the Uther/Igerne episode, Layamon impresses us with the insignificance of individual human passions in the perspective of Destiny. This is the contrary of the 'courtly' viewpoint, in which whatever transcendental issues may arise must be reached through the experience of two individuals in a complex relationship.

Layamon makes one more tantalising alteration to the story. After the duke's death, Uther tells Igerne the truth about their night in Tintagel — and Igerne, though Uther repeats what they said to one another in bed, refuses to believe him! (9592-9). There is the seed of a first-class psychological drama here: what must be Igerne's bewilderment and revulsion at the story, what must be her feelings at being forcibly married to a man who is either a sinister seducer or an abominable liar? Layamon gives the seed no time to grow, but he alerts us to the possibility of developing the aftermath of the story, a possibility which Robert de Boron and his successors exploit to the full.

Of all the writers on the Uther/Igerne theme, Layamon is the only one to give a genuine mythic quality to its essential constituent, the engendering of Arthur. Layamon's approximate contemporary, Godfrey of Viterbo, offers a complete contrast: a version of the story in which Arthur is scarcely mentioned. His *Pantheon* (c.1186) is a compendium of world history, a combination of Latin prose and verse, the former being intended for clarification and the latter for relaxation (col. 878). Book 18 is concerned with Britain, and consists of a mangled account of the *Historia* which stops short at the death of Uther. (It is curious that Godfrey should reject what most readers of the *Historia* have always considered to be the most interesting part.) The story of Uther and Igerne greatly attracts Godfrey, particularly as he considers Uther (stretching a point as far as it will go, col. 1002) a 'princeps italicus'. He tells it entirely in verse — that is, for entertainment — and makes it into a lascivious Ovidian fabliau. This is the exact opposite to the sternly moralistic approach of the Variant Version. Uther is neither a warrior nor an embryonic courtly lover, but a lecher who, at the feast, strips Igerne with his eyes:

> nexi sunt pectore visi,
> femineas latebras tactus amore sitit.   (col. 1003)

The scene is comical, as the other ladies seethe with jealousy of Igerne and Uther brings the feast to a hurried close — at which the duke leaps up 'territus', presumably lest the king should leap on his wife there and then! Uther, however, is as naive as he is lecherous. Not only does he describe his lust as an illness, as in Geoffrey, but also believes that it is one, and sends for his doctors, who are baffled until Merlin supplies the correct diagnosis. Uther's visit to Tintagel, no longer a lonely, sea-girt fortress, but a full-scale *bourg*, is, unusually, described in detail, and Godfrey heartlessly savours the irony of Igerne's deception. The effect is most unpleasing, for Igerne, unlike Alcmena (her probable original), is too intrinsically pathetic a figure to fit into a comedy. Uther's words to her when he demands the surrender of her castle are the acme of callous insensitivity:

> ingratum cognosce ducem iugulatum.
> Desere morte datum, melius iam percipe fatum.   (col. 2006)

The final touch of absurdity comes when Igerne actually accepts this advice. Like a true *fabliau* author, Godfrey is determined that no character should emerge with credit. Here, in fact, the Uther/Igerne story shows us the reverse of the courtly medal.

Godfrey is an isolated freak in the Arthurian tradition, but his treatment of our story is perhaps not the unique example it seems at first sight. Alexandre Micha, discussing the story in his study of Robert de Boron's *Merlin*, decides that it shows some courtly elements, but lapses into 'fabliau, voire en vaudeville' (p.176). The grotesqueness of Boron's version is mostly due to his stylistic clumsiness: his style throughout his work fails to complement the interest of his material. However, even when Boron affronts our aesthetic sensibilities, he repays detailed study, for he never fails to give new turns to old themes, and he allows himself more room to work than other adapters. Boron, of course, changes the perspective of the Arthurian story from the secular history of Britain to the spiritual history of the grail. It is through the Round Table set up by Uther and fostered by Arthur that the grail is to be achieved: Uther and Arthur are centrally important because of this. Thus, Arthur's engendering is very much a *felix peccatum*. (Later, at his coronation, he appears as a messiah.) Things are not as simple as that, however, because in Boron's story Uther is scarcely ever responsible for his own actions. He is guided by Merlin, whose task it is to manipulate history towards the achieving of the grail. Merlin, with his diabolical ancestry, can carry a certain amount of odium; nevertheless it seems strange that this minister of God should calculatingly engineer the rape of an innocent woman. Boron is aware of the problem, and — as often — the difficulty elicits from him a brilliant narrative twist. Instead of glossing over Merlin's guilt, he emphasises it, and uses it to motivate a sequel to the seduction which is of considerable psychological interest. At the same time, Boron keeps Merlin out of the way during Uther's own amorous intrigues, thus keeping some of the blame from Merlin, and maintaining the interest of the seduction story by allowing Uther, for once, a free hand.

So is the actual seduction a fully developed 'courtly' story? The answer is that it is more so than any version we have yet seen, though Boron is of course developing hints given to Wace, as Micha shows.[17] The main innovation is that the court intrigue drags on for over a year (edition, pp.197-226). This greatly dilutes the violence which Geoffrey and, following him, Wace gave to Uther's feelings and actions. Boron retains exactly the same elements, the feast, the 'iocosa verba', the proffered cup, the duke's withdrawal from court, but by spinning them out he gives Uther much more the air of a patient courtly lover, whose devotion ought by courtly 'rules' to be rewarded. Time and again, whilst sheering away from the subject of physical seduction, he attempts to force on Igerne the role of consenting *domna*. But — and here the story breaks the standard courtly mould, as it must do

---

[17] Ibid., 172-7. References to the *Merlin* are to Micha's edition, Textes Littéraires Français (Geneva, 1980).

if it is to remain faithful to its source — Igerne refuses to play the courtly game although she is perfectly aware of what Uther is up to. Like Fenice or Iseult, and like any real-life *dame* (however courtly), she is forced to take account of physical and social reality, and finds the position of *domna* totally incompatible with that of wife. Boron emphasises this at some length in conversations between Igerne and Ulfin, Uther's pander. Through these, Igerne's character, a rather negative element in other versions, becomes clear and admirable. She arouses pity not only through her situation, but also by her courage, delicacy, and (in the simpler sense) her courtesy. And yet the very realities to which she clings bear her to her doom. If she insists on her 'true' role, that of virtuous wife, Uther will insist on his: the role of king. In his final conversation with Igerne, Ulfin begs her: 'Dame, por Dieu, aiez merci dou roi et de vos meimes et de vostre seignor' (p. 206). His use of the word 'merci' here marks the exact moment at which he passes from courtly to political vocabulary: either Igerne surrenders willingly and bears her shame (which in courtly terms is none) in secrecy, or the king will force her, whatever the consequences for her and everybody else. This threat is followed by the gift of the golden cup, which Igerne's husband, in blissful and ironic ignorance, encourages her to accept (p. 208). Igerne feels herself to be committed by this acceptance. (We remember that, according to Capellanus, 'vascula' were one of the things which Marie de Champagne considered acceptable gifts from acknowledged lover to lady, Walsh, p. 268.) Unable to endure the choice between personal shame and public calamity, Igerne does what most women would do: she takes refuge in tears, so that her husband has to question her and thus take responsibility for the frightful confession (pp. 209-10). From afar we are reminded of Phèdre's avowal to Oenone. Boron's psychological observation here is good.

With Igerne's confession, the whole intrigue becomes public (as it does in Layamon), and this changes its nature. Uther and the duke, both of whom have law on their side,[18] assume their *Historia* roles as mighty opposites. Uther, who has won some sympathy from the reader for his relative patience and restraint through the previous year, now forfeits it. He is unable to endure rejected *amor de lonh*, and his sufferings during the siege are ignoble, not ennobling in the courtly way. Even Ulfin, his former sympathiser, now accuses him: 'Vos estes molt de foible cuer et de lasche, quant vos cuidiez morir por l'amor d'une femme' (pp. 216-17). And when Merlin reappears, he promptly reduces the whole question to one of lust: 'je vos feré gesir en sa

---

[18] Ibid., 197 (part of a study by H. Micha incorporated into the *Étude*).

chambre avec lui tout nu' (p. 224). Is there a disjunction here between the earlier part of the story, which is largely Boron's own invention, and the siege, where he rejoins the *Historia*? One could say so, but there is a defence against the charge. Boron's whole intention is to teach scorn for earthly passions except when they serve divine ends. By first granting, and then withholding, a courtly colouration to Uther's passion, Boron reveals the foolish self-deception and helplessness of human beings who believe that they are masters of their own fates. Whether or not Uther really believes himself to be a refined courtly lover is immaterial here. What matters is that the — very genuine — lust which he now feels can be turned to Merlin's ends. Boron, while faithfully following his source, gives the impression that Merlin has kept away just long enough to ensure that the suffering Uther will obey his lightest word. For in Boron's version, Merlin does not allow nature to take its course and bring about the birth of Arthur and his eventual coronation. Nature needs a little help, and to this end Merlin obtains from the lusting king an unnamed boon or *don contraignant*,[19] later revealed as the child which Igerne is to bear. Thus is the complex Uther/Igerne intrigue to be connected once again with Boron's central theme, the destiny of the grail. For a few pages, however, the reader, like Uther, is mystified by Merlin's request, and so both are delivered into Merlin's power: we must trust him to bring good out of apparent evil.

For the moment, the evil is very apparent. This is because Boron, unlike other authors, keeps the pathetic and noble figure of Igerne constantly in mind. He makes Merlin acknowledge her virtue, as Layamon does (*Brut*, l. 9402); but whereas in Layamon this is a dignified compliment from one great soul to another, in Boron it is the cackling boast of a naughty Terentian pander: 'ele est molt saige feme et molt loial vers Dieu et vers son seignor. Mes or verroiz quel pooir j'aurai de lui engignier' (p. 225). As in all accounts, the actual seduction is not described. Boron remains silent, I think, because he wants to leave both Uther and Igerne some dignity. Micha describes Boron's Uther as 'Un Jupiter auprès d'Alcmène privé de toute auréole, un amour de mousquetaire fâcheusement accommodé de relents bourgeois' (*Étude*, p.176). This, though delightfully phrased, is inaccurate, for when Uther drops the role of courtly lover he assumes that of king, while the enigmatic (and for the moment unattractive) figure of Merlin is interposed between Uther and the worst aspects of the deception.

---

[19] On this notion see J. Frappier, 'Le motif du don contraignant dans la littérature du Moyen Age', *Travaux de Linguistique et de Littérature de l'Université de Strasbourg* 7 (1969), 8-44, repr. in id. *Amour Courtois et Table Ronde* (Geneva, 1973), 225-64.

Nor does Boron want us to see Igerne happy in the arms of her supposed husband, lest she seem complaisant. From now on he is going to represent her as a martyr, the antithesis of the all-powerful *domna*. First as the widow of a feudal magnate, then as a mother, she feels the full weight of male power.

Like the 'courtship' before the war, the marriage negotiations afterwards, which balance the courtship, are Boron's own invention. Hugues Micha has given an elaborate discussion of their legal aspects, which are acutely realistic;[20] this dry realism throws into relief the plight of Igerne. She is in the same position as Laudine after her husband's death. Indeed, some of the discussions are not unlike the scenes in *Yvain* where Lunete and Laudine persuade Laudine's counsellors that what she would do anyway — marry Yvain — is politically necessary.[21] But Igerne herself is no Laudine. Though technically mistress of her estates until she remarries, she follows the advice of her wisest friends without demur, as a feudal magnate should. But Boron, by the barest of hints, allows us to guess at her feelings as the man who, she knows, has lusted after her and betrayed her (she does not know how completely) claims her in marriage with the joyous approval of her *gent*. Ulfin 'demande a la dame cui parole el disoit et as paranz le duc: "Loez vos ceste pais?" (i.e. the marriage, which will end the war). *La dame se taist* et li parent parolent . . .' (pp. 243-4). In that silence lies all the pathos of woman as victim.

In all earlier versions of the story, her marriage is the last we hear of Igerne. We are left to assume that she lived happily ever after, unlikely as that may seem. But Boron carries on, making Merlin's guilt over the deception of Igerne the motive for the smuggling away of her newborn child. (His other reasons for doing this are too complex to go into here.)[22] It is ironic that Merlin's determination to make amends for the first deception of Igerne should lead him straight into another. In both cases, Merlin and Uther collaborate with Merlin as ringleader; in both cases Merlin gets what he wants (Arthur); and the incidents are linked not only by Merlin's guilt, but also by the *don contraignant* which was his condition for helping in the first deception, and which is his prize in the second. In short, Igerne must now be bullied into surrendering the child which, in all innocence of mind, she conceived on the night of the seduction. In Boron it is this scene, rather than the seduction itself, which shows Uther in a repulsive light, torturing Igerne through her deepest instincts as obedient wife

20 *Étude*, 121-4; edition, 231-44.
21 *Yvain*, ed. M. Roques, CFMA 89 (Paris, 1960, repr. 1971), ll. 2040-144.
22 See *Character of Arthur*, 29-30.

and mother. A few months after their marriage, he speaks of her by now obvious pregnancy and asks who the father is, since it cannot be he or her first husband. She too has realised that her visitor on the fatal night was not the duke, and Uther accuses her of being a whore, lying with another man while her husband was away at the war. The only way to avoid public humiliation is to hush up the pregnancy and birth. By thus withholding the truth, Uther plunges Igerne into a confusion of feeling which is well conveyed (p. 246). Terrified at Uther's accusation, she is at first 'molt liez' to realise that he is not going to repudiate her, then hopelessly resigned to obeying his cruel command to give up the child: 'Sire, et de moi et de quant que a moi ataint poez faire vostre volenté, que je suis vostre'. We have to imagine her feelings when the child is born, but Boron, bald as his descriptions are, enables us to imagine with sympathy. She is to bear a child to a man she does not know. Since this man bore the form of her husband, he clearly had supernatural powers; judging from the analogy of Merlin's birth, and the range of medieval demonological belief, she would be justified in fearing that the father was a demon. (She actually says this in the post-Vulgate *Merlin*, to which we shall return.) On top of that, she must fear the wrath of her husband, though knowing herself innocent. On top of that, her child is torn from her as soon as born. In this context, Boron's remark that 'la mere plore comme mere qui grant dolor a' (p. 253) is scarcely adequate to the case.

At this tragic juncture we may pause a moment to recall the Alexander legend. The Latin romances have scenes analogous to this of Boron's (he may have drawn on them), and the comparison illuminates Igerne's pathos as victim. Olympias too must bear a child to a man with demonic powers, or a god-demon; she, too, must fear the wrath of an outraged husband, Philip of Macedon, who was away at the wars when the seduction took place (Bergmeister, pp. 15-21). But Olympias remains in control of the situation. She has a good idea of who the father really is, and instead of the enchanter colluding with the husband to deceive the wife, the enchanter (Nectanebus) colludes with the wife (Olympias) to deceive the husband (Philip). Thus the child (Alexander), instead of being sent away from the household as the putative father (Philip) was minded to do, is accepted into it as the true parents wish — whereas Arthur is sent *away* from the household as his real father wishes. Boron, in fact, gives us a reverse image of the Alexander story. The parents' characters are also reversed. Philip is a deceived husband (to put it brutally, a cuckold); Olympias is a cunning minx. Uther is a cunning deceiver; Igerne is a deceived wife. Since Uther at this point is obeying Merlin's orders, and Merlin's ends are noble even if his means are not, I would say that Arthur comes better out of the tangle than Alexander does. This may be one of the points which Boron, anxious to give his hero the highest position in the hierarchy of medieval legend, is trying to make.

Having made his point, and prepared the story of Arthur's epiphany, Robert de Boron loses interest in Igerne. Now, Boron's enormous expansion of the story has given Igerne a far greater importance than she had in earlier versions, and his desertion of her is felt by the reader to be a loose end. In the cyclic development of Arthurian romance which Boron initiated and which thirteenth-century prose authors expanded to colossal proportions, loose ends are seldom left trailing. They get woven into the story, often to the enrichment of its meaning. It can also happen that the same thread is woven in different ways by different continuators.[23] This happened with Igerne. The first continuator merely tucked in the loose end. He was a scribe who added to his MS of the Boron *Merlin*: 'Si li (sc. Uther!) avint une mout grant mescheance au chief de .vii. anz, car sa fame Yguerne s'adola si de son anfant que perdu avoit en son cuer que ele en prist une si grant maladie qui li dura deus anz et demi et plus, si que a morir l'en convint.'[24] This stark conclusion is perfectly convincing, given the faithful and loving nature of Boron's Igerne, but it leaves us with a sense of injustice. Could not Igerne be undeceived at the last, and be reunited with her child? The answer, of course, is yes, if the narrative demands it. This demand does not arise until we come to the so-called 'post-Vulgate' *Merlin*.[25] This work lays great stress on the tragic nexus in which Arthur is caught when he commits incest with his sister and engenders Mordred, his future destroyer. For the tragedy to be initiated, it is essential that Arthur should be ignorant of his identity when he meets his sister; for the tragedy to be brought home to him, it is equally essential that he should learn his identity when it is too late. It is the latter event which brings Igerne back on the scene. There is no absolute need to produce her, as Merlin could simply tell the story. But by doing so, the author accomplishes two things. He pleases us by making Igerne happy at last, and he establishes a parallel between Uther's conscious sin of lust, from which comes good (Arthur's birth) and Arthur's unconscious sin of incest, from which comes evil (Mordred's birth). Thus is forged a link of common sin which dooms Arthur's family through three generations.

[23] On these methods see *Character of Arthur*, passim; Bogdanow, *Romance*, passim; E. Vinaver, *The Rise of Romance* (Oxford, 1971), 53-67.

[24] MS BN fr. 798. Micha, *Étude*, 16, suggests that this passage may be by Boron, but it is the sort of explanation in which remanieurs delight.

[25] Ed. G. Paris, SATF, 2 vols (Paris, 1886), vol. I. On the 'post-Vulgate', see Bogdanow, *Romance*.

The scene in which the truth is finally revealed is based on Boron's scene in which Igerne is bullied into surrendering Arthur. Here, she is bullied by another false accusation, from Merlin: that she made away with the infant. In self-defence, she of course tells the full truth about the birth, as she knows it, after which other witnesses complete the tale, and mother and son are reunited (pp.169-70). Igerne's bearing throughout the accusations is superb. She regains the dignity and resourcefulness which she showed in the courtship scenes of the Boron *Merlin*. Instead of shrinking under Merlin's (assumed) wrath, as she did under Uther's, she accuses Merlin of spiriting away the child — maybe a demon child, like to like! — for his own evil purposes, adding: 'Et se vous le volés noiier que bailliés ne vous eust esté, je vous en feroi honnir dou cors, que ja pour tous vos enchantemens ne remanroit! (p.170). For a reader who has endured the capricious and exacting Merlin from Boron through to the post-Vulgate, the relief of hearing him spoken to in this tone of voice is inexpressible.

The romance development of our tale culminates in the post-Vulgate, though writers like Malory can still add new slants. Notably, in Malory Igerne informs her husband the instant she divines Uther's intentions, and herself advises withdrawal from court, thus giving an even stronger impression of courage and resourcefulness. Malory kindly has Uther tell Igerne the truth about the fatal night when he first alludes to her pregnancy: this destroys the delicate and sinister web which Boron wove around her, but Malory's narrative hereabouts is so brisk that the loss is not noticeable. The change does have one interesting consequence, however: at the recognition scene, instead of being accused of destroying her child, Igerne is accused of causing him a lot of unnecessary trouble by keeping silent while he struggled to defend his throne against the suspicious barons — to which Igerne retorts that, while she knew that her child was Uther's son, she had no idea that he had reappeared as king Arthur.[26] These changes are partly due to Malory's conflation of the Vulgate and post-Vulgate *Merlins*,[27] and they are skilfully made, turning Igerne from a pathetic victim into a self-sufficient lady who, like the great dames of the Wars of the Roses, can survive in a world of power politics — though, unlike many of those ladies, she retains her virtue unsullied. It is fitting that Malory, the last great medieval Arthurian romancer, should achieve a reversal of the trend set by Geoffrey of Monmouth, the first, who made Igerne into the archetypal victim.

26 Malory, *Works*, ed. E. Vinaver (2nd edn, Oxford, 1967), 7, 10, 45.
27 For an outline of Malory's methods of adaptation, see *Works*, Introduction, lxiv-lxxiii.

Malory, however, does not stand at the end of the development of our tale. It receives a startling new twist from the Scots chroniclers, who, led by Hector Boece, turn the intrigue into a sequence of rape and murder worthy of a modern police file. This interpretation is determined by the virulently anti-British (by extension, anti-English) impression given by Boece's skilful manipulation of the *Historia* material.[28] To Boece, the British, in contrast to the virtuous Picts and Scots, are receptive to every kind of corruption, and Uther is representative of them. The period of peace used by Geoffrey to trigger the Uther/Igerne intrigue is similarly used by Boece, but in such a way as to incriminate Uther, not to excuse him: 'Nimium enim otium ac delicie, quibus tum fere Britanni erant immersi, fuit homini in causa, non solum ut adulterium, sed et homicidium, unde cruenta bella Britannis sunt nata, perpetraret' (fol. 154v. The 'cruenta bella' are the struggles between Mordred, seen as the legitimate heir to the British throne, and Arthur, the bastard and usurper.) Boece follows Geoffrey's account of the feast, emphasising Igerne's repulsion: 'et ipsa plurimum regios aversabatur amplexus'. Thereafter, he makes a crushing alteration by dropping the essential datum of Geoffrey's tale, the shape-shift. With the loss of this romantic detail, there is nothing left but a particularly brutal rape:[29] 'interceptam foeminam . . . cupide compressam, pregnantem haud multo post reddidit' (ibid.). Along with the shape-shift, Boece abandons Tintagel, Merlin and the war, so that Gorlois is simply executed on a trumped-up charge of treason. Boece, aware of the general acceptance, even in his (Boece's) own century, of Geoffrey's veracity, does give a cavalier reference to the original version ('sunt qui scribant, Merlini opera, Uterum in Gothlois specie transformatum, eo commento mulieris potitum amplexu', 155r), but its tone makes clear that even if, *per impossibile*, the story were true, it would not mitigate Uther's guilt. Nowhere else is he so nakedly condemned.[30] If ever Arthur's birthtale was exposed as discreditable to him, it is here — ironically, by an author who has stripped it of

---

[28] On the Scots chroniclers see R. H. Fletcher, *The Arthurian Material in the Chronicles* (Boston, 1906, repr. New York, 1968), 237-48; K. H. Göller, 'König Arthur in den schottischen Chroniken', *Anglia* 80 (1962), 390-404; F. Alexander, 'Late medieval Scottish attitudes to the figure of King Arthur: a reassessment', ibid. 93 (1975), [17-34] 17-28. For Boece's *Scotorum Historiae* I refer to the second edition (Paris, 1574). The Uther story is on fols 154-5.

[29] Technically, of course, it always was rape, since Igerne does not knowingly consent to intercourse with Uther: see *Character of Arthur*, 28.

[30] The severely moralistic *Perlesvaus* is disapproving of Uther's sin, but lays the burden more on Merlin: ed. W. A. Nitze and T. A. Jenkins, 2 vols (Chicago, 1932, 1937, repr. New York, 1972), vol. I, 282-3.

almost every identifying element. Boece's last and most significant change is to make Uther, having disposed of Gorlois, illogically neglect to marry Igerne, thus making it impossible for Arthur to be passed off as legitimate.

Many Scottish writers fall gleefully on Boece's account, but his most intelligent follower is George Buchanan, who, in his *Rerum Scoticarum Historia* (1582)[31] makes fascinating use of both Boece's and Geoffrey's data. He does not discount Merlin, for he is interested in the centuries-old debate about the validity of his prophecies,[32] but he considers Merlin a rogue and a charlatan, in contrast to his virtuous contemporary, Gildas (p. 80). Thus we are prepared for deception in the Uther story. In fact, we get a completely new version. Uther is already married. The logical Buchanan thus accounts for the existence of Arthur's sister Anna, Mordred's mother and pretext for claiming the British throne, who must, for the purposes of the Scottish versions, be legitimate; but he also accentuates the infamy of Uther's lust. However, Uther here is no born villain, but a virtuous man damned by one crime. As in Wace (though the resemblance must be coincidental), he has long loved Igerne, but, foiled repeatedly by her impenetrable virtue, he deceives and rapes her with the help of Merlin, the method remaining unexplained, and the intrigue undiscovered. For — and this is a startling difference — Uther *has not yet become king*. In due course his wife dies, and Uther, 'rex factus (ut sibi persuaderet) solutus legibus', kills Gorlois in battle, marries Igerne and acknowledges his son Arthur. Thus, Buchanan makes Boece's political horror-story into a sordid little private intrigue, of a type which many princes had in their past,[33] and rejoins a long tradition by making Merlin guiltier than Uther — without in any way condoning the latter or denying Arthur's bastardy, an article of faith amongst the Scots.

Not even in Buchanan, however, will the original tale lie down and die. He makes an astonishing concluding reference to it:

Ut autem uxoris infamia (quando tegi non poterat) saltem elevaretur, fabulam confingunt, non dissimilem ei quae de Jove et Alcmena in theatris

---

31 In *Opera Omnia*, ed. T. Ruddiman (Edinburgh, 1715), vol. I, 80-1. On the author see I. D. McFarlane, *Buchanan* (London, 1981).

32 On this debate see R. W. Southern, 'History as Prophecy', *Transactions of the Royal Historical Society* (1972), 159-78, especially 168.

33 Buchanan, political theorist and tutor to a prince, was naturally interested in the perpetual question of *rex legibus solutus*: see McFarlane, *Buchanan*, 397-8. Edward IV and Elizabeth Woodforde, Richard III and Ann Neville, engaged in intrigues not dissimilar from Uther's. Buchanan may have been thinking of Bothwell, who virtually raped Mary while she was still married to Darnley, and then arranged for his murder.

saepe actitata fuerat: Uterium scilicet arte Merlini in faciem Gorloidis versum, primam cum Igerne (sic) habuisse consuetudinem. Et erat is Merlinus, qui pravo potius quam nullo facinore vellet nobilitari (p. 81).

From the viewpoint of literary history, the main interest here is the comparison with the Alcmena story. Evidently Buchanan, alone among pre-modern readers except the early thirteenth-century chronicler William of Rennes,[34] had recognised Geoffrey's probable source. Which dramatic enactment Buchanan had seen we cannot tell; the subject, as Giraudoux has reminded us, has long been popular, and Buchanan doubtless saw a university performance at some stage in his academic peregrinations. The transferring of the invention from Geoffrey, or from chroniclers generally (Boece's 'sunt qui scribant'), to the characters themselves fits the shabby psychology with which Buchanan has endowed them, but it raises more narrative difficulties than it solves. Were Merlin, Igerne and Uther all in collusion? How, if not by the shape-shift, *did* Uther deceive Igerne? Igerne's threatened 'infamia' presumably arises from Uther's open admission that Arthur is his child and not Gorlois's, but is it wise to exonerate her by pretending to admit to a wicked deception? And who is going to believe the tale anyway? Presumably the aim is to convince Uther's subjects, the primitive and credulous Britons, that Arthur is indeed of Uther's blood. The main reason for Buchanan's interpretation, however, is his own desire to divide history from fiction — a desire quite alien to high medieval thinking. Of course, Buchanan, like other historians of his time (and many since) commits the error of assuming that when the *Historia* has been purged of incredible incidents, what remains must be the truth. Thereby he creates a new fiction. This fiction, like Geoffrey's, plays on human credulity, but in a different and strikingly 'modern' way. It is about the manipulation of propaganda, the cynical deception of the ignorant masses by their enlightened and ruthless masters. Now, in propaganda a whopping lie has more chances of succeeding than a feeble lie. If Buchanan was involved in the production of the Casket Letters,[35] he would have had every opportunity of discovering the truth of this statement.

This consideration of the Scots writers has brought us very far from the beginnings of courtly literature, but it proves once and for all the essential brutality of the Uther/Igerne legend. To conclude our discussion, we may describe this story as a 'courtly romance' which was aborted. Geoffrey, Wace and Boron supply some courtly

---

[34] On whom see *Character of Arthur*, 25.

[35] This is certainly not proven, though he made abundant use of them: see McFarlane, *Buchanan*, 320-54.

emotions and vocabulary, but they remain on the surface. The Scots, ironically enough, are truest to the *Historia* original. The real fault of that original, from the courtly viewpoint, is that too much happens. The characters have too much to do to have time for refinements of emotion. The Tristan story, always uncourtly in the final analysis, is so for the same reason: things happen. Even the Lancelot/Guinevere story suffers the same fate, as Chrétien doubtless realised it would when he abandoned it. To be complete, it must become that tragedy of a whole world. The real interest of the Uther/Igerne story lies in its rejection of courtliness, for out of this comes the first stirrings of a delineation of real character.

IV

MANUSCRIPTS, READERS AND PATRONS IN FIFTEENTH-CENTURY ENGLAND SIR THOMAS MALORY AND ARTHURIAN ROMANCE

Carol Meale

On 31 August 1422 the victor of Agincourt, Henry V, died in his newly-acquired French territories. His untimely death was followed in October of the same year by that of his father-in-law, Charles VI of France. The demise of these two monarchs meant that, under the terms of the Treaty of Troyes,[1] the ten-month-old son of Henry and his queen, Catherine of Valois, became Henry VI, titular ruler of both countries. The man to whom fell the not altogether enviable task of governing France in the new king's stead was John Duke of Bedford, the eldest surviving son of Henry IV of England.[2] Apparently one of Bedford's earliest acts as regent was to instigate enquiries as to the contents and value of the French royal library, a magnificent collection of over eight hundred volumes assembled with care by Charles V during the fourteenth century.[3] The task of cataloguing the books took from 11-15 April, 1423, but Bedford himself did not visit the library, housed in a tower of the Louvre, until 1425; in June of that year he became its legal owner, the sum of money which was eventually handed over to Charles VI's executors being even less than the modest evaluation of the collection's worth arrived at by the team of assessors.[4]

---

1 E. F. Jacob, *The Fifteenth Century* (Oxford, 1961) pp.184-6.
2 See E. Carleton Williams, *My Lord of Bedford* (London, 1963).
3 On the royal library see especially Léopold Delisle, *Recherches sur la librairie de Charles V*, 2 vols (Paris, 1907); and on Bedford's interest in the library, Alfred Franklin, *Histoire Générale de Paris. Les Anciennes Bibliothèques de Paris* (Paris, 1867-73) 3 vols, vol. 2, pp.129ff, and L. Douët d'Arcq, ed., *Inventaire de la bibliothèque du Roi Charles VI, fait au Louvre en 1423, par ordre du régent duc de Bedford* (Paris, 1867). See also, M. J. Barber, 'The Books and Patronage of Learning of a Fifteenth Century Prince', *The Book Collector*, 12 (1963) 308-15.
4 Delisle, *Recherches*, 1, p.138; Franklin, *Anciennes Bibliothèques*, pp.129-30.

Amongst the MSS which Bedford acquired, according to the inventory which he had commissioned, were thirteen volumes of Arthurian texts, including two *Lancelots*, three *Grails*, a *Tristan*, and two *Merlins*, plus other books described as 'du Saint Graal et du Tristan', 'Tristan et Lancelot et des ses faiz de la Table ronde', and 'un romant de la Table ronde'; all of these were in prose, and in addition there were two copies of 'Perceval le Galois' in verse.[5] It has recently been suggested, by Professor Richard Griffith, that within the next forty years this library passed, almost complete, into the hands of Anthony Wydville, Lord Scales and (from 1469) 2nd Earl Rivers, and that he undertook the patronage of Sir Thomas Malory's *Morte d'Arthur*, probably in the middle and latter part of the decade 1460-70; the line of descent of the books, it is proposed, would have been through Anthony's mother, Jacquetta of Luxembourg, whose first marriage, of only two years duration, was to Bedford.[6] This is an intriguing hypothesis and one which, at first glance, appears to solve as many questions as it

5 Delisle, *Recherches*, 2, nos. 1132, 1133, 1113, 1115, 1116, 1190, 1142, 1143, 1117, 1198, 1189, 1151, 1153. There were also copies of various prophetic texts with Arthurian associations, e.g. 1145, 'Les Prophecies Merlin'; and cf. 1146, 1120. The total number of Arthurian romances at one time in the library seems to have been halved by the 1420s: see also Delisle nos. 1081, 1082, 1114, 1116(i), 1118, 1119, 1131, 1140, 1144, 1152, 1197, 1199, 1200, 1201, 1202; on the depredations to which the library was subject after the death of Charles V, see Delisle, 1, pp.125-39. Many volumes were borrowed and not returned, and others were given away as gifts to visiting dignitaries; a *Tristan* was offered to the Queen of Spain, for example. Queen Isabeau removed several Arthurian texts: e.g. a 'Saint-Graal' in 1390; a 'L'Enserrement de Merlin' in 1392; a 'Tristan' in 1402; and an 'Artus' in 1404; (see pp.137, 132-3). It is of note that many of the volumes which disappeared seem to have been fine productions, as, for instance, 1116, described as 'très bien enluminé et historié'; 1118, 'très bien escript et ystorié'; 1197, 'très bien historié et enluminé'; and cf. 1081, 1119, 1131, 1144, 1201, 1202. Those which remained may not have been so valuable: see 1117, 'très ancien et menue lettre vieille, et n'est point enluminé'; 1133, 'de mauvaise lettre de forme'; 1189, 'très mauvaisement escript en françois'; 1190, 'très ancien et très vieille lettre sanz enluminer'; 1198, 'très bien vieil'. No. 1113, described as 'bien escript et enluminé' (a *Grail*) appears to have been the one exception to this latter rule.

6 See Richard R. Griffith, 'The Authorship Question Reconsidered', in *Aspects of Malory*, ed. Toshiyuki Takamiya and Derek Brewer (Woodbridge, 1981) pp.159-77; also 'Arthur's Author: The Mystery of Sir Thomas Malory', *Ventures in Research*, I (1972) 7-43. On Jacquetta see GEC, *Complete Peerage*, II (London, 1912) p.72 (s.v. Bedford); and XI (London, 1949) pp.21-2 (s.v. Rivers). Also, George Smith, *The Coronation of Elizabeth Wydeville* (London, 1935) pp.41-54. Griffith, 'The Authorship Question', p.172, states that the library contained 'some thirty Arthurian works', but this figure does not seem to take into account those which were lost from the collection; cf. n.5 above.

raises, for a constant preoccupation amongst Malorian scholars has been the issue of where, exactly, Malory could have obtained the large number of French romances needed for his translation and reworking of the Arthurian story.

An early theory, and one dependent upon the identification of the author with the Sir Thomas Malory of Newbold Revel in Warwickshire, was that whilst officially in prison in Newgate, Malory could have had access to the library of Greyfriars Abbey (in which institution he was later buried), founded by Sir Richard Whittington, who had himself donated £400 towards the cost of buying books; however, no convincing argument, or proof, was ever brought forward to support such an idea.[7] More recent, though, has been Professor Griffith's advancement of the claims of Anthony Wydville to be considered, not only as the person responsible for the transference of the work from manuscript into the medium of the printed book (an idea which has received wide acclaim since it was first mooted some years since),[8] but also as the provider of source materials for the author, and as the patron active in the creation of the work, fifteen to twenty years earlier. Professor Griffith is, of course, the most eloquent proponent

---

[7] See Edward Hicks, *Sir Thomas Malory: His Turbulent Career* (Cambridge, Mass., 1928) pp.65-70, on Malory's time in Newgate, and pp.74-6, on his burial; on the latter see also C. L. Kingsford, ed., *Stow's Survey of London* (Oxford, 1908, repr. 1971) I, p.321, and cf. P. J. C. Field, 'The Last Years of Sir Thomas Malory', *Bulletin of the John Rylands Library*, 64 (1982) 433-56, p.440. On the library at Greyfriars see *Stow's Survey*, I, p.318, and Caroline M. Barron, 'Richard Whittington: the Man behind the Myth' in *Studies in London History presented to P. E. Jones*, ed. A. E. J. Hollaender and William Kellaway (London, 1969) p.232.

[8] The idea that political considerations led to the concealment of the patron's name in Caxton's edition of the *Morte* was first put forward by N. F. Blake, 'Investigations into the Prologues and Epilogues by William Caxton', *Bulletin of the John Rylands Library*, 49 (1966) 23-44, pp.39, 40, and cf. Blake, *Caxton and His World* (London, 1969) pp.94-5; see also George D. Painter, *William Caxton: A Quincentenary Biography of England's First Printer* (London, 1976) p.147, and Lotte Hellinga, *Caxton in Focus*, The British Library (London, 1982) pp.89-94. Professor Blake has more recently argued, however, that the events recounted by Caxton in the prologue to the *Morte* were entirely fictitious, and that the story was devised as an advertisement, in which apparent recommendation by 'courtly' readers would increase the likelihood of sales; see 'Caxton Prepares His Edition of the *Morte Darthur*', *Journal of Librarianship*, 8 (1976) 272-85, esp. pp.282-4; and, more generally, 'William Caxton: the Man and His Work', *Journal of the Printing Historical Society*, 11 (1975/6) 64-80, pp.73-5; 'Continuity and Change in Caxton's Prologues and Epilogues: the Bruges Period' and 'Continuity and Change in Caxton's Prologues and Epilogues: Westminster', *Gutenberg Jahrbuch* (1979) pp.72-7, (1980) pp.38-43.

of the theory that the author of the *Morte* can be identified as the Cambridgeshire Thomas Malory, of Papworth St Agnes, and he adduces evidence from many different sources in support of his contention that this man and Anthony Wydville knew one another. But advocates of the claims of the Warwickshire Sir Thomas have also enthusiastically embraced the idea of a connection between their man and Wydville. Hilton Kelliher, for instance, in his essay 'The Early History of the Malory Manuscript', on equally plausible grounds transposes the supposed relationship from East Anglia to the Midlands.[9]

Nevertheless, whilst scholars from both camps have expended considerable energy and ingenuity in establishing that Malory and Wydville lands virtually adjoined each other in both parts of the country (and both parties agree that the two men could have met one another at the siege of Alnwick in 1462),[10] it would seem desirable to step back in order to address some fairly basic questions. For instance, what justification is there for assuming, first, that the French library did remain intact after Bedford's death, and that it did pass to Anthony Wydville? Secondly, can we be sure that there was no comparable collection of potential source materials in England at the time? Thirdly, is it reasonable to assume that, in the context of fifteenth-century England, Malory would have had to rely on either the motivation and/or the resources offered by a patron in order to compose his work? The latter issue, it should be said, is one which reaches beyond the bounds of Arthurian literary history. I cannot pretend to offer conclusive answers to any of these questions, but the hope behind this paper is to reopen the field of enquiry, to suggest ways of approaching the subject, and indicate areas which appear to need a more thorough investigation if we are ever to achieve a fuller understanding of the circumstances under which Malory wrote.

The first step is to consider the evidence concerning the existence and extent of English libraries and collections of books in the fifteenth century; and it is from within this context that it is appropriate to

---

[9] *Aspects of Malory*, ed. Takamiya and Brewer, pp.153-6. This essay is a revised version of the article by Kelliher and Lotte Hellinga, 'The Malory Manuscript', *British Library Journal*, 3 (1977) 91-113, pp.101ff. Cf. Field, 'The Last Years', pp.455-6.

[10] Professor Griffith's case rests in large part upon the assumption that Malory and Wydville met one another at Alnwick during the northern campaign; see 'The Authorship Question', p.172. Kelliher attaches less importance to this possibility; see 'The Early History', p.155. For an analysis of the record which indicates that Malory was at the siege see P. J. C. Field, 'Thomas Malory: the Hutton Documents', *Medium Aevum*, 48 (1979) 213-39, pp.225-9, 235-9; (on p.238 Field makes the point that there may have been 'more than one Thomas Malory' at the siege).

look in greater detail at the possibility that the French royal library was either taken, or sent, to England. The theory, as outlined above, runs that on Bedford's death his books were inherited directly by his young widow, Jacquetta, and hence, it is said, they passed to Jacquetta's eldest son by her second marriage, Anthony Wydville. Leaving aside the fact that both the Cambridgeshire and the Warwickshire Malorys predeceased Jacquetta,[11] scholars on both sides of the channel have long been unanimous in their agreement that the library was broken up either before Bedford's death in September 1435, or immediately afterwards. Although ideas as to the destination of the bulk of the books have varied, the fact that only just over one hundred of the volumes have been traced (the majority of these being now in France)[12] argues for a fairly thorough dispersal. M. J. Barber, for example, in an authoritative survey of Bedford's interest in books and learning in general, makes the point that 'no large body of his official or private papers or possessions' survived in either England or France in the confusion of the years following his death, as the English were driven steadily from their French territories;[13] and the disordered state in which the Duke's personal affairs remained over a lengthy period is attested by the difficulties faced by his executors. Amongst the latter was numbered Sir John Fastolf, and his secretary, William Worcestre, wrote to John Paston I in 1456:

My Lord Bedford wylle was made yn so bryeff and generall termys that yn-to thys day by the space of xx yeer can neuere hafe ende, but allwey new to constrew and oppynable; so a generallté shall ne may be so gode as a particuler declaracion. I wryte blontly.[14]

11 Jacquetta died on 30 May 1472; Sir Thomas Malory of Newbold Revel died on either 12 or 14 March 1471 (see Field, 'The Hutton Documents', p.231 and n.80); and the Thomas Malory of Papworth St Agnes was dead by 1 September 1469 (see Griffith, 'The Authorship Question', p.174 and n.62). Jacquetta's husband, Richard Wydville, 1st Earl Rivers, was executed on 12 August 1469. Given these facts, the theory that Anthony was in a position to supply the author with books from his mother's collection during the 1460s would seem to need further elaboration.
12 See *La Librairie de Charles V*, catalogue of an exhibition held at the Bibliothèque Nationale, Paris, 1968; also Delisle, *Recherches*, 1, pp.142ff.
13 Barber, 'Books and Patronage', p.313; the view favoured by Barber is that the books were removed from Paris in 1429 to Rouen, where repairs to the library were carried out at the Duke's orders in 1433; it is suggested further that Bedford may have 'thought to use Charles V's books as a foundation library for the projected university at Caen' (cf. p.311). E. Carleton Williams, *My Lord of Bedford*, p.198, is also of the opinion that the books went to Rouen when they were removed from the Louvre, in 1429.
14 Norman Davis, ed., *Paston Letters and Papers of the Fifteenth Century*, Part 2 (Oxford, 1976) p.130. See also p.105 for a letter of 11 November 1454 in

In addition, the fate of certain of the books suggests that the erosion of the library which began after Charles V's reign continued even during Bedford's lifetime. Following earlier practice, he evidently gave some volumes away as gifts: his younger brother, Humphrey of Gloucester, in this way came into possession of at least three, a Livy (which, it is noted, he received 'l'an mil quatre cens vingst-sept'), copies of *Le Songe du Vergier*, and the *Queste* with the *Mort*; these are now respectively, Paris, Bib. Ste Gen. 777, London BL Royal 19. C. IV, Brussels BR 9627-8.[15] That other of the books travelled to England (though at an undetermined date) is equally certain. Jean duc d'Angoulême, brother of the poet Charles d'Orléans and, like him, a prisoner of war in England, has left testimony to this fact in his inscription in a copy of Guillaume Durant's *Rational des divins offices* (BN fr. 437) which reads: 'Cest liure est a Jehan conte dengolesme lequel lachete / a londres en engleterre lan de grace 1441'.[16]

which Fastolf wrote to Paston:

> ... I pray yow when ye see tyme that my lord of Caunterbury and my Lord Cromewell may be spoke wyth for the godes of my Lord Bedford beyng yn dyuers men handz be compelled to be brought ynne, as ye shall see more along of thys mater wyth the wrytyngys that y have made mencion ...

Cf. pp. 127-8, 132, 135, 136, 554. Seven years after Bedford's death William Worcestre spent around nine months in Normandy 'trying to straighten out the confusion in which the Regent Bedford had left his affairs'; see K. B. McFarlane, 'William Worcestre: A Preliminary Survey' in *Studies Presented to Sir Hilary Jenkinson*, ed. J. Conway Davies (London, 1957) p. 200. For an abstract of Bedford's will, made 10 September 1435, see Nicholas Harris Nicolas, *Testamenta Vetusta* (London, 1826) pp. 241-2; Jacquetta was his main beneficiary, and for notice of her inheritance and an account of the assiduity with which she and Wydville pursued her claims to Bedford's lands in France, see M. A. Hicks, 'The Changing Role of the Wydvilles in Yorkist Politics to 1483' in *Patronage, Pedigree and Power in Later Medieval England*, ed. Charles Ross (Gloucester, 1979) esp. pp. 61-4.

15 On the Paris MS see Alfonso Sammut, *Unfredo duca di Gloucester e gli umanisti italiani*, Medioevo e Umanesimo, 41 (Padua, 1980) p. 122, Delisle, *Recherches*, 1, pp. 283-4, *La Librairie de Charles V*, pp. 108-9 and pl. VII; on the London volume, Sammut, *op. cit.*, pp. 107-8, Delisle, *op. cit.*, 1, pp. 320-1, *La Librairie de Charles V*, p. 107; and on the Brussels MS, Sammut, *op. cit.*, p. 98. Sammut gives additional bibliographical references on all three MSS.

16 A facsimile of this inscription is given in Franklin, *Anciennes Bibliothèques*, p. 132; on the MS see Delisle, *Recherches*, 1, pp. 156-8, *La Librairie de Charles V*, pp. 101-2 and pl. 24. The history of this one MS led Delisle to think that the collection went to England on Bedford's death and that it was broken up there; he suggests that Louis de Bruges, as well as Charles d'Orléans and his brother, bought volumes which had once been a part of it, whilst he was in England; (*op. cit.*, 1, p. 140). Franklin, on the other hand, assumed that the library was sent to England on its removal from the Louvre in 1429; (*op. cit.*,

The impression created by these cumulative references is of a piece-meal, and haphazard, fragmentation of the collection. There is in fact only one manuscript known to have been in the possession of Anthony Wydville which was owned originally by a member of the French royal family, and this is BL Harley 4431, a volume of Christine de Pisan's works collected together before 1415 for presentation to Charles VI's queen, Isabeau of Bavaria.[17] On a flyleaf are the signatures of Jacquetta, Anthony himself, and Louis de Bruges, seigneur de Gruthuyse, the Burgundian nobleman with whom Anthony and his brother-in-law, Edward IV, stayed whilst in exile from the readeption Lancastrian government in England in 1470/71.[18] The volume is not listed, how-ever, in Bedford's 1423 inventory, and it is unlikely that it formed part of the royal library in the Louvre.[19]

The issue is complicated by the possibility that although Bedford is known to have been active as a buyer and commissioner of MSS, his motives in procuring the collection may not have been solely those of a book lover, as has on occasion been assumed.[20] There is an un-doubted chronological coincidence between the acquisition and dis-appearance from contemporary record of the library, and the acqui-sition and loss of the French crown by the English and, as Dr Jonathan Alexander has recently pointed out, Bedford's purchase may well have been directed by a propagandist desire to acquire 'a prestige

p.129). Since writing this paper, my doubts concerning the possibility of the continued existence of the library after Bedford's acquisition of it have received support in private correspondence from Jenny Stratford; her opinion is based upon research carried out for her edition of the inventories of Bedford's goods, Society of Antiquaries of London, forthcoming.

17 For an analysis of the MS, and an account of the process by which it was assembled, see Sandra Hindman, 'The Composition of the MS of Christine de Pisan's Collected Works in the British Library: A Reassessment', *British Library Journal*, 9 (1983) 93-123.

18 This page of the MS is reproduced as pl.43 in Hellinga, *Caxton in Focus*. Since Jacquetta died in May 1472 (see n.11 above) it is possible that Louis de Gruthuyse was given the volume by Anthony during the former's visit to England in the autumn of that year; see F. Madden, 'Narratives of the arrival of Louis de Bruges, Seigneur de la Gruthuyse, in England, and of his Creation as Earl of Winchester in 1472', *Archaeologia*, 26 (1836) 265-86. However, it may be that Anthony used this MS for his translation of Christine's *Moral Proverbs* which were not printed by Caxton until 1477/78, in which case the transfer is not likely to have taken place as early as this. Anthony's translations are discussed further, below.

19 Delisle discusses Isabeau of Bavaria's books, *Recherches*, 1, pp.132-5, and see also Valet de Viriville, 'La Bibliothèque d'Isabeau de Bavière', *Bulletin du Bibliophile*, 14 (1858) 663-87.

20 E.g. by Franklin, *Anciennes Bibliothèques*, p.121; Delisle, *Recherches*, 1, pp.139-40; McFarlane, *op. cit.*, p.205.

possession of the French monarchy'; and he speculates further that 'As the union collapsed the library was allowed to be dispersed.'[21] A similar understanding of the potential significance of patronage and book-ownership as a political tool could also, perhaps, have lain behind Bedford's commissioning of fine service books and translations from Parisian workshops;[22] it almost certainly dictated the action of his first duchess, Anne of Burgundy who, in a move of undeniable diplomatic flair, presented the magnificent Book of Hours acquired by the couple at the time of their marriage, to Henry VI, when he

[21] J. J. G. Alexander, 'Painting and Manuscript Illumination for Royal Patrons in the Later Middle Ages' in *English Court Culture in the Later Middle Ages*, ed. V. J. Scattergood and J. W. Sherborne (London, 1983) p.161.

[22] The books which Bedford ordered from Parisian workshops included: a Breviary of the use of Sarum (BN Latin 17294, begun in 1426, went after Bedford's death to Philippe de Morvilliers, 1st president of the Parlement de Paris); a Missal completed after Bedford's death for Jacques Juvenal des Ursins, Bishop of Poitiers, (lost in a fire at the Hôtel de Ville, 1871); two Latin translations of the *Pèlerinage de l'Âme* (Lambeth 326, BN fr. 602 — the miniatures in the latter are unfinished); *Le Vif Table de Confession* (no longer extant, but copied by the same scribe as Lambeth 326); *La Somme du Roi Philippe, ou somme des vices et des vertus* (Reims 570); *Scientia de numero et virtute numerii*, written by Roland Lisbon, a master in the medical faculty of Paris (Columbia University, Plimpton 173); Jean Tourtier, *Traduction du commentaire de Galien sur les aphorismes d'Hippocrate* (BN fr. 24246, finished 1429); *Le Livre du jugement des étoiles*, a French translation by Guillaume Harnoys of an Arabian work, commissioned 1430 (BN fr. 1352). On these MSS see Barber, 'Books and Patronage'; Eric G. Millar, *Les principaux manuscrits à peintures du Lambeth Palace à Londres* (Paris, 1924) pp. 74-7 and pl. XLII, repr. from the *Bulletin de la Société française pour reproductions de manuscrits à peintures*, 8e année (1924) and 9e année (1925); M. R. James and Claude Jenkins, *A Descriptive Catalogue of the Manuscripts in the Library of Lambeth Palace* (Cambridge, 1932) pp. 427-31; E. Carleton Williams, *My Lord of Bedford*, pp. 249-52. It has been proposed that the so-called Bedford Hours, now BL Additional MS 18850, once thought to have been commissioned by Bedford to give to Anne of Burgundy on the occasion of their marriage in 1423, might have been, rather, a gift to the couple from Anne's brother, Duke Philip the Good; see Janet Backhouse, 'A Reappraisal of the Bedford Hours', *British Library Journal*, 7 (1981) 47-69. MSS bought by Bedford in England include a psalter with illustrations by Herman Scheere (BL Additional MS 42131); and a Breviary and a prayerbook, both of which are small, and intended, presumably, to be carried by the Duke for use in his personal devotions; (both are now in the possession of Christina Foyle). On these last volumes see: *Catalogue of Additions to the Manuscripts in the British Museum, 1926-1930* (London, 1959) pp. 202-6; *A Catalogue of Illuminated and other Manuscripts*, Bernard Quaritch, 1931, item 24, pp.16-17 and pl. 24; Eustace F. Bosanquet, 'The Personal Prayer-Book of John of Lancaster, Duke of Bedford, K. G.', *The Library*, 4th ser. 13 (1932-33) 148-55. BL Additional MS 42131 later passed into Wydville ownership (see further, below) but it is at present the only one of these MSS known to have done so.

spent Christmas with them at Rouen in 1430.[23] The issue of the public face of patronage has obvious implications for any study of the inception and subsequent dissemination of Malory's work, and it is one to which I shall return in due course.

If the lack of specific evidence should incline us to discount the French royal library as the source of Malory's various texts, this conclusion is reinforced when we examine the rider to it, that there was in effect no alternative available to him. It was Professor William Matthews who, in his book *The Ill-Framed Knight*, came to the conclusion that there was no library in England which could have provided the Arthurian writer with all his materials.[24] Following the line of enquiry prompted by his conviction that the author came from the Yorkshire family of Malorys, he commented upon the 'pitifully few' bequests of Arthurian books in the north, and went on to remark: 'Nor indeed is there any evidence that anyone in England ever owned such a collection. The most that can be proved is that various people owned a copy of this romance or that . . .' On the basis of these observations he concluded that Malory wrote his work abroad, most probably under the auspices of Jacques d'Armagnac, duc de Nemours, whose tastes in the way of Arthurian literature are well documented.[25] This dismissal of the potential of the resources likely to have been held by English book collectors, whilst somewhat abrupt, does serve to highlight the problems which are to be encountered in any study of book ownership in England.

The first of these is the inadvisability of placing too great a reliance upon wills as evidence of ownership. These documents are, in fact, notoriously unreliable as guides either to general interest in literature or to the actual subjects of the books which people possessed. It is by no means uncommon, for example, for known book-owners either not to list a single MS in their bequests, or to omit mention of volumes which, because they are still extant, and bear contemporary *ex libris* inscriptions or other identifying marks, can be confidently assigned

---

23 Henry VI's physician made a note on f. 256r of the MS recording the gift. It is somewhat ironic, in the light of the English acquisition of the French royal library, that this Book of Hours came into the possession of the French crown later in the century; see E. Carleton Williams, *My Lord of Bedford*, p. 250.

24 William Matthews, *The Ill-Framed Knight* (Berkeley and Los Angeles, 1966) pp. 141-2.

25 Matthews, *Ill-Framed Knight*, pp. 145-9; on Jacques d'Armagnac see Cedric E. Pickford, 'A Fifteenth-Century Copyist and His Patron' in *Medieval Miscellany presented to Eugène Vinaver*, ed. F. Whitehead, A. H. Diverres and F. E. Sutcliffe (Manchester, 1965), and *id.*, *L'Evolution du roman arthurien en prose* (Paris, 1959). For a refutation of Matthews' view on historical grounds see Field, 'The Hutton Documents', pp. 224-5.

to them.[26] It is similarly no rarity to find books described collectively, and this applies to other kinds of record, as well as to wills. Thus in 1395, Lady Alice West of Hynton Marcel in Hampshire left all her 'bokes . . . of latyn, englisch, and frensch' to her daughter-in-law, and over a century later, in the inventory of the goods of John de Vere, Earl of Oxford, which was made after his death, although his service books were described in some detail, the contents of 'A chest full of frenshe and englisshe bokes', together valued at £3 6s. 8d., are not specified.[27] Again, books may be described by their appearance rather than their content; in 1415 Michael de la Pole, Earl of Suffolk, bequeathed to his wife, Katherine, 'a little book with tablets of silver and gold', and five years later, Dame Matilda Bowes left 'ye boke with ye knotts'.[28] Another of Dame Matilda's bequests, of 'unum romance boke', is scarcely any more informative, except perhaps about the language of the text contained within it.[29] The reasoning behind the adoption of the latter types of description was, no doubt, pragmatic, in that it would have facilitated identification of volumes for the executors,[30] and the same criterion may have led testators to refer to books by only one of several component texts. Detail such as that found in the will of Arthur Ormesby, made in 1467, in which he left to George Neville, Archbishop of York, 'my boke called boneaventure

---

[26] See K. B. McFarlane, *The Nobility of Later Medieval England* (Oxford, 1973) pp. 236-7; A. I. Doyle, Appendix B to *Stephen Scrope: The Epistle of Othea*, ed. Curt F. Bühler, EETS OS 264 (1970) p. 127. Amongst the members of the nobility who did not mention books in their wills was Henry Percy, 4th Earl of Northumberland; although his will was 'writon . . . wt myn awn hand, and signed wt my signe mannuell, and sealed wt ye seale of my armes and signets', he does not mention any books; amongst those which he is known to have possessed is BL MS Royal 18. D. II, containing Lydgate's *Troy Book* and *Siege of Thebes*. The will, dated 27 July 1485, is transcribed in *Testamenta Eboracensia*, III, Surtees Society, 45 (1865) pp. 304-10.

[27] See F. J. Furnivall, *The Fifty Earliest English Wills*, etc., EETS OS 78 (1882) p. 5; Sir William H. St John Hope, 'The Last Testament and Inventory of John de Vere, 13th Earl of Oxford', *Archaeologia*, 66 (1914/15) 275-348, pp. 341, 342; (the latter example is quoted by McFarlane, *Nobility*, p. 237).

[28] Nicolas, ed., *Testamenta Vetusta*, pp. 189-90; *Testamenta Eboracensia*, I, Surtees Society, 2 (1835) pp. 63-5.

[29] Another of the books left by Dame Matilda was 'j romance boke is called ye gospelles'; 'romance', therefore, in the context of this will, seems to mean that the text was in French; cf. R. M. Wilson, *The Lost Literature of Medieval England* (London, 1952) p. 120.

[30] In other cases elaborate descriptions of the coverings of books can be taken as an indication of the owner's pride in their value, whether this is seen in monetary, or social, terms; see, e.g. the will of Thomas Burgeys, citizen and cissor of London, 1468, H. R. Plomer, 'Books Mentioned in Wills', *Transactions of the Bibliographical Society*, 7 (1902-4) 99-121, p. 117.

de vita xpi and in the same boke a wark called speculum xpianorum and in the end of the same an holy trete in English of contemplacon', is infrequent.[31]

Usually we have no means of checking on particular bequests to see how accurately books have been described by their owners. But there is one case where we do, and it is one which is most appropriate in the context of the present discussion. Sir Richard Roos, in his will made in March 1481/2, left his 'grete booke called saint Grall bounde in boordes couerde with rede leder and plated with plates of laten' to his niece, 'Alianore hawte'. This volume, complete with the signatures of Roos, Alianore, and that of the next owner, Elizabeth Wydville, Edward IV's wife and first cousin to Alianore's husband, survives; it is now BL MS Royal 14. E. III, and in addition to the *Queste* it contains an *Estoire* and a *Mort*.[32] The number of texts within this one book should act as a cautionary reminder, in any assessment of the size of an individual's library, of the possibility that there may well be a marked discrepancy between the actual contents of a given book collection and our immediate perception of it.

It should be stressed that the existence of composite volumes is not an argument that Malory would not have had to consult several books. His major French sources, for example, are generally agreed to have been the *Suite du Merlin*, the *Lancelot*, *Tristan*, the *Queste* and the *Mort*; and the *Lancelot* in particular was a bulky compilation. Still, there is no reason to suppose that he need have found them in so many separate volumes as has usually been thought. It is of note in this respect that Eugène Vinaver indicated the likelihood that Malory had access to such multiple-text volumes in his editorial reference to the authorial comment at the end of the book of *Sir Tristrem*, which reads: 'here ys no rehearsall of the thirde booke'; Professor Vinaver observes that in the two MSS of the French text which are closest to Malory's redaction (BN fr. 99 and Chantilly 316) there is a similar textual division and comment at this stage in the narrative, and that

---

31 Plomer, 'Books in Wills', p.116.
32 See the transcription of this will in Ethel Seaton, *Sir Richard Roos* (London, 1961) pp. 547-50; the will was proved 1 April 1482. Elizabeth Wydville's aunt, Joan Wydville, married Sir William Haute of Kent; their son, Richard, was Alianore's third husband; see Seaton, pp. 52-5. The book seems to have been given to Elizabeth before April 1483, when Edward IV died, since the names of her two eldest daughters, Elizabeth and Cecily, appear on f.1, where they are each described as 'kyngys dowther'. For a description of the MS see G. F. Warner and J. P. Gilson, *Catalogue of Western MSS in the Old Royal and King's Collections* (London, 1921) II, p.140, and IV, pl. 85. Matthews mentions this MS (*Ill-Framed Knight*, p.141) but he does not follow up the implications, which affect his own argument, of the structure and contents of the volume.

in both these books, as in Malory's compendium, the work which follows is the *Queste*.[33]

Problems similar to those encountered when dealing with references to books in wills must be recognised in considering the use which it is possible to make of other kinds of contemporary records, ranging from inventories which might list books to household and other accounts which could be expected to detail expenditure upon them. Again, knowledge of book collections drawn from sources such as these is dependent largely upon the accidents of survival, and we should be wary of drawing too firm conclusions from the evidence which they offer.[34] It has often been assumed, for instance, that an interest in literature is more pronounced amongst the French and Burgundian nobility than amongst the English, but it is not generally acknowledged that a contributory factor to this apparent state of affairs is the paucity of relevant documentation which is extant from this period in England. As Richard Green has remarked:

> Not only royal household records and library inventories, but also the records of a number of seigneural establishments . . . are sparser in England than are their counterparts on the continent. If we possessed a fraction of the information about the day-to-day activities of men like John Montagu, earl of Salisbury, William de la Pole, duke of Suffolk, Humphrey of Gloucester, John Tiptoft, and Anthony Wydville, that we have for the dukes of Burgundy and Orléans, or Jean duc de Berri, or René of Anjou, our knowledge of the literature of the English court and of its social background would be increased enormously.[35]

An illustration of the amount and probable nature of the material which has been lost is provided by the fact that wardrobe accounts for Edward IV are available only for a short period from the latter part of his reign, from 1480-81, and yet these papers give valuable information regarding the rebinding of various of the King's books, and the arrangements which were made for them to accompany him on his travels.[36] The equally fortuitous survival of Queen Elizabeth's

---

[33] Eugène Vinaver, ed., *The Works of Sir Thomas Malory* (Oxford, 1967) III, p.1519.

[34] Cf. McFarlane's comments on the survival of inventories of books belonging to men convicted of treason, for example, Sir Simon Burley, Thomas of Woodstock and Henry Lord Scrope of Masham, which 'are likely to suggest a very unlikely correlation between crime, in particular treason, and literacy'; he adds, 'By comparison, few inventories of the possessions of the law-abiding' have been preserved; (*Nobility*, p.237).

[35] Richard Firth Green, *Poets and Princepleasers: Literature and the English Court in the Later Middle Ages* (Toronto, Buffalo and London, 1980) pp.7-8.

[36] See Nicholas Harris Nicolas, ed., *Privy Purse Expenses of Elizabeth of York: Wardrobe Accounts of Edward IV* (London, 1830, repr. 1972) pp.117, 125-6, 152; and cf. n.77 below.

household accounts for the year following her marriage gives, in turn, a rare, but tantalisingly incomplete, indication of her tastes in books.[37] However, in spite of these constraints, piece by piece an understanding of patronage and book production in England is being built up; that this is so is due partly to the work which is being carried out on cataloguing the medieval contents of modern libraries; partly to the systematic research being devoted to documenting the lives of individuals, from whatever class of society; and partly to discoveries as felicitous as that of the Winchester Malory MS itself in 1934.[38] Thus our knowledge is far from being full and, whilst it may never be possible to build up a definitive picture, it is only reasonable to anticipate further developments which will cause a realignment of present views. I would suggest, therefore, that the assertion that there was no library in England in the mid-fifteenth century from which Malory could have drawn his source texts is unwarranted.

Although it is almost certain that Malory did have recourse to a library, or collection of sorts, for the French books he used, it should not be forgotten that he could well have owned one or more volumes himself. Instances in the fifteenth century of members of the gentry or lesser knightly classes possessing Arthurian romances in French include Dame Matilda Bowes, who bequeathed 'unum librum yat is called Trystram'; and the Mauleverers of Ribston in Yorkshire, who have been associated with Cambridge, UL Additional MS 7071, which contains an *Estoire* and a *Merlin*.[39] Allowing for the fact that owing to their cost, and his relatively low income, Malory is unlikely to have been in possession of more than a few volumes, it still does not follow that a bookowner acting in the capacity of a patron supplied him with the rest of the texts he required.[40] There is ample evidence of books

---

37 See below, p.121.
38 The work which is currently being carried out on the *Index of Middle English Prose* may be cited as the kind of research which will uncover much new information; see the discussion of the aims of the project in *Middle English Prose: Essays in Bibliographical Problems*, ed. A. S. G. Edwards and D. A. Pearsall (New York and London, 1981). Where the literary interests of individuals are concerned, the extent and nature of Edward III's tastes have been reassessed by Juliet Vale, in the light of her work on documentary material from the period; see her *Edward III and Chivalry: Chivalric Society and Its Context 1270-1350* (Woodbridge, 1982) Chapter 3.
39 For details of Dame Matilda's will see n.28 above; on the Mauleverers see Vinaver, ed., *Works of Sir Thomas Malory*, III, pp.1277-80; also Matthews, *Ill-Framed Knight*, pp.108-13. The speculations in the latter work should be treated with caution.
40 Malory's income has been assessed at something over £20, which was fairly low for someone of his social standing; see P. J. C. Field, 'Sir Thomas Malory, M.P.', *Bulletin of the Institute of Historical Research*, 46 (1973) 24-35,

being loaned amongst groups of people who lived within the same social or geographical sphere. BL Royal 17. D. VI, for instance, containing works by Hoccleve (including his *Regiment of Princes*) appears to have been owned by William Fitzalan, Earl of Arundel, and his wife Joan Neville, Countess of Salisbury, who died in 1487 and 1462 respectively; but a number of signatures and mottoes at the beginning of the volume, most of which can be attributed to people who were connected with the Arundels by ties of marriage or friendship, seems to indicate that its use may have been communal.[41] Lower down the social scale, the Lambeth Palace copy of the *Awntyrs off Arthure* (MS 491) contains the names of several individuals who seem to have formed a kind of informal literary circle amongst the Essex gentry in the early sixteenth century; (one of the owners has written on f. 273r, albeit in jest, the popular ownership rhyme 'he that styleth thys boke shall be hangyd on hoke').[42] This form of dissemination of literary texts must have been common in the Middle Ages, particularly before the introduction of printing.[43]

With regard to the English works which Malory apparently knew, even if he did not have them in front of him when he wrote,[44] access

p. 27. It would be helpful in this connection to know what prices Arthurian texts commanded on the second-hand market; half a century before, the inventory of Thomas of Woodstock's books records a *Merlin*, price 3s. 4d., a *Lancelot*, price 13s. 4d., and a 'Treti3 de Roy Arthur', price 4s. 4d.; see Viscount Dillon and W. H. St John Hope, 'Inventory of Goods . . . belonging to Thomas, duke of Gloucester', *Archaeological Journal*, 54 (1897) 275-308, pp. 300-3. Even allowing for the inflation of prices during the fifteenth century, it is not impossible that a knight might own several such books, which could have been cheaper than new ones of comparable length. The cost of producing the MS of Malory's work is estimated below, pp. 115-16.

[41] See Warner and Gilson, *Catalogue of Royal MSS*, II, pp. 251-2 and IV, pl. 101.

[42] I hope to discuss the ownership of this MS in more detail elsewhere. Cf. n. 86 below.

[43] On this subject cf. the introduction to *John Benet's Chronicle for the years 1400 to 1462*, ed. G. L. Harriss and M. A. Harriss, Camden Miscellany Vol. 24, Camden Society, 4th ser. 9 (1972) pp. 172-3. It is possible that access was allowed to the libraries of monasteries, if a writer was engaged upon serious research; see, e.g., Antonia Gransden, *Historical Writing in England, ii, c. 1307 to the Early Sixteenth Century* (London, 1982) Chapter 11, on John Rous and William Worcester, esp. pp. 322, 339. For a survey of the kind of material which might have been made available in this way, see Madelaine Blaess, 'Les manuscrits français dans les monastères anglais au moyen âge', *Romania*, 94 (1973) 321-58.

[44] On the English Arthurian texts which Malory knew, and for suggestions as to other minor sources, see: Robert H. Wilson, 'Malory's Naming of Minor Characters', *Journal of English and Germanic Philology*, 43 (1943) 364-85, 'Malory's Early Knowledge of Arthurian Romance', *University of Texas Studies in English*, 29 (1950) 33-50, 'Notes on Malory's Minor Sources', *Modern Language*

to most of these would have been straightforward. The English translation of the Vulgate *Merlin*, the stanzaic *Morte Arthur*, the *Awntyrs off Arthure*, and the treatise on hunting ascribed to Sir Tristrem (to which Malory seems to be referring at the beginning of his tale of *Tristrem*), were all available in relatively inexpensive booklets, and all were in circulation in London, as well as farther north. Furthermore, the text on hunting and the *Awntyrs* were combined by two stationers or purchasers within the same volume.[45] Amongst the romances, only the alliterative *Morte Arthure* and the *Avowinge of Arthur*, to judge from the evidence of extant MSS (in itself not an infallible guide) seem to have had a more restricted geographical distribution.[46] The extent to which copies of Chaucer's *Canterbury Tales* multiplied throughout the fifteenth century is well documented.[47] Even works like Hardyng's *Chronicle* and the English translation of Vegetius' treatise *De re militari* could have been obtained without too much difficulty, and the audience for both texts seems to have been drawn from a broad social

Notes, 66 (1951) 22-6; E. D. Kennedy, 'Malory's Use of Hardyng's *Chronicle*', *Notes and Queries*, 114 (1969) 100-3; Wilson, 'More Borrowings by Malory from Hardyng's *Chronicle*', *Notes and Queries*, 115 (1970) 208-10; Diane Bornstein, 'Military Strategy in Malory and Vegetius' *De Re Militari*', *Comparative Literature Studies*, 9 (1972) 123-9; E. M. Bradstock, 'The Source for Book XVIII of Malory's *Morte Darthur*', *Notes and Queries*, 124 (1979) 105-7; P. J. C. Field, 'Malory's Minor Sources', *Notes and Queries*, 124 (1979) 107-10; Kennedy, 'Malory and His English Sources' in *Aspects of Malory*, ed. Takamiya and Brewer.

45 On the *Merlin* MSS see below, pp. 113-14. The stanzaic *Morte Arthur* is extant in Harley 2252; the *Awntyrs* in Lincoln Cathedral 91, Lambeth 491, Douce 324, and the Ireland-Blackburn MS (now Mr R H Taylor's MS, Princeton University Library). The *Book on Hunting* appears together with the *Awntyrs* in Lambeth 491, and in the composite volume of which Douce 324 once formed a part; (see K. L. Smith, 'A Fifteenth Century Vernacular Manuscript Reconstructed', *Bodleian Library Record*, 7 (1962-67) pp. 234-41). On the hunting text itself see Rachel Hands, 'Sir Tristrem's "Boke of Huntyng": the case for the Rawlinson manuscript', *Archiv für neuere Sprachen*, 21 (1973) 58-74. *Torrent of Portyngale*, which Kennedy suggested as a source for Malory ('Malory and his English Sources') survives in only one copy, in Chetham A.6.31 (8009), which dates from 1480-1500, but this is, again, in inexpensive booklet format; see Meale, 'The Middle English Romance of *Ipomedon*: A Late Medieval 'Mirror' for Princes and Merchants', *Reading Medieval Studies*, forthcoming.

46 The romances survive uniquely in Lincoln Cathedral 91 and the Ireland-Blackburn MS, respectively.

47 See Field, 'Malory's Minor Sources', p.109 for a comparison of lines in Malory with lines from the *Franklin's Tale*; and for descriptions of MSS of the *Canterbury Tales*, and information on their provenance and ownership, see J. M. Manly and Edith Rickert, *The Text of the Canterbury Tales*, I (Chicago, 1940).

spectrum. Whilst it may be open to doubt whether Henry VI or Edward IV ever read the copies of Hardyng's *Chronicle* presented to them by the author, Hunterian MS V.2.20 is a modestly-produced volume on paper, which would have been well within the reach of someone of limited means, and the same is true of Douce 378.[48] Vegetius' treatise, on the other hand, was owned and presumably read by members of the gentry in Norfolk, Warwickshire and Devon, as well as by Richard III, members of the Hastings family, and the Berkeleys of Gloucestershire for whom Walton made the translation.[49] In short, none of the texts which have been proposed as sources for Malory in his work would have been out-of-the-way for someone of his social standing to acquire, or borrow, without the aid of a patron.

At this point it is appropriate to look more closely at the surviving copies of Malory's work, to see whether they offer any more definite clues as to the circumstances of its composition. With reference to the unique MS of the *Morte*, BL Additional 59678, the first gathering is lost and, as Professor Griffith rightly remarks, calculating on the basis that this would have comprised the same number of leaves as the majority of the other gatherings, there could well have been room for the inclusion of a dedicatory preface, addressed to a patron.[50] But two principal arguments may be brought against this theory. The first of these arises from consideration of the MS version. On those occasions when Malory the author breaks into his translation at the end of certain of the tales, the information which he gives is limited to his name, his social status, and a brief indication of his personal misfortunes.[51] It is true that the last few leaves of the MS are also

48 On Hardyng's life, and his presentation of his work to the two monarchs, see C. L. Kingsford, *English Historical Literature in the Fifteenth Century* (Oxford, 1913) pp.140-4; on Hunterian V.2.20 (400) see John Young and P. Henderson Aitken, *A Catalogue of the MSS in the Hunterian Museum in the University of Glasgow* (Glasgow, 1904) pp.319-20; and on Douce 378 (SC 21953) see F. Madan *et al.*, *Summary Catalogue of Western MSS in the Bodleian Library* (Oxford, 1895-1953) IV, p.613.

49 See, respectively, BL MSS Lansdowne 285 (Pastons of Norfolk); Sloane 2027 (Brandons of Warwickshire); Douce 291 (Chalons of Devon); Royal 18.A.XII (Richard III); Digby 233 (Hastings). A limited amount of information on these MSS may be found in Charles R. Shrader, 'A Handlist of Extant Manuscripts Containing the *De Re Militari* of Flavius Vegetius Renatus', *Scriptorium*, 33 (1979) 280-305, pp.302-5.

50 Griffith, 'Arthur's Author', p.23; cf. Field, 'The Last Years', p.455 and n.2. All the quires save one consisted of eight bifolia; the exception is the present quire 5, which was a six; see the introduction to the facsimile of the MS by N. R. Ker, EETS SS 4 (1976) pp.x-xi.

51 Vinaver, ed., *Works*, books 1, 4, 5, 6, 7, 8; and see the facsimile, ff.70v, 148r, 346v, 409r, 449r.

lost, and that Caxton may have simplified the author's conclusion to a greater extent than we suspect, just as elsewhere he omitted to make any mention of the 'knyght presoner' at all, but it still seems unlikely that a writer, dependent upon the goodwill and the financial recompense presumably in the gift of a patron, should have neglected to record the relationship, or debt, in any of the other, well-marked, breaks in the narrative.[52] It could be countered, of course, that since the MS appears to have been copied at an unspecified number of removes from the author's holograph, all references which were deemed irrelevant to the purposes for which the present copy was being made, were excised. However, this explanation would not account for the retention in the colophons, as they stand in the MS, of highly personal details which could scarcely be said to lend the work any prestige by association, whereas information about a patron who, by definition, has to be in a position of some superiority to the author, would have supplied it for the literary market with a pedigree guaranteeing respectability and, perhaps, even fashionableness.[53]

This social aspect of the appeal of literature to a potential audience should not be underestimated. Indeed, it is a factor which Caxton understood and exploited in his marketing techniques, and the absence from the printer's preface to his edition of the *Morte* of any reference to a patron as being involved in the creation of the work suggests that he had nothing to impart on the subject. It may perhaps be that the one gentleman 'in specyal' who, Caxton tells us, requested publication of the *Morte* was (whether before or after death) in sufficient political disfavour to have made it unwise for the printer to give his name, but Caxton had a habit, wherever he had relevant information to hand,

---

52 On Caxton's excision of personal detail see Blake, 'Caxton Prepares His Edition of the *Morte Darthur*', pp. 277-8. On the relationship of patron to writer generally see, e.g., Green, *Poets and Princepleasers, passim*; and the important article by Peter J. Lucas, 'The Growth and Development of English Literary Patronage in the Later Middle Ages and Early Renaissance', *The Library*, 6th ser., 4 (1982) 219-48.

53 The fact that Lydgate's *Troy Book* was written at the command of Henry, Prince of Wales, later Henry V, seems to have accounted in part for its status as a 'fashionable' text; on the MSS see Lesley Lawton, 'The Illustration of Late Medieval Secular Texts, with Special Reference to Lydgate's *Troy Book*' in *Manuscripts and Readers in Fifteenth Century England*, ed. Derek Pearsall (Woodbridge, 1983) pp. 41-69. See also the retention of the colophon explaining the circumstances which prompted the translation of Vegetius' treatise in, e.g., the Pastons' copy, Lansdowne 285; this is transcribed in *A Catalogue of the Lansdowne MSS in the British Museum* (London, 1819) p. 101. Cf. the retention of details of literary 'pedigree' in a late copy of John Russell's 'boke of kervyng and nortur', Meale, 'The Middle English Romance of *Ipomedon*', n. 64.

of discussing the genesis of the work he was issuing.[54] In this case he is conspicuously silent on the history of the text before it arrived in his shop, and this implies that the copy from which he printed contained no details as to how the work came to be written other than those with which we are familiar.[55] To sum up, the textual evidence, fragmentary though it undoubtedly is, allows for the possibility that Caxton enjoyed the offices of a patron but suggests, rather more strongly, that Malory did not.

The discussion so far has tended to concentrate on the function of patronage in relation to the writer and/or distributor of literary texts; but it is also important to consider the subject from the point of view of the patron. It is reasonable to assume that the activity of patronage implies an expectation on the part of the patron, whether male or female, an individual or a corporate body, that he, she or they would derive reciprocal benefits of some kind, whether in the area of politics, learning, or religion.[56] The essentially public nature of much of the patronage which the Duke of Bedford embarked upon has already been alluded to, and he was not unusual amongst his contemporaries. Thus, when Bedford commissioned Laurence Calot to write a pedigree of Henry VI, which was posted on the walls of the major churches of northern France as part of the English propaganda campaign, Richard Beauchamp, Earl of Warwick, who was a military administrator in France under Bedford, and tutor to the young Henry VI from 1428-1436, commissioned Lydgate, who was also in Paris at the time, to write an English translation of the poem; this can be seen as a politic move in the light of the divisions between the war and anti-war parties which developed in England once the euphoria at Henry V's victories had died with the King.[57] A more obvious desire to enhance personal

54 On the question of whether or not Caxton's one gentleman 'in specyal' actually did exist, see the articles by Blake cited in n. 5 above. The printer's prologues and other writings are edited by N. F. Blake, *Caxton's Own Prose* (London, 1973).

55 For a presentation of the evidence that BL Additional MS 59678 was in Caxton's shop, as well as the copy from which the printer and compositors worked principally, see Lotte Hellinga, 'The Malory Manuscript' in *Aspects of Malory*, ed. Takamiya and Brewer, pp.127-42 and cf. Hellinga, *Caxton in Focus*, pp.90-4.

56 Cf. Lucas, 'English Literary Patronage'. The motives underlying the commissioning of texts and MSS are the subject of an essay by K. D. Harris and C. M. Meale in a forthcoming study of book production in the fifteenth century.

57 See B. J. H. Rowe, 'King Henry VI's Claim to France in Picture and Poem', *The Library*, 4th ser., 13 (1932-33) 77-88, also J. W. McKenna, 'Henry VI of England and the Dual Monarchy: Aspects of Royal Political Propaganda, 1422-1432', *Journal of the Warburg and Courtauld Institutes*, 28 (1965) 145-63; cf. Derek Pearsall, *John Lydgate* (London, 1970) pp.166-7.

reputation lay behind other patrons' encouragement of Lydgate and other writers and artists. For example, Beauchamp's daughter, Margaret, later Lady Talbot and Countess of Shrewsbury, commissioned Lydgate to write the story of *Guy of Warwick*, in celebration of her father's legendary ancestor and his chivalric exploits.[58] A desire to recover political standing, as well as her estates, probably lay behind the production of the beautiful series of drawings with accompanying texts known as the *Beauchamp Pageants*, executed, it has been suggested, at the request of another of Beauchamp's daughters, Anne Neville, widow of Richard Neville, Earl of Warwick, in the mid-1480s.[59] Patrons of Lydgate's religious writings, inspired, no doubt, in part by thoughts of a spiritual reward for their devotion,[60] included Thomas Montacute, Earl of Salisbury (*The Pilgrimage of the Life of Man*), his wife, Alice Chaucer, later Duchess of Suffolk (*The Virtues of the Masse*), and John Whethamstede, Abbot of St Albans (*The Lives of St Albon and St Amphabell*).[61]

Returning to the question of a possible connection between Malory and Anthony Wydville, it is clear that the latter, too, was conscious of how reputation could be enhanced by certain judicious acts of patronage. In November 1473 Wydville was appointed tutor to the young Prince of Wales, his nephew, and the books which he translated himself, and had issued through Caxton's press (the *Dicts and Sayings of the Philosophers*, published 18 November 1477, the *Moral Proverbs* of Christine de Pisan, published 20 February 1477/78, and the *Cordyale*, published 24 March 1478/79) were of a kind to impress with their sober, thoughtful, and didactic intent.[62] In the realm of

58 Pearsall, *Lydgate*, pp.167-8.
59 See Kathleen L. Scott, *The Caxton Master and His Patrons*, Cambridge Bibliographical Society Monograph, no. 8 (Cambridge, 1976) pp.55-66, and for a discussion of the patronage of the volume, pp.61-3. There are two complete facsimiles of the MS: William, Earl of Carysfoot, *The Pageants of Richard Beauchamp, Earl of Warwick* (Oxford, for the Roxburghe Club, 1908); and Viscount Dillon and W. H. St John Hope, *Pageant of the birth, life and death of Richard Beauchamp, Earl of Warwick, K. G., 1389-1439* (London, 1914).
60 Cf. Lucas, 'English Literary Patronage', p.230.
61 On these patrons and the texts they commissioned, see Pearsall, *Lydgate*, pp.172-3 and plate facing p.166; 162; 280; 283-5. For the debate as to whether the translation of Deguileville is actually by Lydgate, see K. Walls, 'Did Lydgate Translate the *Pèlerinage de la Vie Humaine*?', *Notes and Queries*, 222 (1977) 103-5, and R. F. Green, 'Lydgate and Deguileville Once More', *Notes and Queries*, 223 (1978) 105-6. On the cost of producing this copy of the saints' lives see n.75 below.
62 On Wydville's tutorship of the young Prince, and the control he exerted over his affairs in general, see Hicks, 'Changing Role of the Wydvilles', esp. pp.75ff. It has also been suggested that Wydville was Caxton's patron for his edition

chivalric activity, too, Wydville seems to have been well aware, in an age of conspicuous consumption, of the propagandist potential of ordered, but ostentatious, display. This is suggested, for instance, by his involvement in the Anglo-Burgundian jousts held at Smithfield in 1467, which accompanied the negotiations for the marriage of Edward IV's sister, Margaret, to Charles the Bold; and by his participation in the wedding celebrations in Bruges the following year.[63] Given the evident care with which Wydville promoted his interests both in general[64] and in respect of his role as patron, if he had been instrumental in the composition of the *Morte*, it is almost inconceivable, even making due allowance for his family's downfall, that no record of such an involvement should be traceable in either manuscript or printed copies of the text. This contention receives support from the argument outlined above, that the only apparent deliberate omissions of material in either version relate to Malory himself.

The evidence would thus seem to leave Malory with the status of 'gentleman amateur' rather than that of professional writer, a role for which there were ample precedents from the fourteenth century onwards.[65] The suggestion which has recently been put forward, that Malory may have written an apprentice work, *The Wedding of Sir Gawain and Dame Ragnell*, before embarking on his more ambitious project, might be seen as additional justification for placing him within the former category.[66] In order to set Malory as an author more firmly within the context of his age it would be worthwhile to compare his position to that of other translators.[67] Whilst such a task

of *Jason*, which is dedicated to the Prince, but this can only be speculation; see Painter, *William Caxton*, p. 86 and Hellinga, *Caxton in Focus*, pp. 95-8.

[63] See Sydney Anglo, 'Anglo-Burgundian Feats of Arms: Smithfield, June 1467', *Guildhall Miscellany*, 2 (1965) 271-83. A measure of Wydville's success as a self-publicist is the preservation in contemporary MSS of accounts of his deeds, e.g. in the Pastons' MS, Lansdowne 285, ff. 18-22, 29v-42; see *Catalogue of Lansdowne MSS*, nos. 12-15, 20-37; (on the changing relations between Wydville and the Pastons see Davis, *Paston Letters*, Part 1 (Oxford, 1971) p. xlvii). It is also of some note that ten years after the Smithfield jousts Edward IV proposed Wydville as husband for Mary of Burgundy, his sister's step-daughter.

[64] See Hicks, 'Changing Role of the Wydvilles', and on Wydville's management of his affairs, E. W. Ives, 'Andrew Dymmock and the Papers of Antony, Earl Rivers, 1482-83', *Bulletin of the Institute of Historical Research*, 41 (1968) 216-29.

[65] See, e.g., McFarlane, *Nobility*, pp. 241-2.

[66] P. J. C. Field, 'Malory and *The Wedding of Sir Gawain and Dame Ragnell*', *Archiv für neuere Sprachen*, 34 (1982) 374-81.

[67] Malory's style has been compared with that of other prose writers in the fifteenth century by P. J. C. Field, *Romance and Chronicle* (London, 1971),

calls for a closer study than is practicable here, a few observations concerning a near-contemporary Arthurian translation may be of use to emphasise the fact that patronage did not provide the sole means by which writers could work in the fifteenth century. The only other Arthurian romance in Middle English to approach Malory's in terms of physical magnitude is the prose *Merlin*; even so, this work is only just over half the length of the *Morte*, covering in its most complete copy (some leaves are missing at the end) 245 as opposed to the original 500 leaves of the Additional MS.[68] I should add that I do not equate the *Merlin* qualitatively with the *Morte*, since it is a relatively straightforward translation from the French, but quantitatively the comparison does have validity.

The romance survives in two copies. One, almost complete, is Cambridge UL Ff.3.11, and the other, of which only a leaf remains, is in a Rawlinson miscellany in the Bodleian (D.913, f.43). The latter is in the hand of a scribe with a prolific output, who worked in London during the reign of Edward IV. The cumulative researches of Eleanor Prescott Hammond, Dr Ian Doyle and Dr Richard Green have established that he worked on another twelve MSS (this seems unlikely to be a final count), and that he had connections with a London stationer; amongst the other texts he copied are poems by Chaucer, Hoccleve and Lydgate.[69] This fragment of the *Merlin* is of paper, and though the scribe is competent, there is little of note about the quality of the copy. It seems justifiable to conclude that the buying public for this MS would not have needed to be particularly wealthy. The history of the Cambridge MS, on the other hand, appears to have been rather different. Ff.3.11 is a vellum book with some, though not a great deal of, illumination; the opening page of text is framed by a demi-vinet border, and smaller painted initials are scattered through the copy thereafter.[70] It has not proved possible to discover who owned

but a study of the development of prose in relation to audience and/or patronage would be of some interest.

68 The *Merlin* is edited by H. B. Wheatley, EETS OS 10, 21, 36, 112 (1865, 1866, 1869, 1899, repr. in 1 vol., 1973).

69 See Eleanor Prescott Hammond, 'Two British Museum Manuscripts', *Anglia*, 28 (1905) 1-28, and 'A Scribe of Chaucer', *MP*, 27 (1929-30) 26-33; A. I. Doyle, 'An Unrecognized Piece of *Piers the Ploughman's Creed* and Other Works by Its Scribe', *Speculum*, 34 (1959) 428-36, and 'English Books In and Out of Court from Edward III to Henry VII' in *English Court Culture*, ed. Scattergood and Sherborne, p.177 and n.42; R. F. Green, 'Notes on Some Manuscripts of Hoccleve's *Regiment of Princes*', *British Library Journal*, 4 (1978) 37-41.

70 For examples of contemporary usage of the term 'demi-vinet' see Margaret Rickert's chapter on 'Illumination' in Manly and Rickert, *Canterbury Tales*, pp.562-3.

this MS originally, but the volume can be definitely associated around 1500 with a Kent family who rose steadily to prominence throughout the fifteenth century until, during the reign of Henry VIII, various members occupied influential positions at court and within the government.[71] The characteristics of the copyist's hand and the style of the decoration indicates a date of sometime after 1450 for its manufacture and it is, therefore, almost contemporaneous with the Rawlinson copy. The conclusion to which all this evidence tends is that at much the same time copies of the *Merlin* were being executed for different kinds of market, though whether they were made for the retail or the bespoke trade is not clear.[72] This pattern of production in turn throws doubt upon the idea that the translation was made at the behest of a patron. It may be, of course, that a slightly earlier MS, now lost, contained some dedicatory material, but the chances of this do not appear to be strong; the Cambridge MS is complete at the beginning, but there is no reference to the circumstances of composition. Perhaps, as happened in the case of some of the prose redactions of romances issued by Caxton and the printers who came after him, the translation of the *Merlin* was undertaken on a speculative, commercial basis.[73]

Mention of the commercial considerations involved in the production of books leads to a last point concerning the physical make-up of the unique MS of the *Morte d'Arthur*, namely that it can in no way be described as a *de luxe* volume; this fact has considerable implications for an understanding of the kind of ownership for which it was intended. The names of characters and of some places are, it is true, highlighted by being written in red ink, but this sign of careful and thoughtful presentation (the switch between pens would have been a time-consuming process) is not matched by other aspects of its production, in particular the lack of uniformity of lay-out adopted

71 I hope to write about this family and their literary interests, including their ownership of this MS, in greater detail elsewhere.

72 See, for general discussion of this problem, A. I. Doyle and M. B. Parkes, 'The production of copies of the *Canterbury Tales* and the *Confessio Amantis* in the early fifteenth century' in *Medieval Scribes, Manuscripts and Libraries: Essays presented to N. R. Ker*, ed. M. B. Parkes and Andrew G. Watson (London, 1978) pp.163-210.

73 On the rationale behind the translation and publication of romances by de Worde and his associates, see N. F. Blake, 'Wynkyn de Worde: The Early Years' and 'Wynkyn de Worde: The Later Years', *Gutenberg Jahrbuch* (1971) pp.62-9, (1972) pp.128-38. Commercial considerations may have governed the composition of romances in the fourteenth century, as well; see the introduction to the facsimile of the Auchinleck MS by Derek Pearsall and I. C. Cunningham (London, 1977), and cf. Nicolas Jacobs, '*Sir Degarré, Lay le Freine, Beves of Hamtoun* and the "Auchinleck Bookshop"', *Notes and Queries*, 29 (1982) 294-301.

by the two scribes, the overall lack of supervision, and the fact that the volume is composed of paper, and that it contains no illustrations or painted decoration.[74] This is not to say that it would have been a cheap book to buy, as can be demonstrated by an approximate valuation based on contemporary rates of copying. For example, at around the time that Malory was completing his compilation, the scribe John Ebesham was submitting a bill to John Paston II for the numerous pieces of work he had carried out for him, and the charges he made were 1d. for a leaf of verse, and 2d. for one of prose.[75] One of the books which Ebesham copied for Paston is still extant, that is, Lansdowne 285, the 'Grete Booke'. The number of lines to a page and the size of the writing space are roughly equal in this MS and Additional 59678 and so, assuming that rates were fairly standard in different parts of the country,[76] this would suggest that the basic cost of this copy of the *Morte* was £4 3s. 8d., although it is not certain whether this sum would include the cost of the scribal insertions in red ink. On top of this there would have been a charge for rubrication, in this case the addition of around 120 large initials at divisions within the text (only 111 remain, owing to the loss of two quires); this could have been carried out by a separate craftsman. Only two of the initials

---

[74] On the scribes' use of red ink see Ker, introd. to the facsimile, pp. xiv-xv: it seems that, rather than the names being filled in after the rest of the text was copied, a different pen was picked up each time red ink was required. Other features of the manuscript's production are analysed in this same introduction.

[75] See *Paston Letters*, Pt 2, pp. 391-2 and also 386-7; and A. I. Doyle, 'The Work of a Late Fifteenth Century English Scribe, William Ebesham', *Bulletin of the John Rylands Library*, 39 (1956-57) 298-325, pp. 299-307. There are other accounts surviving from the fifteenth century. Abbot Whethamstede paid £3 6s. 8d. for his copy of Lydgate's *Lives of St Albon and St Amphabell* (Pearsall, *John Lydgate*, p. 283); and see Robert Steele and Mabel Day, eds, *The English Poems of Charles d'Orléans*, EETS OS 215, 220 (1941, 1946, repr. 1970) pp. xvi-xvii, for the cost of copying Harley 682. Other MSS with contemporary accounts are noted by Malcolm Parkes, in M. B. Parkes and E. Salter, Introduction to the facsimile of Corpus Christi College MS 61 (Cambridge, 1978) p. 1 n. 2, and cf. Doyle and Parkes, 'Production of copies', p. 197 and n. 84. See also H. E. Bell, 'The Price of Books in Medieval England', *The Library*, 4th ser., 17 (1936) 312-32, and Abbot Gasquet, 'Books and Bookmaking in Early Chronicles and Accounts', *Transactions of the Bibliographical Society*, 9 (1906) 15-30, esp. pp. 28-30 for a record of the charges for the making of a psalter for John Howard, Duke of Norfolk. Comparison is made here between the cost of making Additional 59678 and the charges made for Lansdowne 285 because of the similar nature of the texts being copied and the closeness in date of their production.

[76] It is not clear where the MS of Malory's work was written, although Professor Angus McIntosh has tentatively localised the dialect of the two scribes in West Northamptonshire; see his review of Matthews, *The Ill-Framed Knight*, in *Medium Aevum*, 37 (1968) 346-8.

are at all elaborate; these, on ff. 71r and 409v, occupy five lines and have a pen and ink infilling of a formalised, but rather clumsy, leaf design. Apart from these there is one three line initial on f. 349r, of blue with red pen-work decoration, and the remainder are all plain red lombards either of three, but more usually of two, lines; the execution of all of these is rather crude. John Ebesham charged John Paston 3s. 4d. for 'the Rubrissheyng of Alle the booke', which implies that he did it himself; allowing for the relative lengths of the Additional and Lansdowne MSS, an estimate of 8s. for the rubrication of the former may not be too wide of the mark. A final cost would be that of binding. Charges for this work varied with the size of the book to be covered and with the type of materials chosen. Assuming the covering in this case to have been fairly basic — wooden boards with an outer layer of leather — 2s. to 3s. would be an adequate sum to allow, perhaps.[77] An estimated total cost of around £4. 15s. for the book therefore seems reasonable.

Whoever bought the Additional MS must have had at least a moderate income, but its quality suggests that the purchaser is unlikely to have come from the nobility because, even leaving out of consideration the sumptuous painted books which Edward IV and his close associates obtained from Flemish workshops,[78] the quality of the books commissioned and owned by the nobility at this time is very different from that of the Malory MS. Since the suggestion has been made that the latter may have been commissioned by Anthony Wydville,[79] a particularly apt comparison may be drawn between it and Lambeth 265, the presentation copy of Wydville's translation of *The Dicts and Sayings of the Philosophers*, which was completed on 24 December 1477, and perhaps given to Edward by his brother-in-law as a Christmas gift. In terms of luxuriousness this volume scarcely rivals others which the King owned, but it reveals nevertheless several expensive features

[77] Edward IV paid between 3s. 4d. and 20s. for the 'binding gilding and dressing' of various of his books (*Wardrobe Accounts*, pp.125-6), but the materials used were velvet and silk (p.152). The Duke of Norfolk paid 12s. for his psalter to be bound in 1467, but again this would have been of a quality in keeping with the nature of the volume (see Gasquet, 'Books and Bookmaking', pp. 29-30). The sum of 2s. per volume was charged for the binding of wood and leather which still survives on two books presented to Peterhouse in the fifteenth century, now MSS 114, 154; (see Bell, 'The Price of Books', p.322).

[78] See Margaret Kekewich, 'Edward IV, William Caxton and Literary Patronage in Yorkist England', *Modern Languages Review*, 66 (1971) 481-7; Alexander, 'Painting and Illumination for Royal Patrons', pp.152-3 and additional references cited there; see pl.14 in the latter work for an illustration of a MS typical of those owned by Edward.

[79] Hilton Kelliher, 'The Early History of the Malory Manuscript', pp.155-6.

of production. There is only one illustration (the famous scene in which Wydville presents the book to Edward, who is surrounded by his family and members of the court)[80] but aside from this, large illuminated initials of an unusual design abound and the beginning of each sentence is picked out alternately with a blue mark decorated with red penwork, or a gold mark with blue penwork.[81] The material of the book, which is used lavishly, is vellum, and the pages are attractively prepared with ruling in an ink which is now a light-purplish colour.[82] The text is written in a clear and fluent secretary script.[83] Compared with this MS the Additional volume gives the impression of competent, but routine, production. More telling correspondences with regard to execution can be noted between the *Morte* MS and other late fifteenth-century paper copies of English romances, for example: the MS of *Partenay*, now Trinity College Cambridge R.3.17; the version of *Partonope of Blois* now Additional 35288; and the fragmentary remains of the story of *Ponthus* preserved as ff.1-2 of Douce 384.[84] Moreover, the analogy may be extended to the probable ownership of the various volumes. On the basis of scribbled names which appear in the MS of Malory's work, Hilton Kelliher has presented a convincing case for the ownership in the later sixteenth century to be attributed to a relatively well-to-do family of Northamptonshire gentry. The evidence which he has gathered, together with the conclusions prompted by the physical characteristics of the volume, suggests that the original owners are likely to have come from a similar background.[85] Such a history would be in accord with what

[80] This has often been reproduced; see, e.g., R. Strong, *Tudor and Jacobean Portraits*, 2 vols, National Portrait Gallery (London, 1969) pl.162, and the enlarged detail of the portrait of Anthony Wydville, pl. V in Hellinga, *Caxton in Focus*.

[81] See Hellinga, *Caxton in Focus*, pl. III for a colour illustration of f.17v, and cf. the description of the MS by James and Jenkins, *Catalogue of MSS at Lambeth Palace*, pp.412-14.

[82] There are generous borders around the text: the page measurement is 278mm x 198mm, and the writing space is 176mm x 97mm.

[83] The scribe signs his work on f.105r: 'Apud sanctum Jacobum/in campis per haywarde'; Doyle, 'English Books In and Out of Court', p.181 n.54, describes his work as 'accomplished', and suggests that he may have been a cleric at the hospital of St James in the Fields at Westminster.

[84] See, respectively: M. R. James, *Catalogue of the Western MSS in the Library of Trinity College Cambridge* (Cambridge, 1901) II, pp.66-7, and Julia Boffey, *The Manuscript Context of English Courtly Love Lyrics, c.1450-1530*, D.Phil., University of York, 1983, pp.203-5; Gisela Guddat-Figge, *A Catalogue of Manuscripts Containing Middle English Romances* (Munich, 1976), pp.164-5 (ff.2-19 of this MS are of vellum, ff.1, 20-154 of paper) and pp.268-9.

[85] 'The Early History of the Malory Manuscript'. The MS contains the signature

117

is known about the other romance MSS which have been mentioned.[86]

The discussion so far has emphasised the desirability, in our present state of knowledge, of keeping open as many avenues of enquiry as possible in the approach to an understanding of how Malory was able to write his Arthurian work, despite the problems of interpretation inherent in the nature of the evidence with which we have to deal. Thus, it has been argued, it is not necessary to assume that Malory had a patron in order to account for his access to a number of source texts, since there were several different ways in which he could have obtained them. One of the possibilities raised was that he borrowed, or had access to, books owned by someone with a larger collection than he, in all probability, possessed, and investigation into the contents of the libraries of individuals and families who may have been known to Malory does seem to hold out the offer of potentially rich rewards.

In these terms it is reasonable to re-examine the claims of the Wydvilles to be considered as the providers of books, for the family as a whole has acquired a reputation for cultural interests and Anthony, of course, was praised within his lifetime and immediately afterwards for his erudition and his literary accomplishments.[87] Disappointingly

(repeated several times) of one 'Richard Followell', who can probably be identified as a member of the Follwell family of Litchborough. Kelliher has proved a connection, during the sixteenth century, between this family and the lords of the manor of Litchborough, the Malorys, who were distantly related to the Malorys of Newbold Revel, though whether this series of associations has any bearings on the origins of the MS is, as yet, a matter for speculation only.

[86] Trinity College Cambridge R.3.19 is connected with inhabitants of York and two nearby villages, Elvington and Sutton-on-Derwent, in the late fifteenth century; see James, *Catalogue of Trinity MSS*, and Boffey, *Manuscript Context*. BL Additional MS 35288 contains various names, including: Thomas Altherton, 'frauncissi babisonis' and 'melady babsin', 'Dorythe Couper', and 'Robarte Gascoygne'; none of these individuals has been identified, though inscriptions in Altherton's hand imply that the MS was loaned amongst a group of friends; see Guddat-Figge, *MSS Containing Romances*, p.165.

[87] On Anthony's reputation in his lifetime see the prologues and epilogues to his translations written by Caxton, especially those to the *Dicts* and the *Cordiale* (Blake, *Caxton's Own Prose*, pp. 73-7, 70-2). The *virelai* said by the antiquarian John Rous to have been composed by Anthony the day before his death achieved great popularity at the early Tudor court; it has been printed and discussed most recently by R. H. Robbins, 'The Middle English Court Love Lyric' in *The Interpretation of Medieval Lyric Poetry*, ed. W. T. H. Jackson (New York, 1980) pp. 219-24 (see the notes for additional bibliographical references). The admiration which was accorded Anthony after his death is epitomised in the ?late sixteenth-century note written on f. vi v of Lambeth 265, opposite the presentation verses: 'This Earle was the most/lernyd valyant

few books belonging to members of the family remain, but those which do indicate a fairly high level of literary and aesthetic discrimination on the part of their owners. Three MSS can be associated with Anthony's father, Richard Wydville, 1st Earl Rivers. Perhaps one of the first volumes which he acquired was Royal 19. A. XXII, 'Le Codicile de Jehan de Meun' (actually by Jean Chapuis), a devotional work on the Trinity and the seven articles of faith; this copy has been dated to the mid-fifteenth century.[88] Ownership was tentatively attributed to him on the basis of an erased inscription at the conclusion of the text (f. 31v), and the family's possession of the volume is confirmed by the reading, under ultra-violet light, of the name 'Jaquete' on an end flyleaf.[89] The style of the illumination and border decoration is French, and it seems not improbable that Wydville and his wife acquired the MS whilst they were in France as part of the contingent escorting Margaret of Anjou to England in 1445.[90] Other books which can be linked with Richard are rather later. He noted on a flyleaf of Bodley 264, the fine early-fourteenth-century *Alexander* MS, that he bought the book 'le premier jor de lan a londres' in 5 Edward IV, i.e. 1466,[91] and he must have acquired Bodley 456, containing Rolle's

and/honorable knight of the world for his tyme/yet all was exersid w[th]/ adverse accydentes In/his lyfe, at length cam/to atcheeve the honor/of an vndesarvid death//. Modern judgements on the literary interests of the family are summed up by Cora L. Scofield, *The Life and Reign of Edward IV* (London, 1923) 2, p.440: commenting on the election of Lionel Wydville to the Chancellorship of Oxford University in 1479, Miss Scofield remarks that although flattery of the King, by appointing his brother-in-law to the post, was probably a prime consideration, 'As the members of the Wydville family, both men and women, were endowed not only with good minds, but with literary tastes, the intellectual gifts and attainments of Lionel ... probably fully justified his choice'. On Anthony see also the favourable judgement of Charles Ross, *Edward IV* (London, 1974), in what is otherwise a fairly critical view of the family and their influence.

[88] See Warner and Gilson, *Catalogue of Royal MSS*, II, p.323.

[89] The erased inscription on f. 31v is irrecoverable, even under ultra-violet light.

[90] See Smith, *The Coronation of Elizabeth Wydeville*, pp.45-6, for details of their journey. Richard was also in France from time to time prior to this date, campaigning; see *Complete Peerage*, XI, pp.19-20.

[91] On this MS see *The Romance of Alexander: a collotype facsimile of MS Bodley 264*, with introduction by M. R. James (Oxford, 1933), and Guddat-Figge, *MSS Containing Romances*, pp. 252-4; on the fifteenth-century paintings added to the volume see Alexander, 'Painting and Manuscript Illumination for Royal Patrons', p.149; Gereth M. Spriggs, 'Unnoticed Bodleian MSS Illuminated by Herman Scheerre and His School', *Bodleian Library Record*, 7 (1964) 193-203, p.194; and Richard Marks and Nigel Morgan, *The Golden Age of English Manuscript Painting 1200-1500* (London, 1981) p.109 and pl. 35. James suggests (p.3) that the signature 'Ryverys' which appears under the 1st Earl's note is that of the 3rd Earl, Anthony's brother, Richard.

Emendatione Vite, at around the same time: on f. iii v is a crudely painted representation of the Rivers arms (argent a fess and canton gules) together with the inscription 'Iste liber constat Domino Ricardo wydeuill Comit' le Ryviers Et dn̄s de Wymyngton'.[92] Anthony's connections with Harley 4431 have already been noted, but evidence of his tastes in books during the 1460s is hard to come by.[93] It seems, however, that at a later period he did possess the English psalter (Additional 42131) which had been made for his mother's first husband, Bedford, since the date of birth in 1467 of his second wife, Mary Fitzlewis, has been added to the Calendar (f. 3v).[94] 'Marie Rivieres' left her mark on another of the Royal MSS, 18. D. VII, a copy of Laurent Premierfait's translation of 'Jehan Boccacce de cas des nobles homes et femmes', again a French production dating from c. 1450.[95]

Evidence of Elizabeth's interest in books can also be found. Her ownership of Royal 14. E. III, containing Arthurian texts, has been

---

92 Wydville was created Earl Rivers 24 May 1466; in the Bodley 264 inscription he styles himself 'monseignor richart de Wideuille seigneur de riuieres', a title which was bestowed upon him 9 May 1448. On the MS see Hope Emily Allen, *Writings ascribed to Richard Rolle, hermit of Hampole*, PMLA monograph (London and New York, 1927) p. 232; and M. B. Parkes, *English Cursive Book Hands 1250-1500* (Oxford, 1969, repr. London, 1979) p. 15 and pl. 15(i). For comments on the derivation of the arms adopted by Wydville as Earl Rivers, see M. A. Hicks, *False, Fleeting, Perjur'd Clarence: George Duke of Clarence, 1449-78* (Gloucester, 1980) p. 31.

93 For a discussion of the dubious basis upon which the commissioning and ownership of Longleat 257 have been attributed to Anthony, see Meale, 'The Middle English Romance of *Ipomedon*'.

94 *Catalogue of the Additions to the MSS in the BM, 1926-1930*, pp. 202-6; Wydville married Mary Fitzlewis before October 1480 — she was then aged thirteen. Another addition to the Calendar for 31 March has been erased. The arms of Catesby impaling those of Zouche of Harringworth appear on several folios, demonstrating ownership of the MS by William Catesby, who was appointed by Anthony Wydville as one of the executors of his will; (see the abstract in *Testamenta Vetusta*, ed. Nicolas, pp. 379-81). Catesby became counsellor to Richard III and was executed by Henry VII after Bosworth, but he seems to have been less than scrupulous in his careerism; see J. S. Roskell, 'William Catesby, Counsellor to Richard III', *Bulletin of the Institute of Historical Research*, 42 (1959) 145-74. The Additional MSS catalogue entry corrects the assumption made by E. Carleton Williams, *My Lord of Bedford*, p. 250, that the volume had passed into Catesby ownership by 1450. See Marks and Morgan, *Golden Age*, pp. 104, 106 and pls 33, 34.

95 Warner and Gilson, *Catalogue of Royal MSS*, II, p. 313. It is a possibility that this MS, too, was acquired originally by Richard Wydville and Jacquetta during their time in France; Warner and Gilson note stylistic similarities between the decoration of this volume and that of Royal 15. E. VI, a book of romances and other texts given to Margaret of Anjou by Talbot, probably on the occasion of her marriage, which was also produced in France.

referred to above. She also wrote her name, apparently whilst she was in sanctuary in Westminster Abbey during Richard III's reign, in a fragmentary MS of lessons and collects, dating from c.1300 (*olim* Fitzwilliam Museum, Bradfer-Lawrence MS 15);[96] and amongst the expenses passed through her chamber accounts for the year 1466-67 appears the following: 'per manus Willelmi Wulflete clerici nuper cancellarii universitatis Cantebrigiensis £10 ut in precio unius libri eidem domine regine venditi'.[97] The evidence for her ownership of another two books is, however, less sure. The first of these is the Huntington Library copy of Caxton's 1474 edition of the *Recuyell of the Histories of Troy*. Although the volume is prefaced by an engraving, in the style of the Master of Mary of Burgundy, in which a kneeling figure presents a book to Margaret, Elizabeth's sister-in-law[98] (which might be considered appropriate to Elizabeth's assumed ownership) the inscription on the lining of the cover, reading 'This boke is mine, Quene Elizabet, late wiffe vnto the most noble King Edwarde the Forthe', was made by one 'Thomam Shukburghe juniorem',[99] and the attribution, therefore, is less than fully reliable.[100]

[96] The Bradfer-Lawrence MSS have now been sold; for a description of the MS see Pamela Tudor-Craig, *Richard III*, exhibition catalogue, National Portrait Gallery, 1973, no.156, pp.64-5.

[97] A. R. Myers, 'The Household of Queen Elizabeth Woodville, 1466-67', *Bulletin of the John Rylands Library*, 50 (1967-68) 207-35, 443-81, p.481. Whilst there is no evidence concerning the contents of this book, it is of some interest to note that William Wulflete apparently had a liking for vernacular literature; he owned Corpus Christi MS 496, a copy of Hoccleve's *Regiment of Princes*, which he transcribed himself; see E. B. Emden, *A Biographical Register of the University of Cambridge to A.D.1500* (Cambridge, 1963) p.657. Elizabeth's contacts with the University appear to have extended beyond an acquaintance with Wulflete; for her patronage of Queen's College (founded by Margaret of Anjou) see Ross, *Edward IV*, p.270.

[98] Reproduced as the frontispiece in Painter, *William Caxton*; and as pl.47 in N. F. Blake, *Caxton: England's First Publisher* (London, 1976); the engraving is discussed by Blake, op. cit., pp.132-5, and by Kathleen L. Scott, *The Mirroure of the Worlde — MS Bodley 283 (England c.1470-80): The Physical Composition, Decoration and Illustration* (Oxford, for the Roxburghe Club, 1980) pp.32-3.

[99] A full transcription of this note is given by Blake, *Caxton*, p.133.

[100] A. I. Doyle suggests that Shukburghe may be identifiable as the London draper of that name who inscribed a contemporary MS; see 'English Books In and Out of Court', p.180, n.53. For a sceptical view of the authenticity of this attribution see P. J. Croft, *Lady Margaret Beaufort, Elizabeth of York and Wynkin de Worde: A Description of a Copy of Walter Hylton's 'Scala perfectionis' printed by Wynkyn de Worde in 1494*, etc. (London, 1958) p.4, n.2. The close association of Elizabeth Wydville with Caxton's press which was at one time assumed, is also open to doubt. Professor N. F. Blake, whilst maintaining his belief that she is the 'noble lady' referred to by

There is some dispute as to whether the second book in question, *Horae angeli custodientis* (Liverpool Cathedral MS 6), belonged to Elizabeth Wydville, or to her daughter, Elizabeth of York.[101] The small volume contains an illuminated presentation miniature (f. 5v) in which a kneeling woman presents a book to a queen; dedicatory verses are addressed to 'Lady souereyne princes' and the initials of the first nine lines spell out the name 'Elisabeth'.[102] The attribution to Elizabeth of York was occasioned by the fact that the initial 'D' with which the text opens on f. 6r has within it a white rose superimposed upon a red, but it has been argued on stylistic grounds that the MS is of an earlier date than Henry VII's reign.[103]

This collection of books, whilst of considerable intrinsic interest, is nonetheless uninformative as to the likelihood of any of the Wydvilles having been in a position to give Malory access to material relevant to his work; the only Arthurian texts which have so far been associated with them did not come into their possession until at least a decade after the longest-lived Thomas Malory had died and, whilst not wishing to discount the possibility that further research into the books owned by members of the family might one day provide a link with the writer, I think it should be borne in mind that an appreciation of books and literature was not, in the middle of the fifteenth century, by any means unique to them. Another family whose literary interests might well repay investigation in connection with Malory, for example, is the Nevilles, and this is so, not only because ownership of a number of books has been attributed to them, but also because a persuasive case has been advanced for an association between Sir Thomas Malory of Newbold Revel and Richard Neville, Earl of Warwick.[104]

Caxton in one prologue, is now of the opinion that she did not request the publication, and he concludes that we must accept that the printer is 'not being entirely truthful in his remarks about the translation'; see 'William Caxton: the Man and His Work', pp. 75-7, and for his earlier view, 'The "noble lady" in Caxton's *The Book of the Knight of the Tower*', *Notes and Queries*, 210 (1965) 92-3 and *Caxton and His World*, pp. 92-3.

101 For descriptions see: *A Catalogue of Illuminated and Other Manuscripts — together with some works on palaeography*, Bernard Quaritch, 1931, no. 73 pp. 53-6; *Medieval and Early Renaissance Treasures in the North West*, Catalogue of the exhibition held at the Whitworth Art Gallery, University of Manchester, 1976, p. 29 no. 49 (description by J. J. G. Alexander); N. R. Ker, *Medieval Manuscripts in British Libraries*, III (Oxford, 1983) pp. 165-6.

102 Folios 5v and 6r are illustrated in the Quaritch catalogue, p. 52, and the verses are printed in full on p. 54.

103 Alexander, *Medieval and Early Renaissance Treasures*, p. 29.

104 P. J. C. Field, 'The Last Years', where evidence is presented to show affiliation on a number of different levels; if, however, Malory was a participant in the Cornelius plot, as Mr Field argues, he anticipated, rather than followed,

The only MS which has been assigned definitely to Warwick, on the basis of the occurrence of his badge and arms, is Geneva, Bibliothèque de la Ville MS fr. 166, which is a copy of *L'enseignement de vrai noblesse* made and decorated in Flanders in 1464.[105] Aside from this, the Earl seems to have taken a certain interest in historical matters. Thus he offered to help Jean de Waurin obtain information which he needed for his chronicle of England, although in the event, whilst Warwick was generous in the hospitality he afforded the Flemish writer, he was apparently too 'busy with other important matters' to aid him any further with his researches.[106] Also, Warwick and his wife, Anne Beauchamp, may have shared an interest in the antiquarian researches of John Rous, chaplain of the chantry at Guy's Cliff, which had been instituted by Anne's father; Rous sent Neville a copy of Matthew Paris' account of the legendary foundations of the town of Warwick, and on another occasion, the priest was permitted to consult a law book which was in the possession of the Earls of Warwick, in right of their hereditary position as chamberlains of the royal exchequer.[107] The probable connection of Warwick's widow with the commissioning of the Beauchamp *Pageants* has been alluded to, and perhaps it was for her that the *Rous Rolls* were executed.[108] It is possible, too, that she was in possession of Corpus Christi Cambridge

Neville's involvement with the Lancastrians. The literary patronage and manuscripts of the Beauchamp and Neville families c.1400-c.1500 is the subject of the doctoral research currently being carried out by Lynne McGoldrick at the Centre for Medieval Studies, University of York.

[105] Scott, *The Caxton Master and His Patrons*, p.62 and n.249 (*ex inf.* A. I. Doyle); for a description of the MS see H. Aubert, 'Notices sur les manuscrits conservés à la Bibliothèque de Genève', *Bibliothèque de l'Ecole des Chartes*, 72 (1911) 298-302 (Petau 46 and 47).

[106] On Waurin and his *Recueil des Croniques et Anchiennes Istories de la Grant Bretaigne a present nomme Engleterre* see Gransden, *Historical Writing in England*, ii, pp. 288ff, and on Warwick's proffered help, p.290; (the quotation is taken from a passage of the *Croniques* translated by Gransden). A copy of this text was amongst the books produced in Flanders which Edward IV owned: Vol.I, a presentation copy, is Royal 15.E.IV.

[107] Gransden, *Historical Writing*, ii, p.311 and n.19; on Rous see pp.309ff, also T. D. Kendrick, *British Antiquity* (London, 1950), Chapter II.

[108] Scott, *Caxton Master*, pp.62-3. There are two versions of the *Roll* (which is an illustrated history of the Earls of Warwick and Kings of England); the first, the so-called 'Yorkist' roll, is in English and was written before 1485 (BL Additional 48976); the second, the 'Lancastrian' roll, is in Latin and was written after the accession of Henry VII (College of Arms, Warwick Roll). Dr Scott raises the possibility that the illustrations in the two rolls and in the Beauchamp *Pageants* were carried out in the same atelier; (the view that Rous himself was the artist of the rolls is not now generally accepted, cf. Gransden, *Historical Writing*, p.311, n.17).

MS 61, the finest MS of Chaucer's *Troilus and Criseyde*, since the inscription 'neuer Foryeteth Anne neuill' appears on f.101v. An early Beauchamp association with the MS seems probable, since John Shirley, who was secretary to Anne's father, is known to have handled the volume at some stage,[109] but it should be stressed that there are other Anne Nevilles of the fifteenth century who may be proposed as owners, including an aunt of Richard Neville, who married the Duke of Buckingham, and who is known to have owned several books on her own account.[110] Again, a number of Warwick's brothers and sisters are known to have possessed books: a MS bequeathed to George Neville, Bishop of Exeter and Archbishop of York, has been mentioned, as has the Royal MS of Hoccleve's poems owned by Joan Neville and her husband.[111] Cicely, whose first marriage was to Henry Beauchamp, Duke of Warwick, probably owned the Book of Hours which passed later to Elizabeth of York, and the interests of her second husband, John Tiptoft, Earl of Worcester, require no elaboration here.[112] Two other of Warwick's sisters married noted book owners; the second husband of Catherine was William, Lord Hastings, and the youngest sister, Margaret, married John de Vere, Earl of Oxford.[113] Neither

109 See Parkes, in M. B. Parkes and E. Salter (eds), *Troilus and Criseyde: A Facsimile of Corpus Christi College Cambridge MS 61* (Woodbridge, 1979) p.11 and n.30; Doyle, 'English Books In and Out of Court', p.175 and n.34. The frontispiece to the MS is illustrated in Marks and Morgan, *Golden Age*, pl.37.

110 Parkes, *Troilus*, p.12 is in favour of the MS having been owned by Anne Neville née Beauchamp, but the claim of the Duchess of Buckingham to be identified as the writer of the note is upheld by Salter in Pt 2 of the introduction; see p.23, and n.30 for a list of other MSS owned by this Anne Neville. Cf. the discussion by Doyle, Appendix B to the *Epistle of Othea*.

111 See above pp.102-3, 106. For accounts of the family see *DNB* (s.v. Richard Neville, Earl of Salisbury); and 'Marriage and Politics in the Fifteenth Century: the Nevilles and the Wydevilles', in J. R. Lander, *Crown and Nobility 1450-1509* (London, 1976).

112 Cicely's ownership of Additional 50001 is suggested by an erased inscription on f.147r recording her death; see Marks and Morgan, *Golden Age*, p.110 and pl.36. Henry Beauchamp owned a psalter and hours made for him (New York, Pierpont Morgan MS M.893); Marks and Morgan, op. cit., pp.114, 116, pls 38, 39. On Tiptoft's literary interests see: R. J. Mitchell, *John Tiptoft* (London, 1938) and 'A Renaissance Library: The Collection of John Tiptoft, Earl of Worcester', *The Library*, 4th ser. 18 (1937) 67-83; R. Weiss, 'The Library of John Tiptoft, Earl of Worcester', *The Bodleian Quarterly Record*, 8 (1935-38) 157-64, 'Another Tiptoft Manuscript', *The Bodleian Quarterly Record*, 8 (1935-38) 234-5, and *Humanism in England during the fifteenth century* (3rd ed. Oxford, 1967) Chapter VII. See Warner and Gilson, *Catalogue of Royal MSS*, II, pp.311-12 for a description of Royal 18.D.IV, containing Lydgate's *Fall of Princes*, which belonged to Tiptoft and Cicely.

113 On Hastings see Scott, *Caxton Master*, pp.52-3, also the facsimile of the

were these interests confined to a single generation: in 1426 Richard Neville's paternal grandmother Joan Beaufort was left a 'Tristram' by her brother, Thomas Beaufort, Duke of Exeter;[114] and his maternal grandfather, Thomas Montacute, as mentioned earlier patronised the translation of Deguileville's *Pèlerinage*.[115] Members of the Countess of Warwick's family, too, are well established as literary patrons and bookowners,[116] and it may not be without significance to the present discussion that when Guy Beauchamp donated forty books to Bordesley Abbey in 1305, amongst which were 'le premier livere de Launcelot', 'un Volum del Romaunce Iosep ab Arimathie, e deu Seint Grael', 'Un Volum del Romaunce deu Brut, e del Roy Costentine' and 'Un Volum de la Mort ly Roy Arthur, e de Mordret', he stipulated that the Abbey should not sell or otherwise dispose of them, and that he and his heirs should continue to have access to them, 'pur solas aveyr'.[117]

This brief indication of the book-owning and commissioning activities of the Nevilles is not offered here with the intention of promoting the claims of one family over another to be considered as the suppliers of Malory's sources, but rather to re-emphasise a point made earlier,

Hastings Hours (Additional 54782) with introduction by D. H. Turner (London, 1983). On John de Vere see p.102 above.

[114] For Exeter's will see J. Nichols, *Royal Wills* (London, 1780) p.254. Joan had to sue Henry V's executors for the return of two books on the Crusades which she had lent the King; see Nicholas Orme, *English Schools in the Middle Ages* (London, 1973) p.25; Hoccleve dedicated one of the holograph MSS of his poems to her (now Durham University V.III.9).

[115] Above, p.103; for a list of books owned by Montacute's third wife, Alice Chaucer, see *HMC* 8th Report, Appendix I, ii, 629a; cf. Green, *Poets and Princepleasers*, p.96.

[116] Anne's father, Richard Beauchamp, owned a copy of Froissart's poems, BN fr.831, and a copy of Trevisa's *Polychronicon*, Additional 24194; see Parkes and Salter, *Troilus*, p.22, n.26, Doyle, 'English Books In and Out of Court', p.175. Richard Beauchamp's first wife, Elizabeth Berkeley, was patroness of Walton's translation of Boethius, and her father was patron to Trevisa. Beauchamp's third wife, Isobel, Lady Despenser, was the recipient of Lydgate's *Fifteen Joys of Our Lady*. See Pearsall, *John Lydgate*, p.71. It may be noted that the association once presumed to have existed between Malory the author and Richard Beauchamp, on the basis of a Thomas Malory having served under Warwick in France during the reign of Henry V, has been discounted by P. J. C. Field, who has established that it is not the Sir Thomas Malory of Newbold Revel who is mentioned in the 1415 retinue roll; see 'Thomas Malory and the Warwick Retinue Roll', *Midland History*, 2 (1979-80) 20-30.

[117] Madeleine Blaess, 'L'Abbaye de Bordesley et les livres de Guy de Beauchamp', *Romania*, 78 (1957) 511-18, p.514; I am grateful to Miss Blaess for pointing out this clause of the agreement to me.

that to focus too narrowly upon particular families or individuals is, in the present state of our knowledge, premature, and that much groundwork remains to be done which will, it is anticipated, significantly alter previous ideas concerning book ownership and literary composition in the fifteenth century. What can be asserted now, however, is that the attempt to place Malory's achievement as a writer within a true historical perspective depends upon collaborative research being undertaken by scholars working in several different areas — historical, codicological and bibliographical, as well as literary.[118]

118 A shorter version of this paper was read at the conference of the British Branch of the International Arthurian Society held at the University College of North Wales, Bangor, from the 19-21 July, 1983.

V

ERNEST CHAUSSON'S 'LE ROI ARTHUS'

Tony Hunt

Arthus, désespéré, laissait tomber ses armes. Dans l'or et la pourpre du couchant, les voix invisibles appelaient vers les îles mystérieuses le roi déçu par la destinée. La mélodie grave et consolatrice s'élevait de toutes parts pour bercer la douleur du vaincu et célébrer son apothéose. Et nous, nous songions à celui qui avait mis tout son coeur dans ces chants de gloire et de tristesse. Nous le plaignions d'avoir été, lui aussi, comme le vieux roi, arraché à sa tâche.[1]

In the words with which André Hallays greeted the first performance of Chausson's one and only opera, 'Le Roi Arthus',[2] given at the Théâtre Royal de la Monnaie in Brussels on the 30th of November, 1903, we already find an acknowledgement of that affinity between the composer and the central figure of his lyric drama which was to become a *locus communis* of critical writings on the work. Begun in 1886 as Op. 23, 'Le Roi Arthus' was to cause its composer much heart-searching and protracted struggles before his death in 1899 in a bicycle accident. A draft scenario had been sent to Paul Poujaud in 1886, but it was not until nine years later that Chausson made heroic efforts to complete the work, at San Domenico di Fiesole, putting the final touches to Act Three on Christmas Day, 1895. Thereafter, there were constant attempts to have the opera staged, beginning with proposals by the Belgian violinist Ysaÿe[3] for a production in Geneva and

1 A. Hallays, *'Le Roi Arthus'*, *La Revue de Paris* 6, déc. 15, 1903 [pp.846-58] 846.
2 'Drame lyrique en 3 actes et 6 tableaux', it follows the Wagnerian pattern of continuous music and vocal writing, separated only by orchestral interludes, thus eschewing the more traditional sequence of recitative and aria. For a list of ten projected theatrical works by Chausson see Jean Gallois, *Ernest Chausson. L'homme et son oeuvre* (Paris, 1967; repr. 1981), pp.113f. *La Vie est un songe*, adapted from the most celebrated of Calderon's dramas, *La vida es sueño*, was planned as an opera of which the libretto was completed (1899), but not a note of music written.
3 A friend of the composer, who dedicated the widely performed *Poème* op. 25

continuing with representations by the conductor Nikisch for a performance in Dresden, the Spanish composer Albeniz[4] for one in Prague, and Felix Mottl for its staging in Karlsruhe. Discouraged, Chausson had talked of leaving the field to 'Bruneau et Wagner' (!). In the event, his sudden death was to delay performance yet further, though his widow lived to attend the first night. Lacking confidence and afflicted with the severe self-criticism that also assailed Dukas, Duparc and Maurice Emmanuel, Chausson would scarcely have been prepared for the enthusiastic reception his work received in Brussels, an enthusiasm unfortunately not shared by Paris, where his publisher Choudens had high hopes. In his review of the first performance Hallays wrote,

> Le Roi Arthus a forcé l'admiration générale par la grandeur chevaleresque de la conception poétique, la grâce et l'originalité des thèmes, la richesse de l'orchestration, le superbe lyrisme du rôle d'Arthus.[5]

In another notice of the Brussels production Gustave Samazeuilh was warmly appreciative, whilst expressing some reservations about the orchestration of Act One:

> Nous ne nous évertuerons pas non plus à dresser le catalogue des thèmes, toujours expressifs et caractéristiques, sur lesquels s'échafaude la polyphonie orchestrale du Roi Arthus. Nous nous en voudrions néanmoins de ne pas louer l'éclat et la chaleur de l'instrumentation, peut-être un peu opaque au premier acte pour les voix, ainsi qu'il advient souvent dans d'autres ouvrages contemporains d'Arthus. Il est certain que l'auteur, s'il vivait aujourd'hui, serait des premiers à rechercher une atmosphère instrumentale allégée et plus propice à la perception des paroles chantées.[6]

Particularly laudatory and perceptive were the remarks of Georges

---

to him, Ysaÿe not only gave the first performance of that work, but played it as a tribute to his dead friend, a week after his death, on 17 June, 1899. Today the Poème is the best known of Chausson's works and was the subject of an unforgettable recording by the lamented Ginette Neveu in 1946 (with Issay Dobrowen and the Philharmonia Orchestra). Ysaÿe was also the dedicatee of the remarkable, if not totally successful, Concert in D major for piano, violin, and string quartet (1889-91).

4 Albeniz himself planned an operatic trilogy King Arthur, of which only the third part, Merlin, was composed. A vocal score was published in Paris in 1906, but I know of no public performance.

5 art. cit., 847.

6 G. Samazeuilh, 'Ernest Chausson et Le Roi Arthus (Théâtre de la Monnaie, 30 novembre)', La Revue Musicale 3e année, no. 18, 15 décembre 1903, [pp. 699-705] 704. Gustave Samazeuilh, who died as recently as 1967, was, like his friend and teacher, Chausson, a law graduate and distinguished himself as a composer and critic, as well as preparing the French version of Tristan und Isolde. In 1947 he published a sketch, 'Ernest Chausson', in Musiciens de mon temps.

Eekhoud several months later, printed in the influential *Mercure de France*:

> La critique fut unanime à louer la ferme et noble tenue de la partition du *Roi Arthus*. Le travail orchestral, très fouillé et opulent sans surcharge, les riches harmonies, l'écriture élégante et recherchée quoique toujours aisée et lumineuse; les exquises combinaisons de timbres, le chromatisme si attachant, les modulations infinies, l'originalité et la valeur expressive des thèmes mélodiques, l'allure et le style des récits, la justesse de l'accent, le commentaire symphonique des gestes et des sentiments des personnages, et surtout les admirables préludes et interludes descriptifs, sans oublier le prestigieux ensemble choral du dénouement; tous ces éléments concourent à faire de cette oeuvre une des plus belles dont s'enorgueillera la jeune école française.[7]

There is no doubt that Chausson was fortunate in the circumstances and choice of venue of the first performance of his opera. The Théâtre Royal de la Monnaie in Brussels had an enviable record of operatic first performances, including Reyer's *Sigurd* (7 Jan. 1884) and *Salammbô* (2 Feb. 1890), Chabrier's *Gwendoline* (10 April 1886), d'Indy's *Fervaal* (12 March 1897), and Blockx's *La fiancée de la mer* (1902). Albeniz's *Pepita Jiménez* was performed there. It was the first theatre to give the French versions of *Aida* (1871), *Tannhäuser* (1873) and *Meistersinger* (1885) and had performed Bellini, Donizetti and Verdi before Paris did. Chausson's early teacher, Massenet, whom he left to study exclusively with Franck, had his *Hérodiade* performed at the theatre, the première taking place on 19 December 1881. The production of *Le Roi Arthus*, meticulously supervised by d'Indy, was in fact the fulfilment of a promise given by one of the directors, Maurice Kufferath, shortly before the composer's death and evidently no efforts were spared to ensure the work's success. Georges Eekhoud wrote 'Le succès de l'ocuvre a été considérable et s'est confirmé aux représentations suivantes. On est à la dixième et tout fait prévoir que la pièce fournira une carrière des plus brillantes'.[8] According to Gustave Samazeuilh the first performance was marked by 'un triple rappel à la fin de chaque acte'.[9] The musical direction was in the hands

---

[7] 'Chronique de Bruxelles', *Mercure de France* 49 (1904), 256-61. It should be pointed out, in fairness to Eekhoud, that the chapter on the opera in Jean-Pierre Barricelli and Leo Weinstein, *Ernest Chausson. The Composer's Life and Works* (Norman, 1955; repr. Westport, Connecticut, 1973) pp.187-202 contains the most deplorable plagiarism, being a tissue of unacknowledged literal translations of Eekhoud's review which the authors have the audacity to pass off as their own opinions. To add insult to injury, there is no mention of Eekhoud's review in their bibliography.

[8] *art. cit.*, 256.

[9] *art. cit.*, 700.

of Sylvain Dupuis, a Belgian composer (1856-1931), a friend of d'Indy and a Wagnerian enthusiast, who conducted at the Théâtre Royal de la Monnaie throughout the period 1900-11. The tenor taking the role of Lancelot was the highly gifted Frenchman Charles Dalmorès (1871-1939), who began his musical career as a horn player and made his operatic début at Rouen in 1899. After singing for a time in Brussels, he was in England taking part in the British première of *Hérodiade*, the *Hélène* of Saint-Saëns, and Charpentier's *Louise*. In the role of Lancelot he was acclaimed for his 'jeu dramatique et vibrant' which it was generally thought could not be improved on. Great critical praise was also accorded to Mme Paquot-d'Assy in the part of Genièvre[10] and Henri Albers as Arthus.[11] The production was given lavish material assistance and moral support by the directors of La Monnaie, Maurice Kufferath and Guillaume Guidé. Kufferath (1852-1919) was a director of the theatre from 1900 to 1914 and besides being a prolific writer on Wagner, also conducted Dukas's *Ariane et Barbe-Bleue* and Debussy's *Pelléas et Mélisande*. Kufferath made sure that the best artists were engaged in the production. The costumes, designed by Fernand Khnopff, were praised for their 'archaïsme assez discret' and the artist Dubosq and producer De Beer were both complimented on their substantial contribution to the effectiveness of the opera.[12] Alas! *Le Roi Arthus* did not achieve the brilliant future predicted for it.[13] There were several subsequent performances of Act Three alone, including one at the Paris Opera in March 1916 and a radio broadcast on 25 April 1934.[14] The whole

---

[10] In a letter of 1899 to Henry Lerolle, Chausson had suggested that Georgette Leblanc, whom he had visited on 30 March, 1895 and who had sung the lead in his *Légende de Sainte Cécile*, would make an ideal interpreter of the role. This gifted woman, long time companion of Maeterlinck and heroine of his dramas, possessed, like so many of Chausson's friends, both musical and literary talent.

[11] Samazeuilh, *art. cit.*, 704, praises his artistry, whilst regretting 'quelques défectuosités vocales'.

[12] The scenery was painted by Henry Lerolle. For Khnopff's involvement in opera productions see J. W. Howe, *The Symbolist Art of Fernand Khnopff* (Ann Arbor, 1982), p.10: ('Khnopff's theatre designs deserve more study in themselves.')

[13] As has often been mentioned, the Brussels journal *Théatra* conducted a poll of Belgian opera lovers in 1909 to discover which works would be most welcomed at the Théâtre de la Monnaie. The first four choices were *Tristan* (1273 votes), *Pelléas et Mélisande*, *Götterdämmerung* and *Le Roi Arthus* (1199 votes).

[14] A pre-war recording of two excerpts from Act Three ('Pommiers verts, pommiers fleuris' and 'Ne m'interroge plus') was made by the baritone Arthur Endrèze in the role of Merlin (Pathé PCX 5006).

work was revived for a broadcast on 24 June 1949 and in 1981 Lionel Friend recorded the work complete for French Radio, the recording being broadcast by the BBC in the following year.

The literary interest of *Le Roi Arthus* stems in part from the fact that Chausson, an extremely cultivated and widely-read man, wrote the libretto himself and displayed the same anxiety and meticulous care in its preparation and constant revision as he showed in the composition of the music. Hallays remarked that for this *poète-musicien* 'son goût et sa culture lui rendaient aisée la tâche d'imaginer et d'écrire un livret'.[15] Painters[16] and sculptors, musicians and writers flocked to his home in the Boulevard de Courcelles:[17] the list of his guests reads like a roll-call of the major cultural figures of late-nineteenth-century France.[18] With many of these artists he shared his doubts and hopes, seeking their advice and explaining his difficulties, whilst offering constant encouragement to others who sought his assistance or requested his opinions. His correspondence with a number of musicians, including Debussy, Duparc and d'Indy, as well as with his lawyer friend Paul Poujaud and his wife's brother-in-law Henry Lerolle, provides a fascinating documentation of his struggles with the composition of *Le Roi Arthus*, which was a constant preoccupation from 1886 to 1895.

Chausson's interest in medieval literature is attested as early as 1882 by the writing of his symphonic poem *Viviane* Op. 5.[19] This

15 *art. cit.*, 853.
16 For Chausson's own collection of paintings see Ralph Scott Glover, *Ernest Chausson. The Man and his Music* (London, 1980), pp.225-7 and compare Chabrier's collection of Impressionists, described in R Meyers, *Emmanuel Chabrier and His Circle* (London, 1969), pp.146-54.
17 See Barricelli and Weinstein, *op. cit.*, pp.34-6 and Glover, *op. cit.*, pp.17-18, 34-5. It may be noted that Chausson wrote a novel *Jacques* (1877), which he destroyed, and that Camille Mauclair dedicated to him his novel *Le Soleil des morts*. There would be value in a study of the literary relations of Chausson and his contemporaries along the lines of Arthur B. Wenk's *Claude Debussy and the Poets* (Berkeley etc., 1976). On Chausson's reading see Gallois, *op. cit.*, pp.75-6.
18 For surveys of his musical contemporaries see G. Samazeuilh, *Musiciens de mon temps: chroniques et souvenirs* (Paris, 1947); J. Tiersot, *Un demi-siècle de musique française 1870-1919* 2nd edn (Paris, 1924); Romain Rolland, 'The Awakening: A Sketch of the Musical Movement in Paris since 1870' in id., *Musicians Today* transl. M. Blaiklock (London, 1915), pp.246-324, also in R. Rolland and G. Jean-Aubry, *French Music of Today and Musicians of Today* [transl. E. Evans] (London, n.d.), pp.246-324. The regular visitors to Chausson's home are listed by Glover, *op. cit.*, pp.17f.
19 The work was dedicated to Jeanne Escudier who shortly afterwards became Chausson's wife. A piano transcription of the piece was made by Samazeuilh (as well as by d'Indy) and published by Bornemann. The music is much superior

enchanting piece, so unjustly neglected in the modern concert hall, was not a great success on its first performance (31 March 1883), but underwent successive revisions and was well received when the definitive version was given by Lamoureux on 29 January, 1888. It was subsequently played in places as far apart as Glasgow, St Petersburg and Barcelona, so that in 1895 the composer was able to write to d'Indy:

> Cette Viviane est vraiment infatigable. Elle fait la province et l'étranger. Et voilà encore qu'elle repique sur Paris! C'est égal, il me semble qu'il est grand temps de lui donner une compagne de route. Patience. Tout de suite après *Arthus*, on s'y mettra.[20]

For the performance of this work Chausson reports that he had had made a special pair of antique cymbals in F and C, which had unfortunately been lost, and then draws d'Indy's attention to the marking of the score:

> Le titre exact, c'est: Viviane, poème symphonique. Le topo se trouve en tête de la partition.

The 'programme' to which Chausson refers as prefixing the score was as follows:

> Viviane et Merlin dans la Forêt de Brocéliande
> Scène d'Amour
> Les envoyés du Roi Arthur parcourent la forêt à la recherche de l'Enchanteur. Il veut fuir et les rejoindre.
> Viviane endort Merlin et l'entoure d'aubépines en fleurs.

A langorous introduction on muted strings, with its characteristic avoidance of a fixed tonality, establishes the sense of mystery which is so essential a feature of Chausson's style.[21] The forest setting is evoked throughout by a memorable motif on the horn. The theme of love is presented in bold, passionate themes on the violins and on the cellos, which are then contrasted with the individual voice of a solo violin. A most effective use is made of trumpet calls, including off-stage echo effects, to indicate the spatial movements of Arthur's men within the forest. Despite the occasional exploitation of certain

---

to Guy Ropartz's *La Chasse du Prince Arthur* (1912).

[20] See 'Lettres inédites à Vincent d'Indy' in the special number (1 déc. 1925) of *La Revue Musicale* devoted to Chausson [pp.128-36] 132.

[21] Writing to Poujaud in 1886, sending him the scenario of *Le Roi Arthus*, Chausson reflects on the appearance of Merlin in Act 2, 'L'apparition de Merlin me tente beaucoup. Vous pensez bien que l'antique *Viviane* va renaître de ses cendres et se refaire une virginité. On pourra objecter que cette scène n'est pas préparée, pourtant à la manière dont elle arrive, je crois qu'elle peut être défendue'. See 'Lettres inédites à Paul Poujaud' in *ibid.* [pp.143-74] 155.

Wagnerian devices, the piece is remarkable for its avoidance of clichés and for the young Chausson's masterly command of a dazzling range of atmospheric effects together with strong melodic lines.

Outside the Arthurian legends Chausson also showed a great attachment to the *Chanson de Roland*. In 1888 he wrote to his friend Poujaud from Biarritz:

> Depuis longtemps je veux faire une expédition à Roncevaux. Venez donc. Nous la ferons ensemble. J'ai la *Chanson de Roland*, que nous lirons dans les auberges.[22]

Some time later (the letter is undated) Chausson writes again, from Ochaberrietra, that he has visited Saint-Jean-Pied-de-Port and Roncevaux:

> ... pendant quatre jours, je ne me suis servi que de mes yeux, je ne pensais plus à rien. Sauf pourtant à la *Chanson de Roland*, en étant à Roncevaux. J'ai vu la fontaine près de laquelle il est mort et le ruisseau où Turpin alla chercher de l'eau. Aimez-vous férocement la *Chanson de Roland*? Oui, sans doute. Je trouve le second chant beau comme de l'*Homère*. C'est bien à cause de lui que j'ai fait le voyage de Roncevaux.[23]

There is no indication, however, that Chausson ever contemplated a musical composition based on the *Roland*.[24]

A brief study of the genesis of *Le Roi Arthus* will clarify its central position in Chausson's *oeuvre* and demonstrate the pains which he took to refine his conception of the tragedy and to deal with the dangers posed by the inevitable analogies with *Tristan*. In 1886 whilst in Cannes Chausson sent Paul Poujaud a sketch of the scenario for the opera:

> Le sujet me plaît beaucoup, malgré les nombreuses analogies avec *Tristan* qui m'effrayent ... Le plus gros défaut de mon drame est sans doute l'analogie du sujet avec celui de *Tristan*. Cela ne serait rien encore, si je pouvais arriver à me déwagnériser. Wagnérien par le sujet et wagnérien par la musique, n'est-ce pas trop à la fois?[25]

Despite numerous difficulties, Chausson's attachment to the work could not be broken:

> Quant au pauvre *Roi Arthus*, Bouchor me l'a si rudement éreinté, j'y ai tant vu de difficultés de toutes sortes, que pour un moment j'en ai désespéré. Je

22 *ibid.*, 160.
23 *ibid.*, 172.
24 The Italian composer Luigi Dallapiccola set a number of passages in his *Rencesvals* (*Chanson de Roland*) for mezzo-soprano/baritone and piano (1946). He had earlier written *Rapsodia, studio per la morte del Conte Orlando* for chamber orchestra (1932-3).
25 *art. cit.*, 150/155.

me remets à y songer. Malgré tout ce qu'on en dit, *je l'aime*, comme dirait le bon Franck.[26]

Already the composer, inclined to pessimism, foresees the uncertainties which might frustrate the development of a new lyric theatre and ruefully reflects that it would be his luck to submit his work to a company or theatre on the eve of their bankruptcy proceedings! — 'Et qu'importe après tout? Le principal n'est-il pas d'abord de faire ce que l'on sent de son mieux, sans s'occuper d'une réalisation plus ou moins problématique?'[27] In another letter of dejection in which he explains the depression which has delayed his writing ('C'est *Arthus*, toujours, qui en est la cause'), Chausson informs Poujaud,

> *Arthus* avance lentement et je ne sais trop qu'en penser. Il y a des endroits où je vois clairement que c'est mauvais. Il y en a d'autres où je ne sais plus que dire. C'est même pour cela que je vous écris en attendant l'heure du déjeuner . . . Je commence à avoir un peu de confiance, non dans ce que j'ai fait, mais dans ce que je ferai de ce drame. Je me reproche même de trop aimer mon sujet.[28]

Chausson received much valuable advice from Duparc in a document which we shall examine later and this had included suggestions about how to arrange Genièvre's death. In a letter of 3 September 1893 Debussy inquired 'Avez-vous fait décidément mourir cette pauvre Genièvre? La dernière chose que vous m'avez montrée me fait présager d'excessivement belle musique de vous!'[29] Chausson was concerned with more than musical and dramaturgical considerations, however, for he was constantly revising the text of his libretto. To Debussy he confides, of *Le Roi Arthus*,

> Il me cause toujours beaucoup de malheurs. Et des malheurs renaissants. Car quand je crois que j'ai terminé une scène, je m'aperçois après quelques mois de repos qu'il y a des tas de choses dans les paroles qui ne vont pas; je les change, et naturellement, il me faut aussi changer la musique. C'est toujours à refaire, et cela finira-t-il jamais? Il le faudrait pourtant . . .[30]

---

[26] *ibid.*, 156. The poet Maurice Bouchor (1855-1929), who had varied interests in music and the theatre (esp. the Petit Théâtre des Marionnettes) successfully collaborated with Chausson on a number of occasions. The beautiful setting of his *Poème de l'amour et de la mer* is one of Chausson's most inspired compositions. Chausson also wrote the music for Bouchor's translation of Shakespeare's *The Tempest*, for his drama *La Légende de Sainte Cécile*, the four *Chansons de Shakespeare* (Bouchor's translations) and the *Quatre Mélodies* (verses by Bouchor).

[27] Letter to Poujaud, *art. cit.*, 156.

[28] *ibid.*, 157.

[29] F. Lesure, *Claude Debussy, Lettres 1884-1918* (Paris, 1980), p. 52.

[30] 'Correspondance inédite de Claude Debussy et Ernest Chausson', *Rev. Mus.* 1 déc. 1925 [116-26] 119.

Debussy, in trying to alleviate his friend's burden, advises Chausson to avoid 'la préoccupation des "dessous"', a Wagnerian temptation, and to take as a model the music of Bach 'où tout concourt prodigieusement à mettre l'idée en valeur, où la légèreté des dessous n'absorbe jamais le principal'.[31] Chausson, as usual, is not reluctant to act on the suggestions of his friends:

Moi, j'ai repris, et sans trop de peine, mon troisième acte. Je ne suis pas mécontent de ce que j'écris en ce moment. Il me semble que ça se clarifie et déwagnérise. Ma femme à qui j'ai joué la première scène m'a dit qu'elle ne me reconnaissait presque pas ... Vous avez mille fois raison dans ce que vous me dites de la préoccupation des 'dessous'. Pendant que vous m'écriviez je pensais à peu près la même chose, le commencement de mon troisième acte en est une preuve. C'est je crois, surtout à l'esthétique de la Société Nationale que je dois cette préoccupation.[32]

The most successful period of work on *Le Roi Arthus* appears to have been 1895 when Chausson was working at San Domenico di Fiesole, near Florence. He writes to Poujaud,

Cet interminable *Arthus* avec le temps avait sûri et m'avait comme empoisonné. Après quelques explications violentes, j'ai fini par avoir le dessus et maintenant je l'enterre fort gaîment sous un monceau de pages d'orchestre (le second acte seul a 235 pages de brouillon)![33]

And to d'Indy,

A force de travailler à l'orchestre d'*Arthus*, je m'aperçois avec étonnement qu'il avance et parfois l'envie me vient de le terminer avant de rentrer dans cette capitale des fiacres et des marchands de journaux ... J'espère entamer l'orchestre du troisième acte le 1er janvier.[34]

[31] Lesure ... p.58. Debussy himself planned an opera on Tristan, using a libretto by Gabriel Mourey and based on Bédier's *Le Roman de Tristan*, which had already inspired the composer on its first appearance. The project remained in Debussy's mind from 1907 till 1916 when he abandoned it. See R. Orledge, *Debussy and the Theatre* (Cambridge, 1982), pp.251-3. On Frank Martin's Tristan oratorio, also based on Bédier, see U. Müller, 'Mittelalterliche Dichtungen in der Musik des 20. Jahrhunderts III: Das Tristan und Isolde-Oratorium von Frank Martin (nach Joseph Bédier) ...', in *Tradition und Entwicklung. Festschrift Eugen Thurnher zum 60. Geburtstag* ed. W. M. Bauer et al., Innsbrucker Beiträge zur Kulturwissenschaft, Germanistische Reihe Band 14 (Innsbruck, 1982), pp.171-86. A brilliant production by Paul Hernon was presented at the Jeannetta Cochrane Theatre, London in January, 1983.
[32] Letter to Debussy, *art. cit.*, 123. This is an undated reply to Debussy's letter of 24 Oct. 1893.
[33] *art. cit.*, 171. According to Gallois, *op. cit.*, p.51 Act Two was finished by the end of 1892. Chausson worked on the battle scene of Act Three in the company of Debussy at Luzancy in 1893.
[34] *art. cit.*, 171.

The opera was completed in the knowledge that Act Three was the most successfully reworked part of the drama and that there remained weaknesses in the first two acts which the composer did not feel he had the stamina to deal with. It is, indeed, the Third Act which has drawn the most favourable critical response since the first performance[35] and which alone was the subject of the few attempts in more recent times to perform part of the work.

Before undertaking an analysis of *Le Roi Arthus* it remains to consider briefly the question of Wagnerian influence on Chausson. The neglect of many of the latter's most beautiful compositions is not a little due to exaggerations like Martin Cooper's sweeping statement that Chausson's opera is 'impeccably Wagnerian from beginning to end'.[36] It is certainly not Wagnerian in spirit, as we shall see.[37] Chausson's anxiety about the influence of Wagner stems from the days (1883-6) when he was labouring on his lyric drama *Hélène* Op. 7 (two acts, after Leconte de Lisle), of which only a female chorus has been published.[38] Chausson had attended a performance of *Tristan* in 1880 which made a great impression. Yet, a few years later he was to write complainingly of 'ce spectre rouge de Wagner qui ne me lâche pas ... J'en arrive à le détester.'[39] Later, after the completion of *Le Roi Arthus*, he wrote contemptuously that 'le besoin de trouver des ressemblances [avec Wagner] est devenu une sorte de passe-temps. Triste passe-temps, et très vain.'[40] These words were written in a review of the first performance of the medieval and 'Wagnerian' *Fervaal* by

---

35 See, for example, the comments of L. Davies, *César Franck and His Circle* (London, 1970), p.198 'Act 1 is overburdened with a pallid and derivative love duet, as well as a bardic chorus that harks back suspiciously to the days of Grand Opera ... The moving farewell which Arthur bids must rank among the best finales in modern French opera.'

36 M. Cooper, *French Music from the Death of Berlioz to the Death of Fauré* (London, 1951), p.66. Cooper's judgement is strongly contested by Glover, *op. cit.*, p.185. In the *Revue Musicale* 1 déc. 1925 Maurice Bouchor argues that *Le Roi Arthus* marks little advance on Wagner and that it 'devait apparaître, aux yeux mêmes de son auteur, comme l'oeuvre d'un épigone' (p.181). The same prejudice concerning alleged Wagnerian influence has deprived us of the chance of hearing any of Karl Goldmark's operas with the exception of *Die Königin von Saba*. His opera *Merlin* was performed at the Vienna Opera on 19 Nov. 1886 and was revised in 1904.

37 A. Hallays justly wrote in the *Revue de Paris* déc. 15 1903, p.852 'Ernest Chausson admirait beaucoup Richard Wagner. On en surprendrait difficilement la preuve dans ses oeuvres musicales: il est un des rares compositeurs français de son temps à peu près indemnes de toute imitation wagnérienne.'

38 See the brief assessment of this work in G. Samazeuilh, *Musiciens de mon temps. Chroniques et souvenirs* (Paris, 1947), pp.126-8.

39 In a letter of 1884 to Poujaud, *art. cit.*, 144.

40 See 'Fervaal', *Mercure de France*, sér. mod. 22, avril 1897, p.135.

his friend d'Indy and this notice shows him reflecting on the nature of 'influence' and defending the opera *Fervaal* against the charge of Wagnerism:

> Les plus grands artistes ont toujours subi l'influence des maîtres qui les ont précédés, mais l'idée empruntée, passant par leur cerveau, subissait l'empreinte de leur propre tempérament. C'est dans cette mesure seulement qu'il est légitime de dire que l'auteur de *Fervaal* est wagnérien. Ce qui individualise surtout un artiste, c'est sa sensibilité. Les procédés par lesquels il la manifeste importent beaucoup moins.[41]

Henri Duparc was no less percipient in the fifty-one pages of commentary on the libretto of *Le Roi Arthus* which he wrote at the end of 1888 when he was struggling with his own opera *Roussalka* (later destroyed) and sent to the composer with the comment that, whether it should prove useful or not, he had himself learned much in assembling his remarks:[42]

> Il est certain que pour nous débarrasser de la préoccupation de cet homme [i.e Wagner] et de ses oeuvres, il faut un effort surhumain; mais cet effort, il *faut le faire*, sous peine de n'écrire que des oeuvres impersonnelles, car ce serait une grande erreur de croire que, s'il y a des ressemblances dans le drame, la musique ne s'en ressentira pas ... Wagner a merveilleusement réalisé ses conceptions, et, dans des conceptions analogues, aucun de nous ne peut espérer l'égaler: notre seul mérite sera donc d'avoir su faire de belles choses en les concevant autrement.[43]

Duparc gives an example from *Le Roi Arthus* of the way in which an artist may be misled by the tyrannical power of Wagner's achievement. He argues that in his presentation of Lancelot and Genièvre Chausson has slipped too easily into the trap of conceiving them to be like Tristan and Isolde. The latter retain their capacity to move us, despite the disloyalty and adultery, because they act under fatality, symbolised by the potion. In this way Wagner could avoid alienating the audience and could preserve some sense of the lovers' honourable qualities. Chausson's Lancelot and Genièvre lack any justificatory equivalent to the potion and do not have the advantage of familiarity to the audience:[44]

[41] *loc. cit.*
[42] This fascinating document is printed, with an introduction, in Charles Oulmont, *Musique de l'amour* t.2 *Henri Duparc ou de 'L'invitation au voyage' à la vie éternelle* (Paris, 1935), pp.109-73.
[43] *supra*, p.127. He also remarks (p.126) 'Un très grand défaut, qu'il me semble *absolument nécessaire* de faire disparaître ... c'est l'obsession des drames de Wagner et surtout de *Tristan*'.
[44] A typical example of Duparc's forthright style in this connexion is his claim that we condemn adultery 'à moins qu'il ne nous soit bien prouvé que les deux confectionneurs de cornes n'ont pas pu faire autrement'.

> Mais nous, spectateurs, nous ne connaissons pas les légendes de la Table
> Ronde, et nous sommes bêtes: nous voulons qu'on nous explique tout.[45]

At some point in the opera, not necessarily at the very beginning (which Duparc finds satisfactory as it was submitted to him), we must be brought into a sympathetic relationship with Lancelot ('Je trouve indispensable que . . . tu nous attaches à Lancelot'). As it is, he appears as 'un très vilain monsieur, qui n'aura pas volé le châtiment, – quel qu'il soit, – qu'il va recevoir': we know too little about his virtues and have little reason to excuse his vices. We must be shown, therefore, that he is initially esteemed by Arthur's knights and that he is capable of revolting against his own conduct – 'l'amant ne peut pas avoir tué complètement le héros en lui'. In addition, there must be a final transfiguration of the hero through the triumph of conscience over passion, a 'réveil complet' of his true self.[46] This is what will best explain his refusal to fight against Arthur, and Duparc suggests that it would be fittingly inspired by a treacherous deal offered by Mordred which renders the hero indignant (Chausson does not adopt this procedure). *Le Roi Arthus* thereby becomes a *drame de conscience*, exploring the effects of shame, remorse and renunciation. What Duparc calls 'ces nuances' will not only generate true human tragedy, but, even more important, 'leur mise en oeuvre éloignera toute idée de rapprochement avec *Tristan*'. And Genièvre? She earns Duparc's complete approval – 'elle est très femme'.

Chausson acted on most of Duparc's suggestions and consequently the implications of his drama are far removed from Wagner's. The apotheosis of the lovers in the *Liebestod* stems from the acknowledgement, as in Gottfried von Strassburg, of the transcendental nature of passion, which exceeds the bounds of social order and sexual morality. In Chausson the love of Lancelot and Genièvre is sterile, destructive of individual integrity through conflict with conscience, and symptomatic of the human weakness which will lead to the breaking up of the fellowship of the Round Table. What we have is a drama of Christian repentance, incorporating the power of guilt, the value of renunciation and the expiatory role of death. Paul Dukas, shortly after the first performance of *Le Roi Arthus*, made the following shrewd observations on the nature of Chausson's drama:

> La préoccupation évidente de Chausson, en écrivant ce drame lyrique, a
> été de produire une oeuvre non pas symbolique ou philosophique, mais

---

[45] *op. cit.*, pp.129-30.

[46] L. Davies, *op. cit.*, p.198 argues that Chausson does not really make the theme of betrayal convincing and that the remorse of Lancelot in Act Three rings more truthfully than his earlier turpitude.

directement engendrée par l'émotion qui naît du contraste des situations et des caractères; en un mot, un drame au sens propre du mot, et non pas un poème musical plus ou moins scénique, comme en a fait éclore à foison l'imitation du drame wagnérien. A certains points de vue, le *Roi Arthus* répond à ce but, principalement par la façon dont l'action externe réagit sur le moral des personnages, au contraire des oeuvres conçues selon l'esthétique du maître de Bayreuth, dans lesquelles l'action nous est présentée le plus souvent comme le reflet du monde des apparences sur des êtres de physionomie intérieure préconçue et dont le jeu des événements est surtout destiné à rendre sensible les variations conscientes ou inconscientes.[47]

Lancelot's tragedy, a sort of Christian morality, is played out against the contrasting presence of Arthus, who stands for heroic perseverance, noble stability and unflinching faith, all of which set in relief the vicissitudes of ignoble passion and emphasise the need for redemption. Perhaps Chausson remembered here the role of Charlemagne in his beloved *Chanson de Roland*. It is also difficult to deny that Arthus embodies some of Chausson's own characteristics — generosity, faith in constant effort,[48] equanimity, and acceptance of death. Some critics have even gone so far as to see in the fellowship of the Round Table a poetic transposition of the companionship enjoyed by 'la bande à Franck'. Much of all this can be detected in the last moving exchange of monarch and knight:

Arthus	Mon honneur!
	Crois-tu donc qu'il dépende
	d'un autre que moi-même?
	. . .
	Ah! J'ai cru à la puissance
	De l'effort, a l'énergie de la volonté.
	Sans relâche, j'ai lutté.
	Et maintenant, que reste-t-il
	De toute ma vie?
	Espérances déçues!
	Inutiles, inutiles efforts.
Lancelot	Qui peut connaître la force
	Des pensées et la durée des choses?
	A travers les âges, ton nom peut-être périra,
	Mais, plus durable que son éclat sonore,
	Ta pensée, Arthus, est immortelle.
	L'amour, dont ton coeur s'enivra,
	Jaillit de la flamme éternelle.
	Tu vivras! Tu vivras!

[47] Quoted from his essay 'Le Roi Arthus et le Wagnérisme' in *La Revue Musicale* 1 déc. 1925, p. 215.

[48] See his letter of August 1888 to Poujaud, *art. cit.*, 161 and Debussy's letter to him of 26 Aug. 1893, Lesure p. 47.

> Pour d'autres, la mort est l'éternel oubli.
> Ils disparaissent pour jamais,
> Hélas! hélas! comme moi . . .

The centrality of Arthus and the moral reawakening of Lancelot (Hallays found his death 'le chef-d'oeuvre' of the piece), who finally recognises the supreme values represented by the man he has betrayed, form a unity which was overlooked by some of the opera's earliest commentators. André Hallays complained,

> Ce livret a pourtant un défaut très grave, et très inattendu pour qui connaissait le goût classique d'Ernest Chausson: il manque d'unité. A vrai dire, il renferme deux drames: celui de Lancelot et celui d'Arthus. Au lever du rideau, nous entrevoyons Arthus dans le palais de Carduel. Puis, tout de suite, Lancelot et Guinèvre sont les protagonistes. Les remords de Lancelot et la passion de Guinèvre paraissent le fond même de la tragédie, lorsqu'au milieu de l'action, au quatrième tableau, Arthus revient au premier plan et dès lors domine tout drame. Cette erreur dans le dessin et dans la conduite du poème déconcerte un peu le spectateur. Peut-être explique-t-elle aussi certaines incertitudes de l'oeuvre musicale.[49]

A more accurate judgement came from Gustave Samazeuilh:

> On sait les analogies extérieures qu'il [= Le Roi Arthus] présente forcément, surtout dans sa première partie, avec celui [= 'le poème'] de Tristan et Yseult, emprunté au même cycle légendaire. Mais il importe, par contre, de faire ressortir à quel point la signification en est différente. Tandis que chez Wagner le personnage du Roi Marke est relégué dans l'ombre de ses lamentations et tout l'intérêt concentré sur la passion triomphante des deux amants, c'est au contraire ici la grande figure d'Arthus, fondateur de la Table Ronde et défenseur de la Bretagne, qui devient prépondérante, donne son nom à l'oeuvre et contient en elle toute la philosophie du drame. A côté de la sienne, auréolée de gloire, les destinées de Guinèvre, toute à sa folle passion, et de Lancelot, sans cesse hésitant entre son amour et sa vénération pour son roi, disparaissent et s'éteignent dans une fin sans honneur. Ils n'ont recherché dans la vie qu'une satisfaction égoïste et trompeuse; pour eux, la mort sera l'éternel oubli, et une oeuvre noble et grande ne fera pas vivre, comme celle d'Arthus, leur pensée à travers les âges. C'est sur cette idée vraiment personnelle et d'une grande élévation grâce à laquelle les dernières pages de l'oeuvre atteignent au sublime, qu'ont été établis les trois actes du Roi Arthus . . .[50]

Chausson's libretto is itself a poetic drama. Even in its early stages Duparc had recognised its beauty of form and expression:

> Le langage est excellent, tout à fait ce qu'il doit être, noble et naturel: quant à tes vers, je t'avoue franchement qu'ils m'ont espatrouillé, et que, malgré la très haute estime en laquelle je te tiens, je ne te croyais pas capable

[49] art. cit., 856.
[50] art. cit., 701-2.

d'en faire d'aussi beaux. Tu *m'épates*! La marche générale du drame est parfaite: j'aurais dû commencer par te le dire, avant de te chicaner si long-temps pour des détails et des nuances ...[51]

In the analysis which follows we shall try to show how carefully Chausson attended to the language and form of his lyric drama, particularly under the guidance of Duparc, who announced the sending of his fifty-one page 'colis' in a letter dated 29 December 1888.

The opera opens with an animated prelude, the first theme of which is a boisterous, galloping figure of triplets in C minor (later echoed in *Soir de fête*), which suggests the putting to flight of the Saxons.[52] In a shift to the dominant, a vigorous dotted rhythm in the basses beneath high trills in the violins is reminiscent of Wagner's *Die Walküre* (see p. 2, bars 9 *et seq.*)[53] and provides a tempestuous transition to the stately, triumphal theme in E♭ major (p. 4, bars 11-21), given out on trumpets, and associated throughout the rest of the work with Arthus and the Round Table. The tempo picks up again and a theme of martial character, exploiting triplets over a striding bass, brings us to another statement of the Round Table theme on full orchestra (p. 8, bars 1-3) and the prelude ends with an unmistakable reminiscence of the *Meistersinger* overture (p. 8, bars 4 *et seq.*). The turbulence of battle and the noble strains of victory are admirably conveyed through strongly characterised themes and orchestration which is rich without being thick.

The curtain rises and Arthus sings 'Gloire à vous tous' against harp and solo trumpet. The setting is magnificent: a large hall in the royal palace at Carduel (Kamelot in the scenario sent to Poujaud). The first performance imitated the indications already contained in the early scenario: 'Grande salle, avec colonnades en pleins-cintres. Première époque du style roman'. Beneath Romanesque clerestory and arcade, to the left, is the royal throne. Beside the King sits Genièvre and her ladies. The hall is full of knights, squires and pages, the most prominent of the knights being Lancelot and Mordred. On either side of the set stand bards in long white robes. Arthus seems to be concluding an oration to mark the victory celebrations (the invading Saxons have been resoundingly defeated by the Bretons). In the hour of victory Arthus acknowledges the Round Table and the help of God ('Et, surtout, gloire à Dieu') 'dans nos communs efforts'. He thinks of the absent Merlin and there is a resurgence of the stately, triumphal theme at the words 'Où que tu sois, du moins ton âme vibre/au cri de guerre

---

51 Oulmont, *op. cit.*, p.170.
52 Page and bar numbers refer to the vocal score published by Choudens in 1900.
53 I cannot agree with Glover, *op. cit.*, p.173 who says 'It would be difficult to find anything less Wagnerian than the Prelude to Act I'.

141

des Bretons' (p.14, bars 3-6). The attendant knights cheer and the opening theme of the prelude is introduced, followed by a quieter section celebrating peace. The colourful, confident opening is completely different from the one sketched in the early scenario sent to Poujaud. There Scene 1 depicted Lyonnel, 'écuyer de Lancelot (entre 16 et 23 ans)', watching anxiously by the Queen's bedchamber. The final version makes clear how seriously Chausson took Duparc's suggestions that we must early on be provided with a sympathetic portrait of Lancelot and an indication of the jealousy of some of the knights (in preparation for Mordred's treachery and rebellion). Since Chausson followed them so closely, it is worth quoting Duparc's directions:

> Le moyen me paraît bien simple: je ferais de lui [= Lancelot] le héros de la journée: c'est grâce à lui que la bataille a été gagnée, et Arthus le lui dirait avec enthousiasme: 'pourquoi sembles-tu triste, quand nous célébrons notre plus grande victoire, une victoire *dont tu es le héros* . . . (Un peu plus de développement encore ne nuirait pas [e.g. the bards singing of Lancelot's victory] . . .) Cela expliquerait 1° que Lancelot, au lieu d'être mêlé aux autres chevaliers, se tienne seul près du trône d'Arthus, à une place d'honneur, et que Genièvre descende de son trône pour lui offrir la coupe, – ce qui, au point de vue scénique, n'est pas sans importance, – 2° cela justifierait clairement (point essentiel) la rage jalouse des chevaliers, que je voudrais un peu plus développée; il faudrait, pour préparer la trahison de Mordred au 3e acte, que celui-ci eût déjà une sorte d'influence sur eux, que leurs propos l'irritassent, et que dès maintenant, à part, il grommelât quelque vague désir de vengeance personnelle.[54]

Accordingly, Arthus instructs the bards to sing the praises of Lancelot, the true victor (E minor chorus, p.25, bars 8 *et seq.*). Mordred mutters darkly 'C'en est trop. Toujours Lancelot' and a separate group of knights echo the words, complaining 'Pour le Roi, nous ne sommes plus rien', all of which leads to Mordred's 'Bientôt, je vous vengerai tous . . .' and the knights' 'Oui, oui, vengeons-nous'. After the Round Table theme rings out again on the trumpets (p.34, bars 2-6), Arthus comes down from his throne and asks Lancelot 'Quel nuage assombrit ton front?', whilst Mordred delivers a sarcastic comment, which his monarch silences with the rebuke 'Ne soyez pas hautain ni railleur, je vous prie,/envers l'insigne fleur de la chevalerie'. At this point Genièvre, her vocal part marked 'doux, avec grâce', leaves her throne and presents a cup to Lancelot ('Recevez de mes mains cette coupe vermeille'). However, Mordred hears her whispered intimation to Lancelot ('Cette nuit . . . le signal . . . viens') and jealously reflects on how the Queen rejected his love. Genièvre and her ladies now exit.

---

[54] *apud* Oulmont, *op. cit.*, pp.136-7.

Duparc proposed an ending which clearly did not find favour with Chausson, namely, that Arthus should retire and that we should see the Queen in the doorway of her room looking for Lancelot and giving Lyonnel instructions to keep watch:

> Cette fin de scène ferait un contraste saisissant avec ce qui précède, et rendrait beaucoup plus clair le tableau suivant . . .[55]

It is possible that Chausson found this direct evocation of the adultery so soon after Arthur's celebrations and his thanks to Lancelot distasteful. He complains in one of his letters to Debussy: 'J'ai assez vécu avec l'adultère et le remords. Je suis fort tenté d'exprimer d'autres sentiments, moins dramatiques'.[56] At any rate he dropped the opening scene of the early scenario, replacing it with the court celebrations.

Following Wagnerian practice, the second scene is preceded by an interlude, beginning with the turbulent C minor theme of the opening of the opera and using fragments of Genièvre's 'aria' as well as other motifs of the prelude. The final section marked 'lent' (p.47), with its oboe and cello solos, especially the beginning in rising fifths and a descending chromatic scale, irresistibly calls to mind *Tristan* (which gives so much scope to solo instruments, often in the same way that Chausson treats them). There is also (p.44, bars 2-8) a brief, passionate suggestion of impending action, which, as Glover has argued,[57] is a quotation from the Prelude to Act 2 of *Tristan*.

The second scene is set on a terrace of the castle, with a porch in the foreground, behind which are the Queen's apartments. It is night and the moon is up. Lyonnel, Lancelot's squire, is seated on the steps of the porch in the role anticipated for him by Duparc in the first scene. Chausson pruned Lyonnel's monologue, at Duparc's suggestion, only to be told that he had shortened it too much! Lyonnel's words depict Lancelot's fall from honour:

> Hélas! Faut-il que mon coeur
> Malgré moi te condamne?
> Amour fatal, amour sacrilège et maudit!
> Lancelot, toi, l'ami d'Arthus,
> Son frère d'armes et de gloire,
> Parjure, déshonoré, félon!
> Comment cela peut-il être?
> Son amour l'a pris tout entier,
> Il vit comme en un rêve,
> Sans comprendre son crime.

[55] *ibid.*, p.139.
[56] *La Revue Musicale* 1 déc. 1925, p.119.
[57] *op. cit.*, p.177.

Duparc's recommendations again were carefully heeded here, several lines of the final version stemming from him; 'Je n'aime pas beaucoup la fin: je voudrais Lyonnel plus accablé de voir Lancelot coupable que préoccupé de son rôle de veilleur'.[58] The music is poignant. There is a melody, marked 'modéré' (p. 50, bars 3-6) of almost Elgarian tenderness introducing the words 'J'espérais un jour recevoir de ta main les armes de chevalier' and this is used as a motif to express the affection that Lancelot inwardly bears for Arthus (see Act 2, sc. 2, p.163, bars 1-2 and Act 3, sc. 1, p.232, bars 5-7). The reference to Mordred's jealousy is followed by the Tristanesque rising fifths and descending chromatic scale (p.55, bars 1-6). Against a high C# on strings and flute we hear the cries of the nightwatchmen and then all is light as harp and clarinet in Ravelian combination (p.55, bars 7 *et seq.*) introduce the lovers. The famous Ab major duet, whilst failing to reach the heights of its counterpart in *Tristan*, cannot conceal the latter's influence.[59] There is a certain lack of rhythmical subtlety in the way that the voices move together in Chausson's duet, but there is much to admire (Duparc found the whole scene 'admirable'). The duet begins:

> Délicieux oubli des choses
> De la terre, rêve enchanté,
> Rêve d'amour et de clarté
> Parfumé de suaves roses,
> Profond et doux enivrement
> Où nos deux âmes confondues,
> Muettes d'extase, éperdues,
> S'étreignent amoureusement . . .

There is no trace of 'Courtly Love', Genièvre declaring to Lancelot, 'Je suis à toi,/je suis ta servante et ta femme' (later, in Act 2, sc. 1, 'Je suis ton butin, ta proie'). There is an obvious irony in the words 'Les amants sont d'éternels vainqueurs./L'amour est le seul maître . . .', sentiments which are completely negated by the conclusion of the opera. In a more peaceful section ('Paisiblement entre les bras s'endort mon coeur'), against a background of harp arpeggios (p.69, bars 1 *et seq.*) the lovers sink into each other's arms, oblivious of their surroundings, and Lyonnel approaches to warn them of daybreak, an event beautifully evoked in graded orchestral colouring (p.80, bars 9 *et seq.*, p.85, bars 5 *et seq.*, p.87, bars 8 *et seq.*). Suddenly Mordred enters, sees the lovers and shouts for assistance. Lancelot strikes him, arranges to meet Genièvre in the nearby forest, but is already stricken with remorse:

[58] Oulmont, *op. cit.*, p.140.
[59] See Glover, *op. cit.*, pp.175-6.

Chevalier déloyal, j'ai tiré mon épée
Pour soutenir mon mensonge.

Returning to her apartments, the Queen finds Mordred alive. Soldiers arrive.

In the scenario sent to Poujaud there were four scenes in Act 1, the love scene being followed by a scene in which Mordred, thinking it to be Lyonnel who has visited the Queen, fights with him. In a fourth scene, Arthus arrived, received explanations from the two men, whilst Lancelot, observed, but unrecognised, made good his escape. Duparc found the third scene too long and suggested incorporating elements of it in the second scene. In addition, he observed, 'Je supprimerais cette évolution craintive de Genièvre, qui fait penser bien inutilement au duo de l'alouette'.[60] Chausson adopted Duparc's suggestions. The rest of the material forming scene 4 of the early scenario was dropped, as was revised material of this section submitted to Duparc.

Act Two begins with a short prelude in which a calm, reflective theme in B major, played on the whole orchestral range in octaves, evokes a still, sunlit, rural landscape. Once again, Chausson makes use of solo instruments, here a solo cello in its high register (p. 89, bars 4 *et seq.*). The scene is the edge of a pine forest, a large expanse of fields forming the background. The sun is shining through the trees and to the right a moss-covered rock provides an area for sitting. The song of a distant ploughman is heard. Lancelot is agitated, anxious to discover whether he has been recognised and whether Mordred is truly dead. He is already overcome by remorse, for he has betrayed 'Arthus! Arthus!/ Le plus grand, le plus saint des rois!/Lui, le chevalier du Christ,/ Le vainqueur des Saxons!' Despite having fallen so low, defiling his honour, word and name, he nevertheless recognises 'A jamais, je resterai lié,/Je le sens bien, à celle qui m'enfièvre./Tout, loyauté, serment, honneur est oublié/Dès que mes bras étreignent ma Genièvre.' The music is sombre and, with Genièvre's arrival, characterised by nervous agitation (see dotted rhythms and offbeat notes at p.106, bars 8 *et seq.* and, later, p.117, bars 1 *et seq.*). Genièvre informs Lancelot that Mordred is not dead and has accused him of treachery, Arthus alone defending, albeit hesitantly, his trusted knight. Lancelot is now caught in a terrible dilemma in the face of Genièvre's mounting insistence that he save her by returning to Arthus and brazenly denying everything ('Un moyen te reste, l'audace!'). Throughout this scene much greater use is made than before of chromaticism and rising sequences

60 Oulmont, *op. cit.*, p.140.

145

to indicate great surges of emotion (often culminating in the *Tristan* chord). The more Lancelot hesitates, the more unsympathetic Genièvre becomes:

Lancelot	Mentirai-je à mon noble maître?
Genièvre	Un mensonge de plus, qu'importe?
	N'es-tu pas déloyal
	Et traître en m'aimant?
	. . .
Lancelot	Mais froidemont tromper
	Sa noble confiance
	Quand, malgré l'évidence,
	Il me veut innocent.
	Genièvre, est-ce possible?
	N'exige pas de moi
	Ce sacrilège horrible.
	. . .
Genièvre	C'est odieux, je le sais,
	C'est infâme, mais il le faut:
	Mon honneur le réclame: le tien aussi.

Lancelot prefers to die, but this cannot save Genièvre. Increasingly desperate, she calls him 'ingrat', 'lâche', in the most insensitive terms: 'Un inepte scrupule/t'interdit aujourd'hui/de sauver mon honneur'. Chromaticism and agitated rhythms abound (p.112, bars 5 *et seq.*, p.124, bars 9 *et seq.*). Exhausted, Genièvre finally dismisses Lancelot: 'Notre amour fut un mauvais rêve,/Je ne veux plus te voir./Je te chasse. Va-t-en'. The crucial step has been taken. Lancelot, immobilised by grief, reflects that he is now no longer loyal even in love (note the typical dotted, chromatic figure in the bass, p.128, bars 11 *et seq.*) and, seeing Genièvre 'pâle comme une morte', he summons up all his strength in a moment of sudden decision, 'Il faut la sauver avant tout. Puis . . .' A trumpet motif (p.130, bars 2 *et seq.*) reminds him of Arthus and the bass clarinet, so distinctive a feature of the melancholy music of Acts Two and Three, introduces the cry of the exhausted Genièvre (p.130, bars 14 *et seq.*). Lancelot will lie to Arthus 'sans baisser la tête' in what will be 'l'épreuve suprême' and then, having saved the Queen, he will seek 'dans les combats . . . une mort noble et prompte'.

Duparc understood 'la situation atroce' in which Lancelot is placed and advised Chausson to remove some of the more tender and sentimental reflexions on his love for Genièvre, also suggesting the intercalation of his ruminations with verses of the ploughman's song, so as to prepare the exclamation 'Arthus! Arthus!' (p.100, bars 11-16):

Voilà, comme je te le disais, le sentiment que j'exploiterais, — sentiment de révolte intérieure, qui fléchira toujours devant la passion, jusqu'au moment de la mort, ou il vaincra la passion. Ainsi compris, il me semble que le caractère de Lancelot serait profondément vrai, émouvant, et tout à fait différent de Tristan.[60a]

Now there is a great resurgence of passion, as Genièvre begs forgiveness for her 'injuste parole' and 'mots odieux', emphasising their common fate, and proposing flight to a refuge where they can 'aimer librement au grand jour'. Lancelot is won over: 'Il me semble que c'est un rêve que je fais ... ne vivre que pour notre amour ...' Genièvre responds:

> Nos corps sont à jamais
> Enchaînés l'un à l'autre,
> Comme nos deux coeurs sont unis!
> Nul amour n'est semblable au nôtre.
> O délices d'aimer!
> O transports infinis!

From this scene Duparc cleared two elements. The first was Genièvre's account of Mordred's love for her, which Duparc directed should be in Act One. Then Duparc wanted Lyonnel out of the way:

> Mais une chose que je trouve tout à fait inutile et refrigérante, c'est l'intervention de Lyonnel: on y sent la préoccupation de faire de temps en temps reparaître cet adolescent: je n'en vois nullement la nécessité: à ta place, j'en ferais un personnage tout à fait épisodique et secondaire, sans quoi tu tomberais forcément dans une espèce de Kurwenal qui n'a pas sa raison d'être ... ici ... il est tout à fait cheveu dans soupe. Et puis, pourquoi offre-t-il sa vie? Lancelot serait bien avancé s'il perforait cet éphèbe![61]

Duparc's outspoken and earthy style is continued in his criticism of a number of passages in which he finds the lovers' reflexions too sentimental:

> Me pardonneras-tu si je te dis sans périphrase que je *déteste* la cavatine: 'O beaux jours écoulés'? et l'espèce de madrigal mélancolique qui la suit: 'Où porter mes pas irrésolus' ... 'qu'est-ce Lancelot sans Genièvre ...' (qu'est-ce que Tristan sans Iseult?) — 'Mais toi, Genièvre, sois heureuse' ... non: j'avoue que ce parfum d'opéra comique me donne de tièdes régurgitations: je m'imagine même que le sacrifice de ces deux ou trois mièvreries ne te rendra pas fou de douleur.[62]

Chausson was not slow to act on these suggestions and the result is almost invariably a more impressive simplicity.

An interlude now brings an animated, passionate climax, dying down to a more sombre section (with bass clarinet again) which anticipates Arthus's anxiety and concludes with a sort of funeral march (p.159, bars 6 *et seq.*).

60a Oulmont, *op. cit.*, p.146.
61   *ibid.*, pp.147-8.
62   *ibid.*, pp.148-9.

In Act Two Chausson finally interverted the two main tableaux as he had sketched them in the scenario sent to Poujaud, so that the second scene comprises material which formed the first scene in that scenario. In an atmosphere of gloomy foreboding we are introduced to an inner, cloister-like courtyard at Carduel. Arthus enters and joins a number of knights already talking together in hushed voices. On learning that Lancelot has not appeared, he dismisses the knights and ruminates on his growing anxiety against a musical background of sombre, rising chromatic scales and the ominous beat of the tympani:

> Toujours, toujours, cette pensée . . .
> La paix fuit mon âme angoissée,
> Je ne puis retrouver ma foi.
> Comment mettre fin à ce doute horrible?
> Genièvre! Lancelot!
> Non! Non! C'est impossible.

A motif associated with the friendship of Arthus and Lancelot here makes its second appearance in the opera (p.163, bars 1-2). The martial theme representing the Round Table also makes an appearance (p.165, bar 4) as Arthus piteously foresees the end of the institution which he founded:

> J'ai fondé la Table Ronde.
> Et je croyais mon oeuvre immortelle et féconde!
> Hélas! J'y découvre un germe de mort.
> Les chevaliers entre eux luttent de jalousie,
> Ils ne supportent plus sans un pénible effort
> La règle austère qui les lie.
> Ils écoutent Mordred
> Qui les pousse en secret à la révolte.

Arthus's distrust of Mordred makes him wonder whether there is a plot against Lancelot. As he sees less and less clearly, he yearns for the advice of Merlin. Suddenly, the trees separate and in a greenish light Merlin is seen half reclining on a bed of apple tree branches.[63] He is old, with a long, flowing white beard, and attracts Arthus's attention by calling to him. There, in the garden of the cloister, Merlin sings the celebrated 'Pommiers verts, pommiers prophétiques' in which he announces that 'les jours marqués sont accomplis'. Faced with these enigmas, Arthus responds 'Ta parole est sombre comme le rire de la mer' and receives the stark message:

---

[63] This scene is referred to in a letter from Debussy of 24 August 1893. Chausson describes changes he has made in it in a letter to Henry Lerolle, see *La Revue Musicale* 1 déc. 1925, p.177 (letter dated 1892).

> N'espère rien de l'avenir,
> Notre oeuvre commune est brisée:
> Dégénérée et méprisée,
> La Table Ronde va périr.

Arthus now realises that 'notre oeuvre impérissable' is doomed, but he still desperately searches for an explanation ('Suis-je le jouet d'un rêve?'). Merlin replies, 'Aveugles que nous sommes,/nous avons trop compté/sur la vertu des hommes':

> Si l'emplacement consacré
> Est envahi par les orties,
> C'est qu'un crime encore ignoré,
> L'orgueil, les basses jalousies
> Ont fait mentir les prophéties.

He declines to reveal more, but in a poetic diction which evokes Celtic verse, he predicts Arthur's eventual rebirth:

> Mais, quand viendra
> Le jour du glorieux réveil,
> O fils de Pendragon,
> O guerrier sans pareil,
> Alors, les chênes, dans leur joie,
> De rouges fleurs se couvriront,
> Vêtus d'argent, d'or et de soie,
> Les guerriers morts s'élanceront,
> Et le clair soleil qui flamboie
> De son disque éclatant
> Couronnera ton front.

This is followed by an energetic statement of the Round Table theme on the full orchestra (p.184, bars 4 *et seq.*). There is nothing left to Arthus but to accept his coming death and at the same time to continue his anguished questioning about Genièvre and Lancelot. No reply is vouchsafed him and Merlin abruptly vanishes, leaving Arthus shouting for the Queen. A crowd of knights forms and soon divides into supporters of the rebellious Mordred and the champions of Lancelot. The curtain falls swiftly on this ugly scene of dissension.

The prelude to Act Three begins with a sombre theme in D minor first given out on bass clarinet over a tremolo background and then passed to cellos and brass. Battle is evoked in an animated passage of dotted and triplet rhythms. The final act opens on the summit of a hill overlooking a battlefield. There are rocks and pine trees in the foreground; in the background, the sea. Genièvre appears anxiously observing the battlefield, convinced that Lancelot, having had the courage not to flee, will be victorious in battle. Mordred has proclaimed himself king and many of the knights of the Round Table have gone over to him. Doubts assail Genièvre — does Lancelot still love her? Just as, at the beginning of Act One, Arthus asked Lancelot 'Quel nuage assombrit ton front?', Genièvre now, filled with foreboding, reflects on Lancelot's joylessness: 'Un farouche désespoir assombrit son visage'. The conflict of Act Three is already expressed in her words,

> Ah! S'il était vrai!
> Si le remords qui dompte son âme
> Avait tué son amour?

Suddenly, Lancelot, unarmed, is seen approaching and confesses to Genièvre that he has fled, unable to bear arms against his monarch:

> Je l'ai vu, lui, Arthus!
> Alors, une soudaine et terrible clarté
> Envahit mon âme, une indicible honte me saisit.
> J'ai jeté mes armes, j'ai fui, j'ai fui, j'ai fui!

Genièvre revives the passionate vituperation of Act Two, calling Lancelot 'ingrat' and referring to the 'inutile lâcheté/d'un coeur pusillanime'. Lancelot's sole duty is to defend to the death their 'indomptable amour', but he refuses to 'combattre en rebelle' and determines to go, if possible with Genièvre, to seek out his king and stop the fighting:

> Et j'obéis à la voix qui parle dans mon coeur.
> Genièvre, accepteras-tu de partager mon sort?
> . . .
> Unis dans l'amour,
> Unis dans le péché,
> Le serons-nous aussi
> Dans l'expiation?

There follows Genièvre's death scene. She is 'Trahie! Abandonée! Méprisée!' She has lost to the 'lâcheté d'un coeur tout éperdu d'amour'. The noise of battle dies down. Genièvre realises that Lancelot must be dead: 'Il a pu l'accomplir,/le suprême abandon!' Determined to die, she strangles herself with her own tresses:

> Ornaments d'une vaine beauté,
> Cheveux sombres et bleus
> Comme la nuit, vous,
> Qui n'avez pas su retenir Lancelot
> Dans vos filets soyeux,
> Prêtez-moi votre secours ami!
> Vous fûtes mon orgueil
> Dans des jours heureux;
> Maintenant, aidez-moi,
> Aidez-moi à mourir.

The first conception of this scene, in the scenario sent to Poujaud, was completely different. Genièvre, after Lancelot's death, is packed off to a convent! This feature evidently survived in the version submitted to Duparc, who does not seem to have expressed any reservations about it. In the early scenario Lancelot, mortally wounded, returned from the field of battle and died in Genièvre's presence. Duparc commented on the Queen's suicide as follows:

> A moins de se serrer le cou assez fortement avec ses cheveux pour se casser la colonne vertébrale — ce qui demanderait de rares qualités athlétiques — elle est obligée de s'acharner: et plus elle réussit, plus elle perd ses forces; par conséquent son suicide est forcément long, et il me paraît indispensable qu'il soit très rapide.[64]

Duparc suggests than Genièvre might employ a scarf with which she had indicated their assignations to Lancelot, or, better, Lancelot's own arms which he might lay down after his refusal to fight.[65]

Duparc also had more general criticisms of Act Three in the version submitted to him:

> Dès la première lecture, la partie dramatique du 3e acte m'a paru inférieure au reste du drame ... je serai bien étonné si tu ne penses pas comme moi qu'il est nécessaire, après avoir empoigné le spectateur par des situations très dramatiques, de l'attacher par des sentiments d'affection ou de mépris à chacun de tes principaux personnages ... les situations, même les plus tragiques, ne suffisent plus; c'est le coeur même du spectateur qui doit, pour ainsi dire, entrer en scène.[66]

Above all, claims Duparc, Arthus, with nothing more to lose, must direct a word of forgiveness to Genièvre. Lancelot's death must be not merely materially more poignant than that of any of the other characters, but must be qualitatively so, as a result of a final 'réveil de son vieil honneur'. Lancelot must be dominated, not by his love, but by anger at Mordred's treachery to Arthus. In fact, in the final version Chausson cut entirely the appearance and explanations of the traitor, whose role is reduced to a brief appearance in the two tableaux of Act One. Chausson worked hard to simplify Act Three after Duparc had made of it what he himself called 'un *monstre* en forme de scénario'. Duparc thought that Lancelot's return to honourable indignation might best be motivated by an attempt on the part of Mordred to win him over to the side of the rebels and he even designed a plan in which Mordred struck Lancelot with his sword.[67]

[64] Oulmont, *op. cit.*, p.111.
[65] The published score contains the directions 'Elle se lève, semble chercher une arme ...'
[66] Oulmont, *op. cit.*, pp.150-1.
[67] Duparc's proposals included the words 'Ah! Mordred, cet homme jadis sans

Chausson rightly sensed that the action was becoming too complicated.

The prelude to the second scene combines the sombre rumination of the bass clarinet over timpani beats with offstage trumpets evoking the battle and with the Round Table theme. The scene is set at the end of the day, on a plain near the seashore. Lancelot lies dying. He could not stop the fighting and threw himself between the combatants. Arthus is griefstricken:

> Je n'ai plus rien d'humain que ma douleur.
> Tout, tout s'écroule à la fois, tout s'effondre.
> L'oeuvre de ma vie est brisée!
> Au cri de mon coeur blessé,
> Nul coeur ne peut plus répondre.

Lancelot urges Arthus to avenge his honour and kill him. There now takes place the exchange, which we quoted earlier, between the King and his vassal in which Lancelot fully recognises the merits of his monarch and predicts that his 'pensée ... immortelle' will last for ever. With Arthus's words

> Mon courage est vaincu;
> Je n'ai plus d'espérance.
> Dans un sommeil sans lendemain,
> Endormez, s'il se peut,
> Endormez ma souffrance.

there are introduced two wordless choirs offstage, which are then joined by five soprano soloists in long, undulating, chromatic patterns, until finally the choirs take up the words,

> Viens!
> Celui qui nous envoie
> T'assigne un sublime sort.

The stage directions read,

> Au fond du théâtre, au milieu des lueurs roses et dorées qui entourent le soleil couchant, on voit apparaître et s'avancer sur la mer une nacelle remplie de femmes. L'une d'entre elles, debout à l'arrière de la nef, étend de grandes ailes en guise de voiles.

Gradually, Arthus takes his leave of life ('Les temps sont accomplis des grandes aventures') whilst the choirs sing of an island 'caressée par des flots d'or et d'azur'. The Round Table theme is heard again (p. 327, bars 1-2; p. 332, bars 12-13; p. 337, bars 2 *et seq.*) and Arthus enters the barge and is borne into the sunset, apparently asleep on a

tache, que l'amour d'une femme a pu me faire oublier, ton infamie l'a enfin réveillé en moi ...' (Oulmont, p. 155).

couch within the boat.[68] In a calm and peaceful finale (C major) the choir sings:

> Comme un sublime manoeuvre,
> Sur terre, tu reviendras
> Pour reprendre ta grande oeuvre
> Et livrer de fiers combats!
> Arthus! Arthus!
> Sur ton front royal
> Qu'a dédaigné la victoire,
> Plane la suprême gloire
> D'avoir cru dans l'idéal!

In this final scene Chausson seems to have distilled musically that 'tristesse majestueuse' which Racine saw as the true pleasure of tragedy.

It is a paradox that an opera which enjoyed so markedly successful a first production should have been so entirely neglected since. Vincent d'Indy, who supervised preparations for the production with loving care, expressed himself delighted and surprised when he first heard parts of the score converted into real sound: 'Ce premier acte que je croyais le moins bon est simplement un éblouissement; il est tout à fait scénique, et paraît court malgré ses 42 minutes de durée'.[69] The rewards of Chausson's painstaking attempts to simplify the action of the drama and of the minute attention which he paid to the practicalities of staging are still, in the absence of modern performances, perforce unappreciated. It is also a paradox that this work, which of all Arthurian operas[70] most clearly has Arthur himself as its central subject, should treat exclusively of the dissolution of the fellowship which he founded. Yet the gloominess of much of the music of Acts Two and Three is relieved by the harmony and tranquillity of the finale in which pessimism gives way to a serene resignation. After the

---

[68] In the scenario sent to Poujaud (*art. cit.*, p.154) Chausson described the ending in the following terms: 'Une force irrésistible l'entraîne [= Arthus] vers la barque enchantée. Les appels deviennent plus pressants et plus doux. Le choeur lui promet l'oubli et l'éternel repos. La barque reste toujours dans le fond du théâtre, elle semble même s'éloigner. Arthus s'avance et pénètre dans la mer. Déjà, l'eau lui monte jusqu'a la poitrine, puis, tout à coup, la barque disparaît. On entend un cri; Arthus disparaît sous les vagues'. For Chausson's hesitations concerning the first scene of Act Three see his letter of 1894 to Henry Lerolle, *Rev. Musicale* 1 déc. 1925, p.177.

[69] Quoted in Oulmont, *Musique de l'Amour* t.1, p.187.

[70] Space does not permit anything like a listing, but in addition to those already cited in the notes above, mention might be made of Tom Cooke's *King Arthur and The Knights of the Round Table* (1835), Frederick Corder's *La Morte d'Arthur* (1877-8), Rutland Boughton's Arthurian 'choral dramas' (1908-45), Luboš Fišer's *Lancelot* (1959-60), and Richard Blackford's *Sir Gawain and the Green Knight* (1978).

'passion' of Arthur, as Oulmont rightly described the central portion of the opera, comes the apotheosis which enshrines the values exemplified by Arthur in a transcendental ideal which will endure, though the Round Table pass away. It is easy to understand how Chausson's best energies were engaged by this subject, for despite his constant striving for perfection, he often experienced the discouragement of isolation and neglect. Yet two years after he completed his opera and only the same number of years before his death Chausson wrote one of the jewels of French chamber music, the A major Piano Quartet (Op. 30) in which the composer, in the words of d'Indy, 'free at last from his doubt and his distress, thinks only of a flight to new and loftier regions of art'.[71] As the Arthurian ideal lives on, so Chausson endures through compositions which have been increasingly appreciated with the passage of time.

[71] Quoted in Glover, *op. cit.*, p. 93.

Editorial note The French Radio recording referred to on p. 000 above is available on record. MRF-174-5 (MRF Records, available from specialist dealers only).

UPDATE

VI

GEOFFREY OF MONMOUTH AND GILDAS REVISITED

Neil Wright

In the course of preparing a new edition of Geoffrey of Monmouth's *Historia Regum Britanniae*,[1] I have noted a number of borrowings from Gildas which were not recorded in my previous article on that subject.[2] None of these borrowings is extensive; most are verbal echoes, often of a subtle nature, consisting of a few words. In order to give a complete picture of Gildas's influence on the *Historia Regum Britanniae* and of Geoffrey's habits of literary adaptation, I have collected these borrowings, as well as some others omitted from my prior study for reasons of space, in the present update.

Let us begin with the *Prophetiae Merlini* (*Historia Regum Britanniae* 109-18) which were probably published in the form of a *libellus* before the completion of the *Historia* itself. As I have demonstrated, the *Prophetiae* contain clear echoes of the *De Excidio Britanniae*.[3] To the borrowings which I have already collected should be added the following: *insulani dracones* (*Historia Regum Britanniae* 113.17) and *insularis draco* (*De Excidio Britanniae* 33.1); *tota superficies insulae* (*Historia Regum Britanniae* 115.20), *superficiem totius insulae* (*Historia Regum Britanniae* 115.36),[4] and *cunctam paene exurens insulae superficiem* (*De Excidio Britanniae* 24.1); and *mare*

---

[1] The *Historia Regum Britannie of Geoffrey of Monmouth I: A single-manuscript edition from Bern, Burgerbibliothek, MS. 568* (Cambridge, forthcoming); however, for the sake of consistency with my previous article the text quoted here is that of Edmond Faral, *La Légende Arthurienne* (3 vols, Paris, 1929) III, pp. 64-303. Similarly, the *De Excidio Britanniae* is quoted from the edition of Michael Winterbottom, *Gildas: The Ruin of Britain and other works* (Chichester, 1978).

[2] 'Geoffrey of Monmouth and Gildas', *Arthurian Literature* II (1982), 1-40.

[3] *Ibid.*, pp. 16-17.

[4] In the second example, I have preferred *superficiem* (the reading of Bern, Burgerbibliothek, MS. 568) to *super faciem* (printed by Faral) not only because of the Gildasian echo, but also because it supplies the object required by the transitive verb *obumbrabit*.

quo ad Galliam navigatur (*Historia Regum Britanniae* 116.48) and *freto . . . quo ad Galliam Belgicam navigatur* (*De Excidio Britanniae* 3.1).

Moreover, one of the *Prophetiae* is itself derived directly from the *De Excidio Britanniae*.[5] Gildas records that the first English to arrive in Britain were encouraged by a favourable augury: 'secundis velis omine auguriisque, quibus vaticinabatur, certo apud eum praesagio, quod ter centum annis patriam cui proras libraret insideret, centum vero quinquaginta, hoc est dimidium temporis, saepius vastaret' (*De Excidio Britanniae* 23.2). Similarly, Merlin makes the following prophecy about the white dragon, which signifies the English: 'Terminus illi positus est quem transvolare nequibit: centum namque quinquaginta annis in inquietudine et subiectione manebit, trecentum vero insidebit' (*Historia Regum Britanniae* 112.43-113.2). As often in the *Prophetiae*, Geoffrey's precise meaning is somewhat obscure. Gildas's prophecy is clear: the English will occupy Britain for three hundred years after their *adventus* and will harass the British for one hundred and fifty years of that time. Conversely, Geoffrey appears to mean that after the *adventus* the English would be subject to the British for one hundred and fifty years and would thereafter control the island for a further three hundred years — very roughly, that is, until the time of the Norse incursions, which are the next event foretold by Merlin.[6] Despite this rather opaque recasting on Geoffrey's part, the influence of Gildas upon this prophecy is nevertheless unmistakable.

It is also possible that the *Prophetiae* contain an oblique reference to Gildas himself. One of the prophecies (*Historia Regum Britanniae* 112.20-22) runs as follows: 'et praedicator Hiberniae propter infantem in utero crescentem obmutescet'; 'and the preacher of Ireland will be silenced because of an infant growing in the womb'. Precisely such an incident occurs in the eleventh-century *Vita Davidis*, when Gildas is unable to continue preaching a sermon in the presence of David's pregnant mother Nonnita, because of the greater holiness of her son, as yet unborn.[7] Geoffrey may well have known this *Vita* and be alluding to it.[8] The description of Gildas as the apostle of Ireland

5 This parallel is noted, in passing, by Faral, *La Légende*, II, p.56.
6 For a somewhat different mediaeval interpretation of this prophecy, see J. Hammer, 'A Commentary on the *Prophetia Merlini*', *Speculum* 10 (1935), 3-30, p.13.
7 *Rhigyfarch's Life of St David*, ed. J. W. James (Cardiff, 1967), pp.4-5: the preacher is named as Gildas in some recensions of the *Vita*, but remains anonymous in others.
8 See J. S. P. Tatlock, *The Legendary History of Britain* (New York, 1950), p.246.

(*praedicator Hiberniae*) is, however, problematical. It may provide supporting evidence that Geoffrey was familiar with the Ruys *Vita Gildae*, or something akin to it, which records the story that Gildas spent some time in Ireland.[9] However, it might be argued that for the mediaeval audience the term *praedicator Hiberniae* could mean only one man — St Patrick;[10] but the extensive body of surviving Latin Patrician hagiography nowhere records an episode parallel to that of the *Vita Davidis*. Either Geoffrey confused Gildas with Patrick or, as is far more likely, deliberately left the identity of the *praedicator Hiberniae* uncertain, as befits the mysterious oracular quality of Merlin's pronouncements.

If we turn to the *Historia Regum Britanniae* proper, a number of additional borrowings can be discovered. In my previous article I noted only two verbal echoes in that part of the work devoted to British history prior to the Roman invasions.[11] This total can be expanded by two further borrowings. The first of these is important because it occurs in a context in which the influence of Gildas is hardly to be expected — the story of Lear and his daughters. In Geoffrey's version of this tale, Gonorilla first quarrels with her father because of his large retinue of knights who insult her servants on the grounds that their rations are insufficient: 'convicia ministris inferebant, quia sibi profusior epimenia non praebebatur' (*Historia Regum Britanniae* 31.69-70). The grecism *epimenia* is unusual in Geoffrey's normally business-like Latin. In fact, it (and its epithet *profusior*) are borrowed from Gildas, who employs it when the English mercenaries make a similar complaint: 'item queruntur non affluenter sibi *epimenia* contribui, occasiones de industria colorantes, et, ni *profusior* eis munificentia cumularetur, . . .' (*De Excidio Britanniae* 23.6). This echo affords an excellent example of the freedom with which Geoffrey reworks his source.[12]

---

[9] See 'Geoffrey of Monmouth and Gildas', p.32. Gildas's connection with Ireland is discussed by R. Sharpe, 'Gildas as a Father of the Church', in *Gildas: New Approaches*, edd. M. Lapidge and D. N. Dumville (Woodbridge, 1984), pp.193-205, at p.200.

[10] Such is the reading of one mediaeval commentator (see Hammer, 'A Commentary', p.10); neither interpretation is free from internal chronological difficulties, since the prophecy seems to apply to the reign of Ceredig — long after the time of Patrick and when David himself was already dead, at least according to *Historia Regum Britanniae* 179.7-11. For problems of David chronology, see M. Miller, *Studia Celtica* 12/13 (1977/8), 33-61, at pp.41-50.

[11] 'Geoffrey of Monmouth and Gildas', p.15.

[12] It is interesting that Geoffrey misconstrued the neuter plural *epimenia* as a feminine singular — an error also made by Æthilwald, an earlier imitator of Gildas; see *Aldhelmi Opera*, ed. Rudolf Ehwald, *Monumenta Germaniae Historica, Auctores Antiquissimi* XV (Berlin, 1913-19), p.496.3.

The second borrowing occurs in the account of the feud between the brothers Brennius and Belinus; a temporary agreement is ruined when the former is perverted by *fabricatores mendacii* (*Historia Regum Britanniae* 35.15). As Geoffrey was doubtless aware, this phrase is Biblical, being found at Job 13. 4 ('ostendens fabricatores mendacii').[13] However, it is also used by Gildas in a passage which Geoffrey quotes at length later in the *Historia*:[14] 'amor *mendacii* cum suis *fabricatoribus*' (*De Excidio Britanniae* 21.3). It is most likely, then, that Geoffrey employed this Biblical allusion under the influence of Gildas's text.

The birth of Christ, which constitutes the starting point of Gildas's brief narrative of British history, is also recorded in passing by Geoffrey. Using the rhetorical technique of *praeteritio*, or pointed omission, Gildas asserts that he will pass over the errors, 'quibus ante adventum Christi in carne omne *humanum genus obligabatur* astrictum' (*De Excidio Britanniae* 4.2). Geoffrey's note on the birth of Christ is considerably reworked, but it owes a clear verbal debt to the imagery of its predecessor: 'In diebus illis natus est dominus noster Iesus Christus, cuius pretioso sanguine redemptum est *humanum genus*, quod anteacto tempore daemonum catena *obligabatur*' (*Historia Regum Britanniae* 64.10-12).

As I have noted, Gildas was the prime source for Geoffrey's account of the raids of the Picti and Scoti. In addition to borrowing passages *in extenso*, Geoffrey also included a number of Gildasian echoes in this section of the *Historia Regum Britanniae*.[15] To those which I have already recorded should be added another example, in which Geoffrey retains Gildas's phraseology while modifying the context of the borrowing. Geoffrey ascribes the success of the first attacks of the Picts and Huns under Gwanius and Melga to the fecklessness of the British who, after the departure of Maximianus and Conan Meriadoc for the Continent, were leaderless. The enemy, he tells us, 'invaserunt regnum quod *rectore* et defensore carebat, *vulgus irrationabile* caedentes' (*Historia Regum Britanniae* 88.34-5). Here he is reworking a passage of Gildas in which the construction of a defensive line from turf rather than stone is similarly assigned to stupidity and lack of direction: [a wall] 'qui *vulgo irrationabili* absque *rectore* factus non tam lapidibus quam caespitibus non profuit' (*De Excidio Britanniae* 15.3).[16]

---

13 See J. Hammer, 'Geoffrey of Monmouth's use of the Bible in the *Historia Regum Britanniae*', *Bulletin of the John Rylands Library* 30 (1946-7), 293-311, p.297.

14 See 'Geoffrey of Monmouth and Gildas', pp.12 and 39-40.

15 *Ibid.*, pp.9-10 and 36-8, and 15-16 respectively.

16 This borrowing is partially recorded by Faral, *La Légende*, II, p.196.

In my previous article, I drew attention to the clear parallel between *Historia Regum Britanniae* 151.8, 'ecclesias usque ad solum destructas renovat' (of Arthur's reconstruction work), and *De Excidio Britanniae* 12.2, 'renovant ecclesias usque ad solum destructas' (of the rebuilding after the persecutions of Diocletian).[17] In fact, Geoffrey was more fond of this phrase than I allowed and imitated it in two further passages concerning respectively Aurelius Ambrosius and the bishops Theonius and Tadiocus: 'condolebat, maxime autem propter *ecclesias usque ad solum destructas*' (*Historia Regum Britanniae* 120.25-26); and 'cum omnes *ecclesias* sibi subditas *usque ad* humum *destructas* vidissent' (*Historia Regum Britanniae* 186.9-10).

Also found in Geoffrey's account of Ambrosius's reign is the character Eldad, bishop of Gloucester, who is consulted about the fate of the captive Hengist and his English followers after their defeat (*Historia Regum Britanniae* 125 and 126). He advises that Hengist should be executed, while Octa and the rest of the English should be bound to the British by treaty and settled in the north of the island. In both cases Eldad's decision rests on a Biblical precedent: Hengist is to be executed just as Samuel killed the captive King Agag; a treaty is to be granted by the Britons to the English just as the Israelites granted one to the Gibeonites. The use of the first of these precedents seems to be original to Geoffrey; at least, no source is extant. The treaty with the Gibeonites, however, is also mentioned by Gildas in the preface of his work, as part of a long catalogue of woes visited on the Israelites in the Old Testament: 'Gabaonitarum irritum foedus, calliditate licet extortum, nonnullis intulisse exitium' (*De Excidio Britanniae* 1.4). Gildas's reason for giving this catalogue is to explain his motive in writing, since he draws a parallel between the Biblical narrative and the situation of the British people, whom he elsewhere terms *praesens Israel* (*De Excidio Britanniae* 26.1); the thrust of his argument is that, if God so punished His Chosen People, what will He do to Gildas's own corrupt contemporaries?[18] In the light of this, it seems that Gildas gave prominence to the comparatively minor episode of the treaty with the Gibeonites because it loosely corresponded to that struck between the *superbus tyrannus* and the English mercenaries (*De Excidio Britanniae* 23) — an *irritum foedus* which could certainly be said to have 'brought destruction on some few,

[17] 'Geoffrey of Monmouth and Gildas', p.18. Gildas is himself echoing Rufinus's *Historia Ecclesiastica* (see N. Wright, 'Did Gildas read Orosius?', forthcoming in *Cambridge Medieval Celtic Studies*); there is, however, no evidence that Geoffrey used or even knew Rufinus's work.

[18] Cf. *De Excidio Britanniae* 1.13: 'si, inquam, peculiari ex omnibus nationibus populo ... non pepercit, ... quid tali huius atramento aetatis facturus est?'.

even though it was extorted by trickery'.[19] As a careful reader of the *De Excidio Britanniae*, Geoffrey would have appreciated this allusion; hence, when in his own *Historia* he compared the treaty drawn up on another occasion between Ambrosius and the English with that between the Israelites and the Gibeonites, he was most likely once again following Gildas's lead.

The section of the *Historia Regum Britanniae* devoted to Arthur, Geoffrey's chief hero, contains a number of borrowings from Gildas. Perhaps the most striking of these occurs when Geoffrey pointedly inverts a phrase drawn from Gildas's account of the shameful defeat of the British at the time of the Roman invasions; Geoffrey skilfully reapplies this to the equally shameful rout of the Roman forces after their battle with Arthur at Siesia.[20] Another borrowing, which I did not record, shows the same process at work. On two occasions Geoffrey states very specifically the battle-formation adopted by Arthur's forces: 'pedestres catervae Britannico more cum dextro et sinistro cornu in quadrum statutae' (*Historia Regum Britanniae* 168. 21-22); and 'agmina pedestria cum dextro et sinistro cornu quadrata' (*Historia Regum Britanniae* 178.26-7).[21] Such squares or deep columns drawn up with a right and a left wing (how else? one wonders) are surely more appropriate to the Roman army than the British;[22] why, then, does Geoffrey assert that this formation was traditionally British (*Britannico more*)? It is, I think, another neat inversion of Gildas who, in the passage already mentioned, castigates the lack of military countermeasures taken against the Roman invaders by the British in the following terms: 'non militaris in mari classis parata fortiter dimicare pro patria nec *quadratum agmen* neque

---

19 It is, however, difficult to know how far this analogy should be pressed, since the parallel is not exact. The Israelites were tricked into the treaty by the Gibeonites, but the *foedus* was not broken for many years, and then by Saul who tried to exterminate the Gibeonites; as a result, God punished the Israelites with famine for breaking their word, which led David to hand over Saul's descendants to the Gibeonites for execution (see Joshua 9 and II Samuel 21). Possibly Gildas was covertly suggesting that his contemporaries should keep faith with the English in future; see Patrick Sims-Williams, 'Gildas and the Anglo-Saxons', *Cambridge Medieval Celtic Studies* 6 (Winter, 1983), 1-30, at pp.27-8.
20 'Geoffrey of Monmouth and Gildas', pp.18-19.
21 Because of the Gildasian echo, I have preferred the reading of Bern, Burgerbibliothek, MS. 568, *quadrata* (not reported by Faral), to *quadrato*, printed in Faral's edition.
22 On three occasions (*Historia Regum Britanniae* 168.38-9, 178.20 and 41-2) Geoffrey also mentions British formations composed of six thousand, six hundred, and sixty-six men, the theoretical complement of a Roman legion; see Tatlock, *Legendary History*, p.334.

dextrum cornu aliive belli apparatus in litore conseruntur' (*De Excidio Britanniae* 6.2). In short, the square column and the right wing, whose absence is bemoaned by Gildas, become in the *Historia Regum Britanniae* a characteristically British manner of deployment.

Another Gildasian echo can be detected in the contrasting speeches delivered by the rival commanders before the final battle at Siesia: Arthur praises his soldiers with the words, 'nequaquam tamen ab innata bonitate degeneravistis' (*Historia Regum Britanniae* 169.7-8); his foe Lucius Hiberus exhorts his men, 'ut avitam bonitatem revocetis' (*Historia Regum Britanniae* 170.16-17).[23] Both phrases recall, with variation, Gildas's unfavourable judgement on the descendants of Ambrosius Aurelianus, who have failed to live up to the example set by their ancestor: 'cuius nunc temporibus nostris suboles magnopere *avita bonitate degeneravit*' (*De Excidio Britanniae* 25.3).

Two further Gildasian borrowings from the closing section of the *Historia Regum Britanniae*, the final decline of Britain, complete this list. In my previous study I noted that Geoffrey's description, in his hexameter *Vita Merlini*, of Vortigern as an *infaustus princeps* is indebted to Gildas, since the latter had applied the same epithet – *infaustus* – to the *tyrannus* who invited the English to Britain, 'iubente infausto tyranno' (*De Excidio Britanniae* 23.4).[24] In addition, Geoffrey also employs this term – in a completely different context – of Gormund, the African king who at the instigation of the English defeats Ceredig and forces the remaining British population into Wales and Cornwall: 'Postquam autem, ut praedictum est, *infaustus tyrannus* cum innumerabilibus Affricanorum militibus totam fere insulam vastavit . . .' (*Historia Regum Britanniae* 186.1-3).

In the penultimate chapter of the *Historia*, Geoffrey tells us that after the death of Cadualadr the degenerate Welsh, unworthy of their British descent, never recovered control of the island, but engaged in petty internal and external feuding: 'immo nunc sibi, interdum Saxonibus ingrati consurgentes, externas atque domesticas clades incessanter agebant' (*Historia Regum Britanniae* 207.16-17). I called attention to the debt of the second half of this clause to *De Excidio Britanniae* 19.4: 'augebantur externae clades domesticis motibus'.[25] However, Geoffrey's literary adaptation is again more subtle than I allowed. The first part of the clause is also Gildasian in origin, being a skilful reworking of Gildas's initial criticism of the ungrateful pride of Britannia: 'Haec erecta cervice et mente, ex quo inhabitata est,

---

[23] Again, because of the parallel with Gildas, I have preferred the reading of Bern, Burgerbibliothek, MS. 568, *avitam*, to *habitam*, printed by Faral.

[24] 'Geoffrey of Monmouth and Gildas', p.31.

[25] *Ibid.*, p.21.

161

nunc Deo, *interdum* civibus, nonnumquam etiam transmarinis regibus et subiectis *ingrata consurgit'* (*De Excidio Britanniae* 4.1). It is typical of Geoffrey's playful, even ironic, method of adaptation that the final sentence of his narrative should echo the very first sentence of Gildas's *historia*-section.

In addition to the borrowings listed above (and in my previous article), there are numerous occasions on which the vocabulary of the *De Excidio Britanniae* — particularly that of passages imitated by Geoffrey — also colours the latter's phraseology elsewhere in the *Historia*. I have collected the following examples: *occidentem . . . versus*, *De Excidio Britanniae* 3.1 and *Historia Regum Britanniae* 51.8; *in edito*, *De Excidio Britanniae* 3.2 and 19.2, and *Historia Regum Britanniae* 11.2 and 157.47; *longe positis*, *De Excidio Britanniae* 4.3 and *Historia Regum Britanniae* 53.7, 69.3, 91.27, 154.3,[26] 185.3; *absque cunctamine*, *De Excidio Britanniae* 11.2 and *Historia Regum Britanniae* 95.45-6 and 165.3; *omni armato milite*, *De Excidio Britanniae* 14 and *Historia Regum Britanniae* 31.141, 59.4, 66.2, 80.9, 82.8, 84.4, 88.31, 131.2, 155.6 (with variation);[27] *belli . . . usus ignara*, *De Excidio Britanniae* 14 and *Historia Regum Britanniae* 178.31; *si hostis longius arceretur*, *De Excidio Britanniae* 15.1 and *Historia Regum Britanniae* 56.8, 89.11, 139.11, 207.6-7 (with variation); *non profuit* (placed last in its clause for emphasis), *De Excidio Britanniae* 15.3 and *Historia Regum Britanniae* 149.13 and 207.4; *ambrones*, *De Excidio Britanniae* 16 and *Historia Regum Britanniae* 88.28, 124.14, 132.38, 141.33, 203.26;[28] *domesticis motibus*, *De Excidio Britanniae* 19.4 and *Historia Regum Britanniae* 159.17; *Romana potestas*, *De Excidio Britanniae* 20.1 and *Historia Regum Britanniae* 67.14, 69.5, 73.12, 76.3, 78.5, 83.16, 90.21, 158.17; *retro aetas*, *De Excidio Britanniae* 21.2 and *Historia Regum Britanniae* 52.2; *crebras . . . irruptiones*, *De Excidio Britanniae* 22.3

---

26 *longe positis* is here the reading of Bern, Burgerbibliothek, MS. 568; Faral prints *longe manentibus*.

27 Geoffrey's fondness for this phrase is probably explained by his recognition of its Vergilian origin; see 'Geoffrey of Monmouth and Gildas', p.15, n.40. In connection with Geoffrey's borrowings from Vergil, I noted (*ibid.*, p.6, n.20) that the phrase 'sub aeriis montibus' (*Historia Regum Britanniae* 5.11) has 'a poetic ring'; in fact, it is an echo of *Aeneid* VI.234, '*monte sub aerio, qui nunc Misenus ab illo*'. I should also like to take this opportunity to correct an error in my previous article. At *Historia Regum Britanniae* 165.42-3, the words, 'at ille, quantum humanae naturae possibile est, commotus', are applied not to Arthur, but to Beduerus who on this occasion is acting as Arthur's scout.

28 On the origin of this word, see Faral, *La Légende*, II, p.196, n.2 and Tatlock, *Legendary History*, p.114.

and *Historia Regum Britanniae* 43.58, 87.2, 172.10-11; *quasi pro patria pugnaturus*, *De Excidio Britanniae* 23.4 and *Historia Regum Britanniae* 102.16, 122.12-13, 147.7, 191.28-9 (with variation); *ignis . . . non quievit accensus donec*, *De Excidio Britanniae* 24.1 and *Historia Regum Britanniae* 9.27, 30.9-10, 58.14, 119.39-40, 136.7, 148.17, 165.70, 167.39 (with much variation; this is a favourite expression of Geoffrey's); *non miminae stragis*, *De Excidio Britanniae* 26.1 and *Historia Regum Britanniae* 43.55, 60.17-18, 66.18-19, and 88.39. These parallels of vocabulary serve to emphasise the fact that the *De Excidio Britanniae* influenced not only the structure of the *Historia Regum Britanniae*, but also Geoffrey's style and latinity.[29]

[29] Compare, for example, the conclusions of Jacob Hammer's study of the influence of the Bible on Geoffrey's Latin (cited in n.6 above). I am grateful to Dr D. N. Dumville for reading this article in typescript.

UPDATE

VII

THE MANUSCRIPTS OF GEOFFREY OF MONMOUTH'S
HISTORIA REGUM BRITANNIAE: ADDENDA, CORRIGENDA,
AND AN ALPHABETICAL LIST

David N. Dumville

Since I published a partial revision (*Arthurian Literature* III [1983] 113-28) of Acton Griscom's list of Galfridian manuscripts, several corrections have become necessary and two further additions can be made to the list. I proceed in the same order as last year.

SHELFMARKS

I owe to Dr Vivien Law, Keeper of Manuscripts at Sidney Sussex College, Cambridge, the information that M. R. James's serial numbers have now become the normal form of reference. Read, therefore, '75 (△.4.13)'. And I am obliged to Mr Daniel Huws for pointing out my blunder (p.116) in awarding the Cardiff Central Library to Mid-Glamorgan rather than *South* Glamorgan County Libraries.

DELETIONS FROM GRISCOM'S LIST

Much further work on the textual history of the *Historia* has led to the conclusion that it is clearly more difficult to distinguish between an abridgment and a variant version than was previously admitted. As a result I have retained in a separate section of the list below the East Berlin, London (BL Arundel 220), and Valenciennes manuscripts which were rejected last year. No doubt others on the main list (and yet others still unlisted) should join this category.

PHILLIPPS MSS.

3117
Thanks to the tenacity and ingenuity of Mr Daniel Huws, Keeper of

Manuscripts at the National Library of Wales, the whereabouts and current owner of this book have now been identified. It has in fact remained in the possession of the heirs of Sir Thomas Watson, Bart., currently represented by his granddaughter, the Hon. Mrs John Southwell of Longparish, Hants.. She has kindly supplied a copy of a letter written to her father, Sir Geoffrey Watson (named after Geoffrey of Monmouth), by Jacob Hammer in April 1939 when he had finished collating the text in this manuscript. He assigned it to a French scriptorium of the end of the fourteenth century, and pronounced it to be a copy of the now mutilated Paris, B.N., MS. latin 6432, and therefore not without interest.

9162
After the final proofs of last year's article, this shelf-mark lost its last digit. 9162, not 916, is the correct number. As Mr Huws points out to me, it was in fact already in the National Library of Wales as MS. Llanstephan 176 when Griscom published his list (not containing notice of this book's Aberystwyth location) in 1929.

NEW LOCATIONS OF MSS. KNOWN TO GRISCOM

Manchester, John Rylands University Library, MS. lat. 216
This volume was *not* described by N. R. Ker, *Medieval Manuscripts in British Libraries*, III.

MANUSCRIPTS NOT KNOWN TO GRISCOM

ENGLAND

The references to catalogue-descriptions of nos 5 and 7 have become partially inverted. For MS. Digby 67 (*S.C.* 1668) read Macray, *Catalogi*, IX (1883), cols 73-6; for MS. Laud misc. 592 (*S.C.* 1388) read Coxe, *Catalogi*, II.1 (1858), col. 421.

27. Oxford, Bodleian Library, MS. Digby 196 (*S.C.* 1797)   *s.* xv
    Catalogued by William D. Macray, *Catalogi Codicum Manuscriptorum Bibliothecae Bodleianae*, IX (Oxford, 1883), cols 212-18. Folios 30-34 bear a single, connected extract (beginning with § 6) from the *Historia*, which is described by Macray as item 30, comprising 'I.ii-x'.

SPAIN

28. Madrid, Biblioteca Nacional, MS. R. 202   *s.* xiv
    See [G. H. Pertz], 'Handschriftenverzeichnisse', *Archiv der*

Gesellschaft für ältere deutsche Geschichtskunde 8 (1843) 284-860, at p.798. I owe this reference to Miss Julia Crick (Gonville & Caius College, Cambridge).

The total of known manuscripts rises only to 211, not 212, however, for no. 4 of these manuscripts (Oxford, Bodleian Library, MS. Bodley 585 [*S.C.* 2357], fos 1-48) should not have been described and counted separately from the parent-book (which was known to Griscom), Cambridge, University Library, MS. Dd.6.7 (324).

MANUSCRIPTS WHOSE CURRENT LOCATION IS NOT KNOWN

For Phillipps 3117, still in private ownership, see above. The Lanhydrock volume was sold at Sotheby's on 12 June, 1963, as lot 132, to the Bodleian Library, Oxford, where it is now MS. Lat. misc. b.17. Thanks are due, for help in tracing it, to Mr Oliver Padel (Institute of Cornish Studies, University of Exeter), Mr Michael Trinick (The National Trust, Lanhydrock), and Dr B. C. Barker-Benfield (Dept of Western MSS., Bodleian Library). See also Neil R. Ker, *Fragments of Medieval Manuscripts used as Pastedowns in Oxford Bindings* (Oxford 1954), p.xvi, n.1.

APOLOGY

This is owed to Dr Christoph von Steiger (Bern) who mysteriously was made into 'Christopher' after the page-proof (of p.114) had been corrected.

APPENDIX

It has been represented to me in the past year that a complete, alphabetical list of the manuscripts of Geoffrey's *Historia* would be of service, to ease the student's otherwise unenviable double task of following Griscom's eccentric order and collating with his catalogue the various lists which have emended it. A numbered list of the 211 known manuscripts therefore follows here, with the three 'abridgments' (too hastily rejected last year) added as a supplement.

1. Aberystwyth, National Library of Wales, MS. Peniarth 42
2.   Peniarth 43
3.   Llanstephan 176 (*olim* Phillipps 9162)
4.   Llanstephan 196
5.   Porkington 17
6.   Wynnstay 14

7. Aberystwyth, National Library of Wales, MS. 2005 (Panton 37), fos 63r-72v
8.   11611 (*olim* Clumber 46)
9.   13052 (*olim* Phillipps 32)
10.   13210 (*olim* Phillipps 26233)
11.   21552
12. Arras, Bibliothèque municipale, MS. 583 (871)
13. Auxerre, Bibliothèque municipale, MS. 91 (85)
14. Bern, Burgerbibliothek, MS. 568
15. Boulogne-sur-Mer, Bibliothèque municipale, MSS. 180 + 139 + 145
16. Bruges, Bibliothèque de la Ville, MS. 428
17. Bruxelles, Bibliothèque royale de Belgique, MS. II. 1020 (*olim* Phillipps 11603)
18.   8495-8505
19.   8536-8543
20.   9871-9874
21. Cambridge, Clare College, Fellows' Library, MS. 27 (N '.1.5)
22. Cambridge, Corpus Christi College, MS. 281
23.   292
24.   414
25. Cambridge, Fitzwilliam Museum, MS. 302 (*olim* Phillipps 203)
26.   346
27. Cambridge, Gonville & Caius College, MS. 103/55
28.   249/277
29.   406/627
30.   450/391
31. Cambridge, St John's College, MS. G.16 (184)
32.   S.6 (254)
33. Cambridge, Sidney Sussex College, MS. 75 (△. 4.13)
34. Cambridge, Trinity College, MS. R. 5.34 (725)
35.   R. 7.6 (744)
36.   R. 7.28 (770)
37.   O. 1.17 (1041)
38.   O. 2.21 (1125)
39. Cambridge, University Library, MS. Dd. 1.17 (17)
40.   Dd. 4.34 (209)
41.   Dd. 6.7 (324) + Oxford, Bodl. Lib., MS. Bodley 585 (*S.C.* 2357), fos 1-48
42.   Dd. 6.12 (329)
43.   Dd. 10.31 (590)
44.   Dd. 10.32 (591)
45.   Ee. 1.24 (913)
46.   Ff. 1.25 (1158)
47.   Ii. 1.14 (1706)
48.   Ii. 4.4 (1801)
49.   Ii. 4.12 (1809)
50.   Ii. 4.17 (1814)

51. Cambridge, University Library, MS. Kk. 6. 16 (2096)
52.   Mm. 1. 34 (2295)
53.   Mm. 5. 29 (2434)
54. Canterbury, Cathedral Library, MS. Add. 128/27a
55. Cardiff, S. Glamorgan Central Library, MS. 2.611
56. Dôle, Bibliothèque municipale, MSS. 348 + 349
57. Douai, Bibliothèque municipale, MS. 880 (835)
58.   882 (838)
59. Dublin, Trinity College, MS. 172 (B. 2. 7)
60.   493 (E. 2. 24)
61.   494 (E. 5. 7)
62.   495 (E. 4. 30)
63.   496 (E. 6. 2)
64.   514 (E. 5. 3)
65.   515 (E. 5. 12)
66. Edinburgh, National Library of Scotland, MS. Adv. 18. 4. 5
67. Eton, Eton College, MS. 246 (*olim* Phillipps 25145)
68. Exeter, Cathedral Library, MS. 3514
69. Firenze, Biblioteca Laurenziana, MS. XVII. dextr. 6
70. Firenze, Reale Biblioteca Nazionale Centrale, MS. 2591-A. 4
71. Glasgow, University Library, MS. U. 7. 25 (331)
72.   U. 7. 26 (332)
73. Leiden, Bibliotheek der Rijksuniversiteit, MS. B.P. L. 20
74.   Voss. lat. F. 77
75. Lille, Bibliothèque municipale, MS. 533
76. Lincoln, Cathedral Library, MS. 98 (A. 4. 6)
77. London, British Library, MS. Additional 11702
78.   15732
79.   33371
80.   35295
81.   Arundel   10
82.   237
83.   319
84.   326
85.   403
86.   409
87.   Cotton Cleopatra D. viii
88.   Galba E. xi
89.   Nero D. viii
90.   Titus A. xviii
91.   Titus A. xxv
92.   Titus A. xxvii
93.   Titus C. xvii
94.   Vespasian A. xxiii
95.   Vespasian E. x
96.   Egerton 3142 (*olim* Clumber 47)
97. London, British Library, MS. Harley 225

98.	London, British Library, MS. Harley	536
99.		3773
100.		4003
101.		4123
102.		5115
103.		6358
104.		Lansdowne 732
105.		Royal 4. C. xi
106.		13. A. iii
107.		13. A. v
108.		13. D. i
109.		13. D. ii
110.		13. D. v
111.		14. C. i
112.		15. C. xvi
113.		Sloane 289
114.		Stowe 56

115. London, College of Arms, MS. Arundel 1

116.	London, Lambeth Palace, MS.	188
117.		379 + 357
118.		401
119.		454, fos 28r-123r
120.		454, fos 124r-204r
121.		503

122. Longparish, Library of the Hon. Mrs John Southwell, *s.n.* (*olim*
123. Phillipps 3117)

Madrid, Biblioteca Nacional, MS. 6319 (F. 147)
124. . . R. 202
125. Manchester, John Rylands University Library, MS. lat. 216 (*olim*
Paris, B.N., lat. 4999 A, item 8)

126. Montpellier, Bibliothèque de l'Université (École de Médecine), MS. 92
127. 378

128. New Haven (Conn.), Yale University, MS. 590 (*olim* Phillipps 2324)
129. 598

130.	Oxford, All Souls' College, MS.	35
131.		39

132.	Oxford, Bodleian Library, MS. Add. A. 61 (*S.C.* 28843)	
133.	Bodley	233 (*S.C.* 2188)
134.		514 (*S.C.* 2184)
[41.		585 (*S.C.* 2357), fos 1-48]
135.		622 (*S.C.* 2156)
136.		977 (*S.C.* 27602)
137.	Digby	67 (*S.C.* 1668)
138.		196 (*S.C.* 1797), fos 30-34
139.		Douce 115 (*S.C.* 21689)
140.		Fairfax 28 (*S.C.* 3908)

141. Oxford, Bodleian Library, MS. Jesus College 2

169

142.	Jones 48 (*S.C.* 8956)
143.	Lat. hist. b. 1, fragment 2
144.	Lat. misc. b.17, fo 10
145.	Lat. misc. e. 42 (*S.C.* 36220)
146.	Laud misc. 579 (*S.C.* 1496)
147.	592 (*S.C.* 1388)
148.	664 (*S.C.* 1048)
149.	720 (*S.C.* 1062)
150.	Magdalen College lat. 170
151.	lat. 171
152.	New College 276
153.	Oriel College 16
154.	Rawlinson B. 148 (*S.C.* 11519)
155.	B. 168 (*S.C.* 15441)
156.	B. 189 (*S.C.* 11550)
157.	C. 152 (*S.C.* 12016)
158.	D. 893 (*S.C.* 13659)
159.	Tanner 195 (*S.C.* 10021)
160.	Top. gen. c. 2 (*S.C.* 3118), pp.22-41
161.	Oxford, Christ Church, MS. 99
162.	Paris, Bibliothèque nationale, MS. lat. 4126
163.	5233
164.	5234
165.	5508
166.	5697
167.	6039
168.	6040
169.	6041
170.	6041 A
171.	6041 B
172.	6041 C
173.	6230
174.	6231
175.	6232
176.	6233
177.	6275
178.	6432
179.	6815
180.	7531
181.	8401 A
182.	11107
183.	12943
184.	13710
185.	15073
186.	17569
187.	18271
188.	nouv. acq. lat. 1001

189. Paris, Bibliothèque Sainte-Geneviève, MS. 2113
190. Philadelphia (Pa.), The Free Library, MS. E. 247
191. Reims, Bibliothèque municipale, MS. 1430
192. Roma, Biblioteca Apostolica Vaticana, MS. Ottoboni 1472
193.   3025
194.   Pal. lat. 956
195.   962
196.   Reg. lat. 692
197.   825
198.   Vat. lat. 2005
199. Rouen, Bibliothèque municipale, MS. U. 74 (1177)
200.   3069 (2010)
201. Saint-Omer, Bibliothèque municipale, MS. 710
202. Salisbury, Cathedral Library, MS. 121
203. Sankt Gallen, Stiftsbibliothek, MS. 633
204. San Marino (Cal.), Henry E. Huntington Library, MS. EL 34.C.9 (1121)
205. Sevilla, Biblioteca Colombina, MS. 7.3.19
206. Stockholm, Kungliga Biblioteket, MS. Holm. D. 1311
207. Troyes, Bibliothèque municipale, MS. 273 *bis*
208.   1531
209. Ushaw, Ushaw College, MS. 6
210. Winchester, Cathedral Library, MS. 9
211. Würzburg, Universitätsbibliothek, MS. ch. f. 140

Abridgments noted by Griscom and Hammer

212. East Berlin, Deutsche Staatsbibliothek, MS. Phillipps 1880
213. London, British Library, MS Arundel 220
214. Valenciennes, Bibliothèque municipale, MS. 792 (589)

SUPPLEMENTARY CORRIGENDUM

San Marino, Huntington Library, MS. HM 145, reported by Griscom (p. 571), is a modern manuscript of no relevance to Geoffrey of Monmouth. Griscom must have meant MS. HM 1345 which contains a copy of the *Prophetia Merlini* (fos 107v-111r). But the book actually described by Griscom is (and was in 1929) MS. EL 34.C.9 (1121).

UPDATE

VIII

ADDITIONS TO TWENTIETH CENTURY ARTHURIAN LITERATURE

F   Carmichael, Douglas. *Pendragon: an historical novel*. Hicksville, New York, Blackwater Press, 1977.
     A pseudo-historical recreation of Arthur in sixth century Britain, of more than usual ingenuity and merit.

P   Craig, Alec. *The Voice of Merlin*. London, The Fortune Press, 1946.

F   Deeping, Warwick. *The Sword and the Cross*. London, Cassell, 1957.
     Artorius, Owen, Igerna, Gerontius, Morgan *et al.* — peripheral Arthuriana in fifth-sixth century British setting.

F   Nathan, Robert. *The Fair*. New York, Knopf, 1964.
     A light fantasy with Arthurian allusions and personalities — Arthur, Badon Hill etc. — but not an 'Arthurian novel' in the accepted sense.

F   Newman, Sharon. *The Chessboard Queen*. New York, St Martin's, 1983.
     Not read yet — presumably a sequel with one more to go to make it a trilogy.

F   O'Meara, Walter. *The Duke of War*. New York, Harcourt, Brace, 1966.
     A somewhat pedestrian tale of the cavalry general defending Roman Britain.

F   Roberts, Dorothy James. *Kinsmen of the Grail*. Boston, Toronto, Little Brown, 1963.
     Gawaine and Lancelot in a pseudo-historical setting with underpinnings from the legends of Perceval le Gallois.

F   Seare, Nicholas. *Rude Tales and Glorious: a retelling of the Arthurian tales*. New York, Potter, 1984.
     Blurb says 'bawdy, bouncy, clever, hilarious'.